# MICROWAVE
## FOOD PROCESSOR
### The Twice as Fast Cookbook

# MICROWAVE

## FOOD PROCESSOR

## The Twice as Fast Cookbook

SUE SPITLER

Edited by Margaret Weale

DAVID & CHARLES
Newton Abbot   London

British Library Cataloguing in Publication Data

Spitler, Sue
  Microwave/food processor.
  1. Blenders (Cookery)    2. Mixers (Cookery)
  3. Food processor cookery
  I. Title    II. Weale, Margaret
  III. Spitler, Sue. Twice as fast
  641.5'89    TX840.F6

  ISBN 0-7153-8549-6

Colour photography by Stan Weale
Line illustrations by Mona Thorogood

The publishers are grateful to Moulinex Limited for kindly supplying
the Moulinex Microwave 691 and the Moulinex Masterchef food
processor used in testing the recipes and the colour photography

First published by Contemporary Books Inc 1982
under the title of *Twice As Fast*
© Text: Sue Spitler 1982, 1984
© Colour illustrations, revised edition: David & Charles Limited 1984
© Line illustrations, revised edition: David & Charles Limited 1984

Typeset by MS Filmsetting Limited, Frome, Somerset
and printed in Great Britain
by Butler & Tanner Limited, Frome and London
for David & Charles (Publishers) Limited
Brunel House, Newton Abbot, Devon

# Contents

# Introduction

Chances are that you acquired your food processor and microwave oven separately, with different hopes and plans for each. One appliance would perform chopping, slicing, shredding, mixing and kneading tasks; the other could defrost foods quickly and cut cooking times by more than half. Because of their distinct functions, the two 'kitchen marvels' came to be celebrated in diverse contexts—the microwave oven for quick, simple meals, and the food processor for recipes that otherwise would have required tedious hand labour.

As technological achievements, each appliance merits praise and discussion in its own right. But from a cook's standpoint, it is much more exciting to consider the two together. Separately, the food processor and microwave oven represent two dimensions of speed and convenience. Together, they define a different way of cooking.

You'll find this new approach to food preparation, based on coordinated use of the food processor and microwave oven, detailed in this book. Designed as a resource book for everyone who wants to take advantage of the latest in kitchen technology, *Microwave/Food Processor* contains more than 160 recipes for all kinds of meals and cooking occasions. Browse through and you'll discover a sampling of the possibilities—everything from quick snacks to elegant pâtés and terrines, from hearty stews to Oriental stir-fried entrées, from potato salad to pasta, from chocolate desserts to whole-grain breads. Even at a glance, you'll notice something unusual about all these recipes: they take much less time to prepare than they would without the food processor and microwave oven. And for this reason alone, they can introduce you to a new world of eating.

The proof of the technology lies, of course, in the tasting. But once you start cooking, you'll recognise other benefits as well. For one thing, food processor/microwave cooking is exceptionally clean. Because most of the preparation is done in the food processor workbowl, there are fewer utensils to wash. Since you can microwave and serve food (and refrigerate and reheat leftovers) in the same dish, separate utensils washing-up and pot-scrubbing are eliminated. Moreover, the microwave oven wipes clean with a damp sponge. So when you prepare these recipes, you can look forward to relaxed meals—without dreading the sight of the kitchen afterwards.

Other advantages can be traced to the fact that the functions of the food processor and microwave oven coordinate beautifully. You'll notice this while you're cooking: there is a very comfortable rhythm to the recipe steps. The time required for ingredient preparation and processing fits in with microwave cooking time; so multistep procedures can be accomplished in an efficient sequence, without wasting time between steps.

It shouldn't take you long to get used to the incomparable precision of the appliances. The food processor chops, minces, purées, slices, shreds, blends, mixes and kneads almost instantly, with much more reliable results than you could achieve by hand. The microwave oven heats foods more uniformly than a conventional cooker can, so there is much less danger of overcooking or burning. No doubt you'll have to try a few recipes before you can break the habit of watchful worrying. But then you'll come to realise that predictability is an essential component of kitchen technology. Like all appliances, the food processor and microwave oven can be counted on to perform the same tasks repeatedly, in precisely the same way.

The speed and precision of the appliances add up to freedom for the cook. You can fill a shopping basket with nothing but fresh ingredients—and not worry about having packaged provisions on hand for extra-busy days. You can watch both your diet and your budget more easily, since there is less temptation to buy processed foods or to eat out in restaurants. You can vary menus just by trying different recipes, since all recipes call for the same basic techniques. You can easily substitute ingredients, since the appliances process and cook all foods within certain categories, like leafy vegetables or boneless meats, in virtually the same way.

You'll probably most appreciate the convenience of cooking with a microwave and food processor in the routine of everyday meals. Used together, they make it incredibly easy to serve wholesome, interesting, family-style dinners in less than an hour. And you can plan menus according to appetite rather than cooking schedule, for the appliances make it possible to prepare chilli, Chinese-style beef, or a chicken casserole, for example, within the same time framework. For this reason, this way of cooking can save money, too. You don't have to work hard to turn cheaper cuts of meat or inexpensive vegetables into tempting dishes. In fact, it takes no more time to prepare poultry, fish, or meatless entrées than it does to grill burgers or steaks conventionally—and the results can be low in calories and cholesterol as well as delicious.

If the versatility of this way of cooking recommends it for everyday meals, the sheer speed can prove equally valuable for special occasions and dinner parties. You may decide to surprise guests with specialities you wouldn't have attempted before—such as a delicate vegetable terrine or a French-style fruit tart—just because it is so easy to do. The recipes can tempt and taunt you with all kinds of culinary ambitions, since you never have to worry about getting bogged down in hours of complex preparations. You can serve a complete Chinese dinner, if you wish, or indulge a passion for chocolate mousse pie. You can plan to feature a

flawless Hollandaise sauce or loaves of homemade bread—without fear of failure. In short, you can have a lot of fun—and take a great deal of pride—in cooking with a microwave and food processor.

To make the most of this book, you should note a few things about its organisation. Before you start cooking, read through the chapters on 'Microwave and Food Processor Techniques' and 'Shopping and Serving Shortcuts'; these will clarify recipe instructions and can answer many questions before they arise.

In addition to recipe chapters devoted to meal courses, from appetisers through breads and desserts, there are also special chapters on sauces and various mixes, calorie-counted dishes, and confectionery. Many recipes, however, don't fit neatly into a single category. So do consult the Index for the widest choice of possibilities. If you look under 'Appetisers' or 'Vegetables,' for example, you'll find some recipes that have been included under other chapter headings. Also check the Index if you have a question about an unfamiliar ingredient or procedure, since you are likely to discover an explanation elsewhere in the book.

# Microwave and Food Processor Techniques

All recipes have been kitchen-tested in standard-size food processors fitted with a Steel Knife, a Medium Slicing Disc, and a Medium Shredding Disc, and in variable-power, 650-700w microwave ovens. Your appliances may have extra features, such as an expanded feed tube or a microwave oven temperature probe, that can make the recipes even faster and easier: so you should read the manufacturer's instructions carefully. To use your food processor and microwave oven safely and most efficiently, it is important that you follow the safety, handling and usage procedures outlined in the appliance manufacturers' manuals.

Here is a guide to cooking terms and the techniques needed to prepare recipes accurately and successfully. Explanations are listed according to recipe instructions, so that you can find whatever information you may need as quickly as possible. For example, if a recipe says 'Process (Steel Knife) until chopped', check under 'Process (Steel Knife)' for the appropriate explanation. If you have some food processor and microwave cooking experience, you probably will not have to refer to this guide very often; if not, you should study both these guidelines and those outlined in your appliance manuals before you start to cook.

## Using preparation and microwave times

Each recipe is accompanied by separate preparation and microwave times. The preparation time has been calculated from the time when you assemble the recipe ingredients, through the cooking process and standing time, to the finished dish; it assumes that some steps will be done simultaneously, such as processing one ingredient while another is cooking in the microwave oven. It includes whatever time is required to prepare ingredients, such as peeling potatoes or cutting up meat. It also includes any time needed to make a sauce, pastry, or other important part of the finished dish. (Only optional ingredients are excluded from the time calculations; see 'Sauces and Ready Prepared Mixtures' for additional information.) Each preparation time is necessarily approximate; it might take you slightly more or less time to accomplish each step in the recipe.

The purpose of the preparation time is to let you know about how much time you need to allow before a dish can be served. This information can be especially helpful, for example, when you want to choose a recipe that can be served for dinner within half an hour or an hour. You might also want to check the preparation time when you are entertaining, so that you'll know how long in advance of serving time or guests' arrival you should begin to cook. You should note, however, that preparation time is not always the same as 'work' time; very often, foods need time to cook, stand, or chill but require little attention during that period. A soup or stew, for example, may need to cook as long as an hour, but you can use that time to do other things. So check the preparation time for scheduling purposes, but also read the recipe to determine how much 'time off' it actually allows.

Microwave oven time is both included in the preparation time and listed separately. By letting you know how much time your oven will be in use, the separate microwave time can help you schedule the preparation of several recipes. It is usually inefficient to microwave more than one dish at a time, since length of cooking is directly related to the amount of food in the microwave oven. If you are planning to serve several dishes, you should be aware of how much oven time each requires, so that you can coordinate the cooking sequence. For more detailed information on scheduling menus, see 'Shopping and Serving Shortcuts.'

For several reasons, microwave oven times can only be approximate. Not only do various oven models perform at different speeds, but any two identical ovens are also likely to give varying results. Just a few of the factors that influence timing are the amount of electrical power delivered to your home or geographical area; the time of day, as it affects the amount of electricity being used in the area; and the number of other appliances, if any, that share an electrical circuit with your microwave oven (ideally, the oven should have its own circuit). In this book you will usually find a range of microwave times given, along with a specific way to tell if the food is done. For more detailed information, see the Microwave Oven Techniques section of this chapter.

## Preparing the ingredients

Quantities of ingredients are specified in volume, weight or size, according to the easiest form of measurement. When volume measurement would be impractical, weights are specified; so you should use kitchen scales to ensure accuracy. Precise volume measurements are critical to baking success. Be sure to measure liquids into a clear measuring jug.

Because small quantities of fresh parsley, coriander and dill are difficult to measure, amounts are given in sprigs. A sprig is the small bunch of leaves you can conveniently cut (with kitchen scissors or a vegetable knife) from one small stem. To process fresh herbs effectively with the Steel Knife, you must remove large stems. It is also essential that the herbs be dry; so towel-dry fresh herbs after you wash them.

Prepare all ingredients as directed in the recipes, referring to these explanations as needed.

*Cut into 2.5cm (1in) pieces*
This description applies to foods that will be chopped, minced or puréed with the Steel Knife. Cutting foods into small, uniform-size pieces ensures consistent chopped or minced texture. If you start with pieces that are too large or not uniform in size, the results will be uneven. A mix of large and small cubes of beef, for example, cannot be processed to desired meat-loaf texture; the smaller pieces will become minced before the larger pieces are properly chopped.

*Cut into halves or cut into quarters*
This description applies to small foods, such as hard-boiled eggs, that will be processed with the Steel Knife. Dividing these foods, as directed, into equal pieces ensures consistent chopped or minced texture.

*Cut to fit feed tube*
This description applies to foods that will be sliced with the Slicing Disc or shredded with the Shredding Disc. Use the feed tube pusher as a convenient guide to the length and width of foods that will fit into the tube. Trim potatoes, lemons and other medium-size foods to fit the feed tube, or cut them lengthwise into halves. Cut larger foods, such as aubergines or iceberg lettuce, into wedges to fit the feed tube. Cut meat and cheese into the largest size pieces that will fit into the feed tube. To fit a seeded, cored green pepper into the feed tube, slit it lengthwise and roll it tightly before inserting it into the tube.

Because the bottom of the feed tube is slightly wider than the top, you may find that you can insert some foods, such as a whole lemon or rolled-up green pepper, through the bottom even though they won't fit through the top. For neatest slices and most efficient shredding, trim ends of rounded fruits and vegetables so that they will rest securely between the Slicing or Shredding Disc and the feed tube pusher.

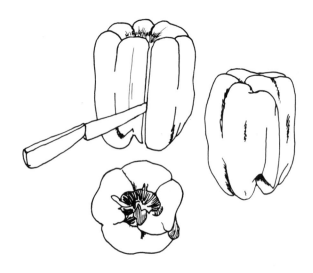

*Chilled or cold*
When applicable, chilling is specified so that ingredients will be firm enough for effective processing. All firm cheeses should be chilled before processing with the Shredding or Slicing Disc. Moist, pliable Parmesan cheese should be chilled before processing with the Steel Knife; dry, aged Parmesan is firm enough to process at room temperature. (Do not attempt to process Parmesan cheese or any other food that is too hard to pierce easily with the tip of a knife blade.) Unless a recipe specifies otherwise, assume that all ingredients are at normal storage temperature; vegetable oil, for example, should be at room temperature, and meat should be at refrigerated temperature.

*Softened*
When a recipe calls for softened butter, margarine or cream cheese, microwave the ingredient to the proper consistency. Remove any aluminium foil wrapping, place the butter or cream cheese on a glass plate or in a glass measure, and microwave at High just until soft enough to spread easily. The time will vary according to quantity and oven. The butter or cream cheese should not lose its shape; so watch carefully, and begin checking at 30 seconds.

*Room temperature*
When egg yolks are used to bind butter or oil with vinegar, lemon juice, or another acidic liquid, as in mayonnaise or Hollandaise-type sauces, the yolks should be brought to room temperature before

processing. To bring yolks to room temperature, place eggs in a bowl of warm water (about 40°C, 105°F) and leave to stand at least 5 minutes before separating them.

*Seeded*

There are two reasons why tomatoes or cucumbers should be seeded before processing. First, the seeded vegetable will give firmer, more attractive chopped pieces or slices. Second, the vegetable won't contribute excess juices to the finished dish. The latter reason is especially important in microwave cooking, because the speed of the process does not allow time for excess moisture to evaporate. To seed a tomato, cut it horizontally into halves and squeeze each half gently until the seeds pop out; if you do this over a strainer or colander placed in a bowl, you can save the juice and substitute it for an equal amount of the water called for in a recipe. To seed a cucumber, cut it lengthwise into halves and scrape out the pulp with a spoon or remove it in strips with a small knife.

To remove seeds from chilli peppers, slit the pepper lengthwise and rinse under cold water; remove the veins with a knife, if you wish. Most of the heat in chilli peppers comes from the seeds and veins; so the flavour will be milder if you remove both. Always be careful not to touch your eyes when you are handling chillies; the volatile oils in the juices can cause irritation. You may want to wear rubber gloves to protect you skin from the oils also.

## Following the recipe

The sequence of steps in each recipe has been designed for maximum speed and convenience. So when you read through a recipe you'll find that the steps follow these general principles:

1 Foods that require a clean, dry workbowl are always processed first, even though they may not be used until later in the recipe. This sequence ensures that you will rarely have to wipe out or wash the workbowl before you finish cooking.
2 Foods that should remain separate from the rest of the ingredients, such as garnishes, are processed in a sequence that prevents them from mingling in the workbowl. If you remove each of these ingredients carefully, using a rubber spatula to scrape the side of the bowl and the blade or disc, you will not have to wipe out the workbowl with kitchen paper.
3 You should empty the workbowl each time you change the blade or disc. But you can process two or more ingredients using the same blade or disc without emptying the workbowl. If the ingredients should be kept separate, the recipe will specify that they be processed separately, even if the same blade or disc is used.
4 In each recipe, the sequence of food-processor steps is coordinated with the sequence of microwave cooking. Usually you can be preparing one part of the recipe in the food processor while another part is in the microwave oven. So read ahead in the recipe to make the best use of your cooking time.

## Food processor techniques

The recipes in this book call for a few very simple food processor techniques. These are the instructions you will find in the recipes, with explanations of how to proceed. Please note that the blade or disc to be used is always indicated in parentheses following the food processor procedure.

*Process (Steel Knife) until blended, mixed or smooth*

This is the most fundamental food processor technique. Position the Steel Knife securely in the workbowl. Add food to the workbowl. Let the machine run until the food has been processed as indicated. Stop the machine and scrape down the side of the bowl at least once during processing to ensure smooth and consistent results.

*Process (Steel Knife) using on/off technique until coarsely chopped, chopped, finely chopped, minced, mixed or blended*

This is the key to controlling food processor action. Position the Steel Knife securely in the workbowl. Add food to the workbowl. Turn the machine on and off until food has been processed as indicated; use the pulse or on/off switch on your machine or rotate the cover, according to manufacturer's instructions. Check the food after 1 or 2 on/off turns for desired texture; continue processing with on/off turns as necessary. Scrape down the side of the bowl with a rubber spatula at least once.

The on/off technique ensures that foods will not be overprocessed. Be especially careful to use the on/off technique, as directed in the recipe, when mixing batters, doughs and pastries for baking, since overprocessing can cause toughness.

*With machine running (Steel Knife), drop or add through feed tube; process or process using on/off technique*

This technique ensures that a small item of food, such as a clove of garlic, will be processed and that a liquid will be entirely incorporated into foods already in the workbowl. Be sure that the Steel Knife is positioned securely in the workbowl. Start the machine. Add food through the feed tube and process as indicated in the recipe.

*Slice (Slicing Disc)*

The standard Medium Slicing Disc that comes with all food processors is used in the recipes. To slice foods with the Slicing Disc, position the disc securely in the workbowl and place food upright in the feed tube. Use the pusher to guide food through the tube.

Efficient use of the Slicing Disc depends on how the food is positioned in the feed tube and how much pressure is applied to the feed tube pusher. Whenever possible, pack the feed tube so that food is held tightly in place. Sometimes you will be able to pack long foods, such as carrots, more securely if you cut them crosswise into halves. You may be able to slice two carrots more efficiently, for example, if you cut them into halves and wedge the four pieces into the feed tube (inserting them through the bottom, if necessary). To slice a single item of food, such as one carrot, position it against one side of the feed tube, opposite the cutting edge of the oncoming disc.

To slice small round foods, such as olives or cherry tomatoes, layer them in the feed tube, filling the width of the tube. Mushrooms can be arranged the same way or they can be stacked sideways with caps placed against alternate sides of the feed tube.

To slice leafy vegetables, such as spinach, arrange the leaves in a neat stack; roll up the stack of leaves and insert the roll vertically into the feed tube. Slice with light pressure on the pusher.

When raw meat is to be sliced, the recipe will direct you to freeze the meat until slightly frozen; the meat should be frozen only until firm—not until it is too hard to pierce with the tip of a sharp knife. Slice with firm pressure on the pusher. Some sandwich and salad recipes call for cooked roast beef. If you wish to slice leftover beef with the food processor, be sure that it is well chilled (not frozen); then cut it to fit the feed tube and slice with firm pressure on the pusher. Pieces of raw or cooked meat should be cut with the grain and inserted with the grain parallel to the feed tube, so that the Slicing Disc will cut across the grain.

Apply pressure to the feed tube pusher according to the texture of the food. Press firmly on hard foods, such as potatoes, and lightly on delicate foods, such as mushrooms. Use light pressure with cheese.

Most recipes do not require perfectly even slices; so don't worry if yours aren't. Cut up any scraps that remain on the disc and add them to the food in the workbowl. If a scrap of food gets caught in the disc, stop the machine immediately and carefully remove the scrap from the disc before you continue.

*Slice (Slicing Disc), arranging food horizontally in the feed tube*

Some foods, such as carrots and courgettes, can be positioned upright or sideways in the feed tube for slicing. If you position the food sideways, you will get longer slices. Long slices of fresh vegetables are especially useful when the vegetables will be served with dips. Green beans are arranged horizontally for slicing when French-cut beans are desired. Mangetout peas are sliced horizontally to give long, delicate strips in Chinese-style entrées.

*Shred (Shredding Disc)*

To shred foods with the Shredding Disc, position the disc securely in the workbowl and place food upright in the feed tube. Use the pusher to guide food through the feed tube. To use the Shredding Disc efficiently, position food in the feed tube and apply pressure on the feed tube pusher as directed above under *Slice (Slicing Disc)*.

Some foods can be positioned upright or sideways in the feed tube. Upright positioning gives short shreds; sideways, long shreds. Ingredients specified in the recipes should be positioned upright for shredding. Firm blocks of chocolate can be shredded to garnish desserts; arrange chocolate in feed tube whichever way it fits most securely and apply firm pressure on the feed tube pusher.

*Using the food processor workbowl*

In some recipes, the workbowl is used as a cooking utensil. By microwaving some of the recipe ingredients in the food processor workbowl, you often can avoid the inconvenience of transferring ingredients back and forth from the food processor to a cooking container. You'll find this procedure used for melting chocolate and letting yeast dough rise, as well as for cooking vegetables, eggs, Hollandaise sauce, and Béarnaise sauce. This procedure is not used when prolonged contact with hot foods might damage the bowl. It is also avoided when microwave use of the bowl would interfere with other food processor steps in the recipe. Since there are occasions when you could be microwaving one ingredient in the workbowl while processing another ingredient in a second workbowl, you might wish to purchase a second bowl; however, the recipes in this book assume that you have only one bowl.

NB Be sure to take these precautions when using the food processor workbowl in the microwave oven:

1 Remove the Steel Knife (or appropriate disc) before you place the bowl in the oven. You can reinsert the Steel Knife and continue processing after the bowl has been removed from the oven. Be very careful when handling the Steel Knife; grasp it by the handle, never by the blade.
2 Check your manufacturer's manual to make sure that your food processor workbowl is dishwasher-safe. If it isn't, don't put it in the microwave oven; transfer the food to an appropriate-size glass casserole or dish.

# Microwave oven techniques

Microwave techniques do not require any special cookware or oven accessories. But they do require you to know these facts about your oven:

1 *Oven watts* All the recipes were developed and tested in 650-700w microwave ovens. If you have an older model oven, it may be only 400-600w. If it is 400-500w, you will have to increase the recipe cooking times by about 35 per cent. If it is 500-600w you will have to increase cooking times by about 20 per cent.

2 *Power settings* For maximum speed advantage, the recipes are cooked at High, or full power, whenever possible. Lower power settings are used to cook some foods, such as large pieces of meat, more evenly and to prevent delicate ingredients, such as cheese or eggs, from overcooking. The lowest power setting is always used for yeast doughs left to rise in the microwave oven.

The power settings in this book are designated High; 70% (Medium High); 50% (Medium); 30% (Medium Low); and 10% (Low). High indicates 100% power. Check your manufacturer's manual to see which settings correspond to the other power percentages.

If your oven only has one setting, High or full power, you can still prepare the recipes in this book. But you will have to adjust both cooking and standing times. When cooling times are short, reduce them according to the power percentage designated. If the recipe specifies 50% (Medium) for 10 minutes, for example, you could microwave at High for 5 minutes and let the food stand 5 minutes. For longer cooking times, you should alternate cooking and standing times until the food is done. If the recipe specifies 50% (Medium) for 30 minutes, for example, you could microwave at High for 10 minutes, let stand for 10 minutes, and then microwave in 5 minute intervals and let stand until done. Be very cautious with delicate sauces; these should be stirred at least twice as often as specified in the recipe if you are cooking them at High. If you do not have variable-power settings, do not attempt to let yeast dough rise in the oven; you are likely to kill the yeast if you subject it to High power.

Here are explanations of the microwave terms used in the book:

## Glass casseroles and glass baking dish

The recipes specify glass casseroles ranging in capacity from 1-4 litres (1¾–7pt) and a 30 × 20cm (12 × 8in) glass baking dish. These utensils are all you need to prepare most of the recipes. The glass must be heatproof; you can substitute ceramic dishes that do not have a metal trim or a metallic glaze. (Do not place any metal utensil in the microwave oven unless it is specially designed for microwave use.) If you don't have the size specified, you can use a larger dish. However, the food may cook faster when it is spread in a larger container, so check to see if it is done a few minutes before the time specified.

An important point to remember when buying dishes for microwave use is that you can cook and serve foods in the same containers. So you may decide it is worth while to invest in the most attractive microwave-safe casseroles and dishes.

Be careful when removing all dishes from the microwave oven. Although not heated by microwaves, the dishes will hold heat transferred from the food, so use oven gloves.

## Glass measuring jugs

A set of heatproof glass measuring jugs is extremely useful for microwave cooking. These allow you to measure, cook and conveniently stir ingredients in a single utensil. Other containers, including heatproof glass or ceramic mugs and casseroles, can be substituted in the microwave oven, but you will have to use additional measuring utensils.

## Other cooking utensils

Whenever foods, such as an appetiser or a pastry, can be heated and served on the same plate, the recipe will specify a glass plate, but any heatproof (not necessarily ovenproof) ceramic dish, without metal trim, can be used.

Some meat and poultry recipes specify a microwave meat rack or a clay pot. A heatproof plate inverted in a suitable baking dish can be substituted for the meat rack; be sure to remove the plate when you take the meat out of the oven, because a vacuum can form as the dish cools. Substitutions for the clay pot are indicated in tips following the recipes.

Several recipes specify size of cooking dishes; other dishes can be substituted, but you should check timing carefully if using a dish with a larger capacity or surface area, as the food will cook slightly faster. A few recipes specify cups or a quiche dish. Small, heatproof ceramic bowls, without metal trim, usually can be substituted for the cups; a suitable pie dish can be used instead of the quiche dish. In both types of recipes, however, the presentation will be best if you use the container specified. Substitutions for specially designed plastic microwave cake tins are given, whenever possible, in tips following the recipe.

## Arranging food in the cooking dish

Always arrange foods for microwave cooking so that thicker pieces or parts are positioned towards the

13

outside of the dish. Because food placed around the edge of a dish cooks more quickly than the food in the centre, thick and thin parts of chicken or meat, for example, will cook in the same amount of time if arranged as directed. When appropriate, recipes will direct you to fold under thin ends of meat or fish fillets to ensure that they are cooked evenly all over.

### Covered or uncovered

Every recipe specifies whether dishes should be covered before placing them in the microwave oven or left uncovered. The various dish coverings are:

*Covered* When the dish used is a casserole, the directions will just say 'covered,' without any other description. You can use the appropriate casserole lid or clingfilm. If you use clingfilm, cover the dish tightly, but leave one corner open to allow some steam to escape. By doing so you can avoid any build up of steam that might cause a burn when the clingfilm is removed.

*Covered with clingfilm* For oblong baking dishes, the food processor workbowl, and other containers that don't usually come with a tight-fitting lid, clingfilm is specified when a tight cover is needed. Be sure to leave a vent in one corner of the clingfilm to avoid possible steam burns.

*Covered with greaseproof paper* When it is desirable to hold heat near the surface of the food but not to trap too much moisture, the recipe will specify that a dish be covered with greaseproof paper. Lay a sheet loosely over the dish.

*Covered with kitchen paper* Occasionally, kitchen paper is laid over foods to absorb excess moisture or fat. Sandwiches, breads and other baked foods can be wrapped in kitchen paper rather than placed in a dish for microwave cooking; the paper helps to keep the food crisp.

### Arrangement of dishes

When appropriate, the recipes will tell you how to place dishes in the microwave oven. This direction applies when you are microwaving more than one dish at a time; it will tell you to arrange the dishes in a circle or in a triangular pattern. These patterns speed microwave cooking by ensuring that microwaves can reach foods from all directions at the same time. You should rearrange the dishes, in the same pattern, during the cooking time to compensate for any unevenness of microwave distribution in the oven. Arrange foods cooked without dishes, such as potatoes, similarly, but place smaller items in the centre of the circle or triangle.

### Microwave power settings

The recipes will direct you to microwave at a specific power setting. Except for High, which is always full power, the settings are given in two ways. The percentage of power, such as 50% or 70%, will be followed, in parentheses, by the most frequently used label for that power level, such as Medium or Medium High. Please note that the power level settings on your oven may not correspond to the same percentages of power. It is quite possible, for example, that 50% power corresponds to the Low, Simmer, Slo-Cook or Defrost setting on your oven, rather than to Medium. So be sure that the power setting you choose corresponds to the percentage specified in the recipe.

The microwave industry hopes to standardise power settings within the next five years; the settings indicated in parentheses in the recipes correspond to those proposed by the industry. For ovens made up until now, however, the power percentages are the only completely accurate guide.

You will notice that some microwave dishes begin cooking at one power setting and are finished at another. It is not necessary to remove the dish from the oven when you change the power setting, unless the food needs to be stirred or rearranged.

### Microwave times

Most recipes give a range of cooking times or an approximate cooking time, along with a way to tell if the food is done. Because of differences in ovens and amount of electrical power delivered to an area at various times of the day, cooking times cannot be absolutely specific. Start checking to see if food is cooked at the end of the minimum amount of time given; continue cooking as necessary.

It is important to take into account your own oven and tastes. If you have a very fast, 700w, oven, or if you like vegetables very crisp, you should start checking to see if food is cooked about a minute before the time given; you can always cook longer, but you cannot retrieve overcooked delicate foods, such as fish, eggs, sauces or vegetables. Recipes do not specify microwave times for boiling water or melting butter. Times for these procedures will differ according to quantity and temperature and are best judged just by looking at the water or butter.

Remember that there is no substitute for a reliable meat thermometer when you are roasting whole meat or poultry. The only way to be sure that meat is cooked the way you prefer is to test it with a thermometer. Never leave a conventional thermometer in the microwave oven. Use a special microwave meat thermometer, or remove the meat to check if it is cooked with a conventional meat thermometer.

### Stirring

Food near the sides and top of the dish will begin cooking, due to friction generated by microwaves, almost as soon as the oven is turned on; the rest of the food in the dish will cook only as fast as the microwave-generated heat is conducted inward. Therefore, stirring is important in microwave cooking, both to speed up the cooking process and to ensure food is cooked evenly. Always stir from the outside of the dish inward, with a circular motion. Use a wire whisk to stir sauces thoroughly. Other foods can be stirred effectively with a plastic or wooden spoon, a wooden spatula, or a rubber spatula. You can leave a non-metallic stirrer in the dish for short periods of microwave time.

*Rotating dishes*

Virtually every microwave oven cooks somewhat unevenly. Foods heat faster in the oven's 'hot spots' and slower in other areas of the oven. All recipes that aren't stirred should be rotated at least once during cooking to ensure even cooking especially if the oven does not have a turntable.

*Protection*

When you are microwaving large, unevenly shaped pieces of meat or poultry, or baking in a rectangular dish, the thinnest parts, or corners, can become overcooked before the rest of the food is done. To avoid this problem, a few recipes will tell you to protect the thinnest parts with small pieces of aluminium foil before the total cooking time is completed. The foil will prevent further cooking, since microwaves cannot penetrate the metal, but it must not touch the sides or any other part of the oven interior.

*Standing time*

Dense foods and large quantities of food will continue cooking in their own heat after they have been removed from the microwave oven. The internal temperature of meats and poultry will rise 5–10°C (10–20°F) during standing. Baked foods will dry to desirable texture. Therefore, many recipes specify a standing time. This amount of time is considered a critical cooking step and is included in the total preparation time. Recipes for meats and other dense foods often will tell you to let the food stand covered with aluminium foil (it doesn't matter which side of the foil faces the food). Recipes for baked foods will sometimes tell you to let the food stand directly on the worktop, rather than on a rack. Both these directions are designed to maximise heat and moisture retention, so that the centre of the food will be cooked evenly during the standing time.

## Recipes

The best way to master all the techniques in this book is to start cooking. If, after reading the above guidelines, you still feel uncertain of your skills, begin with recipes that will succeed even if you make a few mistakes. A dip, for example, will taste good even if the ingredients are overcooked or overprocessed a little. If you are new to food processor slicing, practise with a soup or stew recipe—nobody will notice a few uneven slices. Similarly, you can test the timing on your microwave oven with a soup or stew; if the food is completely cooked in the minimum amount of time or not quite done in the maximum amount of time, you'll know that your oven is faster or slower than average. You can then use that information to adjust timing on foods where precision is more important, such as fish, vegetables, or sauces. If you keep on cooking, you'll soon lose any uncertainty you have about using the food processor and microwave oven. In fact, you'll begin to wonder how you ever cooked without them.

# Shopping and Serving Shortcuts

The food processor and microwave oven provide incomparable shopping, serving, and storage flexibility. So the following guide to ingredients, preparation times and storage possibilities is designed not only to answer questions about the recipes but also to maximise their convenience in your kitchen.

## Shopping for ingredients

Freshness is the key to flavour in all the recipes. Use of the food processor and microwave oven makes it easy to enjoy the taste of fresh ingredients and save the expense of processed foods. But that's no reason to go out to eat if you don't have all the ingredients specified in the recipe! Nor is it any reason to pay a high price for one ingredient when a suitable alternative is on sale in the supermarket. The alphabetised 'shopping list' can help you to make appropriate substitutions as well as to choose ingredients that will produce the most pleasing results. You'll find more detailed directions for ingredient substitutions in the tips following the recipes.

### Stock cubes and stock

Most of the recipes call for chicken- and beef-flavour stock cubes and water when stock is required. The only reason the recipes specify stock cubes is that most cooks have them available. If you have homemade stock in the refrigerator or freezer, by all means use it—the flavour will be better.

### Bread, breadcrumbs and croûtons

Although bread is a routine purchase, it's worth remembering to buy an extra loaf. Use it to make supplies of Breadcrumbs and Croûtons (see Index). You can make dried, plain or seasoned breadcrumbs and croûtons from any kind of bread and store them for months. Unless a recipe specifies otherwise, you can use either homemade or commercial breadcrumbs.

### Browning and seasoning sauce

Many foods cook too quickly to brown in the microwave oven. So browning and seasoning sauce is called for in a few recipes where deeper colour is desirable for attractive presentation. The sauce can be omitted, or you can substitute other ingredients that would add colour, such as Worcestershire sauce, soy sauce or paprika.

Browning is very rarely needed in the recipes, but you can always choose to brown meat or poultry conventionally in a skillet or under the grill and finish cooking recipes in the microwave oven; you'll still save some time and the food will remain more moist than if completed conventionally.

### Butter and margarine

The recipes were developed and tested with unsalted butter. Margarine can be substituted in almost all cases. If you use salted butter or margarine, taste foods, especially sauces, before adding salt. For the best-tasting butter and seasoned butters, see the Index for Food processor butter and variations. The homemade butter can be stored as commercial butter is, in the refrigerator or freezer.

### Cheese

The world of firm cheeses is wide open to substitutions. In a trice, you can always exchange one cheese for another; Cheddar, Gruyère, Cheshire, mozzarella and Edam all fall into this category. Do exercise caution, though, when substituting more assertively flavoured cheeses—they will smell much stronger when melted! You may find it convenient to shred a whole block of cheese at one time and keep it refrigerated in a tightly covered container.

When Parmesan cheese is specified in a recipe, use whichever kind you prefer. The best grade of Parmesan imported from Italy is stamped Parmigiano Reggiano on the rind; it has a marvellous, slightly nutty flavour. Other imported Parmesan, called *grana*, may come from either Italy or Argentina. The important thing to remember about imported Parmesan is that it can be too hard to process effectively if cold; so bring it to room temperature. (Never attempt to process any food that you cannot pierce with the tip of a knife.) By contrast, some brands of domestic Parmesan are so soft that they cannot be processed to grated texture at room temperature; so be sure that soft Parmesan is well chilled. Do not substitute Romano or another hard cheese for Parmesan unless you are sure you want a much stronger, and often harsher, flavour.

Do not attempt to substitute any cheese for ricotta; when ricotta is specified, its consistency is essential to the recipe.

*Cream*

If cream is to be whipped, you must use whipping cream. When cream is used for flavour, you can substitute single cream or even whole milk, if necessary. But always use the type of cream specified in dessert and confectionery recipes for proper consistency. Food processor whipped cream will be dense and have less volume than cream whipped with a mixer or a whisk, but it doesn't make any difference in the recipes. Cream will whip faster if the food processor workbowl and Steel Knife are chilled, so you may wish to place these in the refrigerator or freezer before processing. However, be careful not to process cream to the point of butter—unless you intend to!

*Eggs*

The recipes were developed and tested with large eggs. If you wish to substitute medium eggs in recipes where volume of eggs is important, such as cakes and soufflés, use 3 medium eggs for every 2 eggs specified in the recipe; if only 1 egg is specified, you can just substitute directly.

*Fish and seafood*

Since the market supply of fresh fish varies almost daily, possible substitutions are specified in virtually every fish recipe. An exception is made for trout, since farm-raised trout usually are available. You can always substitute an equal weight of fish steaks for fillets and vice versa, using the type of fish specified. It's a good idea to choose thick, evenly shaped fillets, since these will microwave more evenly and are less likely to overcook.

You can substitute frozen fish for fresh. The taste and texture will be inferior to those of good-quality fresh fish, but they may be better than those of poor-quality fresh fish. These signs of quality apply to all fish, whether fresh or frozen, whole or filleted: there should not be any strong, fishy odour, and no part of the fish should look dried-out or discoloured. Do not buy any fresh fish and do not use any frozen fish that doesn't meet these standards. Defrost frozen fish by microwaving it according to the manufacturer's manual. Do not overdefrost; the fish should still be cold and firm. Rinse off the last remaining ice crystals under cold running water, if necessary. All fish should be rinsed and patted dry with kitchen paper before cooking.

The question of fresh versus frozen is almost irrelevant to shrimps. Almost all the shrimps sold as fresh have been frozen at some point. So look for the best value, according to the size of the shrimp, before you pay more for fresh. Microwave frozen shrimps to defrost them, according to the manufacturer's manual; do not overdefrost. Shrimps cook so fast, whether in the microwave oven or conventionally, that you have to be very careful not to overcook. It's wise to start checking to see if they are cooked after 1 minute for each 450g (1lb) shrimps; you can always microwave them another minute or two, but you cannot save toughened, overcooked shrimps.

*Flour*

Use plain flour in recipes unless the recipe specifies wholewheat. You don't ever have to sift, but you do need to measure accurately.

*Fruit*

Because fresh fruit is one of the changing pleasures of the seasons, recipes suggest substitutions for all types except citrus fruit and avocados. Avocado can be omitted when used as a garnish. Since most avocados are sold at less than peak ripeness, you should purchase them a few days before you plan to use them; avocados will ripen at room temperature and should be used quickly or refrigerated once they are ripe. Lemons can be substituted for limes, if necessary. To get maximum juice from any $\frac{1}{2} \times 5ml$ tsp ($\frac{1}{2}$tsp) citrus fruit, microwave the fruit at High 15 seconds before cutting. When recipes specify tart cooking apples, you can use other types and reduce any sugar in the recipe to taste; for apple sauce or fruit cobbler, a combination of several kinds of apples will yield optimum flavour.

The food processor allows two easy tricks with fruit. First, you can purée any type of fresh or thawed, frozen berries or peaches to make an instant fruit sauce for ice cream, plain cake, or sliced, fresh fruit; add sugar to taste and a teaspoon or two of a fruit liqueur, if you wish. Puréed raspberries are delicious with peach or strawberry ice cream.

Second, you can keep a supply of shredded or grated fresh coconut on hand, if you wish. Puncture eyes of coconut with a screwdriver; drain milk and discard. Microwave coconut at High 5 minutes; crack coconut open with a hammer. Remove brown skin from coconut and cut into pieces to fit feed tube for shredding or small chunks for grating. Shred with Shredding Disc for long shreds appropriate for toppings and garnishes; or, with machine running (Steel Knife), drop chunks through feed tube to grate. Coconut can be frozen in a tightly covered container up to 3 months.

*Herbs and spices*

Fresh herbs can always be substituted for the dried herbs specified in the recipes; use twice the amount

or more, to taste, and process with the parsley, garlic, or another ingredient chopped in the recipe. Substitute 3–4 sprigs fresh dill for $1 \times 5ml$ tsp (1tsp) dried dillweed and 3–4 fresh basil leaves for $1 \times 5ml$ tsp (1tsp) dried. Food processor chopping power might encourage you to cultivate basil and other fresh herbs on a sunny windowsill if you don't have a garden; the fresh herbs will reward you with incomparable flavour.

Fresh herbs that are widely available, including parsley, dill and coriander are specified in the recipes. Dried can be substituted, if necessary. You can chop a quantity of any fresh herb and keep it refrigerated or frozen in a tightly covered container. Substitute about $\frac{1}{2} \times 5ml$ tsp ($\frac{1}{2}$tsp) chopped fresh herb for each sprig specified in a recipe. Substitute half the quantity of dried for fresh herbs.

Don't substitute dried, powdered ginger for root ginger; omit the latter if not available. There's no need to peel slices of root ginger before processing. To refrigerate longer than a week, place it in a jar, add dry sherry to cover, and cover the jar tightly.

There shouldn't be any need to substitute powdered dried garlic for whole cloves, but if there is, substitute $\frac{1}{2} \times 5ml$ tsp ($\frac{1}{2}$tsp) powder for each clove. You can chop a quantity of garlic, place it in a jar, add olive or vegetable oil to cover, and store it tightly covered at room temperature. Substitute $\frac{1}{2} \times 5ml$ tsp ($\frac{1}{2}$tsp) drained chopped garlic for each whole clove specified in a recipe.

*Mayonnaise*
Unless a recipe specifies otherwise, you can use either commercial or homemade mayonnaise (see Index for Food processor mayonnaise and variations) in the recipes. The homemade product tastes infinitely better and can be refrigerated, tightly covered, up to 10 days.

*Meats*
Take advantage of special offers in supermarkets to build greatest economy into the recipes. You can buy beef pot roasts or steaks and freeze them. Then partially defrost, according to microwave manufacturer's manual, and cut them as needed into 2.5cm (1in) pieces to chop in the food processor for meat loaf, hamburgers or meatballs; larger cubes for stew; or strips for beef casseroles. It is easier to cut up meat by hand if the meat is partially frozen; it is essential that raw meat be partially frozen for food processor slicing. Cuts of chuck beef and sirloin can be used interchangeably in chopped beef and stew-type recipes. Chuck is fattier and therefore more tender; sirloin has the best flavour. For chopped beef, the fat content should be about 10 per cent.

When flank steak or a certain type of beef for roasting is specified, do not make substitutions. These cuts have certain flavours and textures that are important to the success of the recipe.

Any cut of boneless pork can be used in recipes that require boneless pork. Large cuts of both pork

18

and ham can be frozen and cut up as needed for food processor chopping and casseroles, so you may want to stock up at supermarket sales.

If you find it more convenient to cut up meat or chop it prior to freezing, you can do so. But the larger the piece of meat, the longer it can be kept frozen.

### Mushrooms

Look for fresh, unblemished white or brown mushrooms with tightly closed caps. Don't soak fresh mushrooms; clean them with damp kitchen paper or rinse them quickly and dry thoroughly. If you must, you can substitute drained tinned mushrooms in recipes that call for chopped texture.

When a recipe calls for dried mushrooms, it is because these contribute a deeper, more woody flavour than fresh mushrooms. Fresh mushrooms can be substituted but the taste won't be the same.

You can use imported Chinese or European dried mushrooms interchangeably, except in Chinese-style recipes, where you will want the unique flavour of dried Chinese black mushrooms. Soak dried mushrooms before using as directed in the recipes.

### Mustard

Many recipes specify Dijon mustard because a little of this type of mustard can go a long way when a tangy highlight is desired. You can substitute other mustards, but you should adjust the amount according to the strength of the mustard you are using; Dijon is stronger than bright yellow, salad-style mustard but milder than most German-style mustards. You might want to substitute one of the flavoured mustards available, such as tarragon or white wine.

### Nuts

Since the food processor takes the effort out of chopping nuts, you can buy nuts in the most economical form available, whether whole or in pieces. When sliced almonds are specified in a recipe, you can chop whole almonds and use them instead. Purchase hazelnuts blanched for maximum convenience. To toast nuts, spread them in a glass baking dish and microwave uncovered at High 2–3 minutes, rotating the dish every minute.

### Onions

One of the most important seasoning ingredients, onions are also one of the most diverse. They vary enormously in flavour and flavouring potency. There are fresh spring onions and leeks; pearl onions for mildness and small, appealing size; large Spanish onions for mild, sweet taste; and red onions for sweetest, least assertive taste. Common yellow-skinned onions can be substituted for all but the pearl onions; you can substitute a quarter of a small yellow onion for a spring onion that will be chopped. Spring onions used for garnish can be omitted. Six spring onions can be substituted for 1 medium leek.

If the recipe doesn't specify the type of onion, any dried onion can be used; if the onion is very strong and tear-provoking, you may wish to reduce the quantity.

The food processor can give you instant access to this fresh-tasting seasoning mix for tossed green salads: process (Steel Knife) 1 spring onion and top, cut into 2.5cm (1in) pieces, with 4 sprigs parsley until minced; sprinkle over salad greens before tossing with dressing. If you have 2 fresh basil leaves or 2 sprigs of fresh dill, you may wish to process them with the onion and parsley—the fragrance is wonderful!

### Oriental cooking ingredients

You'll find soy sauce, sesame oil, rice wine vinegar, bean sprouts and mangetout peas in a large supermarket or a good delicatessen. You can use any type of soy sauce sold in the supermarket in the recipes; choose a light or medium, rather than dark, soy sauce if you're shopping in a delicatessen. Sesame oil has a very distinctive, nutty flavour; vegetable oil can be substituted. Rice wine vinegar has about half the acidity of other vinegars, so substitute lemon juice.

Fresh bean sprouts and mangetout peas taste much better than tinned or frozen products, but the latter can be substituted in cooked dishes. Drain tinned bean sprouts and refresh them in iced water for at least 10 minutes. Rinse frozen mangetout peas under cold running water to separate them and proceed with the recipe; do not attempt to slice them if they have been frozen.

### Poultry

An equal weight of chicken breasts, thighs or drumsticks can be substituted for a cut-up chicken, and vice versa, in any recipe. Whole and boneless chicken breasts can be used interchangeably unless the boneless breast has to be cut into strips. You can easily bone a chicken breast by inserting the tip of a boning knife through the membrane around the breastbone, cutting the large breastbone from the meat, and inserting your fingers under the small rib bones to release them. So buy chicken according to the best price or your taste and convenience. Cut-up chicken or portions can be frozen, securely wrapped, up to 1 month. Freeze boneless chicken breasts individually wrapped, so that you can easily remove as many as you want. Be very careful to wash all surfaces and utensils that come into contact with raw chicken, as there is the possibility of salmonella contamination.

When you want boneless cooked chicken for salads, casseroles and sandwiches, microwave chicken portions and remove the meat from the bones. Arrange chicken in a glass baking dish with meatier portions towards the outside of the dish; microwave covered with clingfilm at High until juices run clear when chicken is pierced with a fork, 7–9 minutes per 450g (1lb). 450g (1lb) of mixed chicken portions will produce about 150g (6oz) of cooked meat; a 450g (1lb) chicken breast will produce about 300g (12oz) of cooked meat.

Cooked turkey breast offers an economical alternative to cooked boneless chicken in salads and casseroles. To microwave turkey breast, see the Index for Turkey breast with honey-mustard sauce. Turkey breast and duckling can be purchased fresh or frozen; defrost according to manufacturer's manual. To microwave duckling, see the Index for Roast duckling with sweet and sour cabbage. If you microwave duckling for use in your own recipes and then grill the duckling conventionally about 10 minutes, you can enjoy the best of both worlds— fast, moist cooking and crisp, tantalising skin.

### Rice

Long-grain and brown rice can be used interchangeably in the recipes. Microwave whichever kind you want to use as directed in recipes for Rice and seasoned variations or Sherried brown rice with mushrooms and pork (see Index); then proceed with any recipe that calls for cooked rice. The microwave oven does not offer much saved time over conventional rice cookery, but it does save washing-up time.

### Tomatoes

Some recipes display an odd ambivalence towards tomatoes. When full, ripe tomato flavour is needed, the recipe will specify tinned tomatoes; a tip at the end of the recipe will give the amount of fresh tomatoes that can be substituted when they are ripe and full-flavoured. Ideally, all tomatoes used should be fresh and ripe, but it is difficult to find good tomatoes all the year round; so the tinned tomatoes make year-round, flavoursome tomato sauces possible. Fresh tomatoes are specified when texture is as important as taste. You can ripen tomatoes at room temperature, stem ends down, away from direct sunlight—but you cannot instil fullest flavour. When good-quality fresh tomatoes are abundant, you might want to chop and freeze a supply for sauces. Microwave tomatoes at High just long enough to loosen skins, about 15 seconds for each tomato. Let tomatoes stand 1 minute; then peel and core. Cut tomatoes into eighths; process (Steel Knife) just until chopped. Freeze tomatoes in a tightly covered container.

### Vegetable oils

Although some recipes specify olive or nut oils, you can always substitute your favourite kind of vegetable oil. Olive oil can be delightfully light and fruity or heavy and overwhelming, depending on its source and how long it has been standing around. Don't use a heavy, intensely flavoured olive oil full strength; mix it with plain vegetable oil. Fragrant nut oils, such as walnut or sesame, are used only for flavouring, not for all-purpose cooking; so they are almost always combined with vegetable oil in recipes.

### Vegetables

Pick whatever vegetables look freshest and best— and most enticingly priced—in the market. Then check the Index for appropriate recipes. It's wiser to shop this way than to select an expensive or less-than-fresh vegetable just because it fits a specific recipe. If you don't find a suitable recipe, you can always microwave the vegetable, either whole or sliced, and serve it with a sauce from this book or seasoned butter. You will find dozens of sauces that can be made in minutes, including such favourites as Hollandaise and Butter sauce. Microwave green and yellow vegetables covered at High until crisp-tender, about 5–6 minutes per 450g (1lb).

If you wish to serve frozen vegetables, you can microwave them in the packet; cut 1 or 2 slits in the box or bag and microwave at High about 5 minutes. For further information see the Defrosting chart on page 23. Among the few frozen vegetables specified is chopped spinach, which can provide convenience without sacrifice of flavour when used in a sauce. Remember to remove paper wrapping from boxes of frozen vegetables to prevent the printing ink from staining the bottom of the oven.

### Vinegars

Few ingredients can highlight seasonings as easily and effectively as vinegar. Keep several varieties on hand, including red wine, tarragon, white wine, distilled white, and cider vinegars. You can substitute one for another in the recipes, but flavour will be better if you use the type specified.

If you would like to make your own herb vinegars, microwave white or red wine vinegar in a glass measure, uncovered, just until boiling. Pour the vinegar over chopped fresh herbs in a jar; cover tightly and let stand at least 10 days. Use 1 × 15ml tbsp (1tbsp) herbs for each cup of vinegar, or more to taste.

### Wine

When a recipe calls for dry white wine, you can use any appropriate type, such as Chablis or Chardonnay, a French white Bordeaux or Muscadet, or an

Italian Soave. Remember that the flavour of the wine will come through in the finished dish; so don't use a wine that you wouldn't enjoy drinking.

*Yeast*

Recipes for yeast breads call for active dry yeast. Check the date on the packet before you use the yeast to make sure it isn't too old to be effective. Proving yeast enables you to tell if it is still active. Dissolve the yeast in warm liquid (43°C, 110°F)—never hot or cold—as directed in the recipe. If the mixture doesn't begin to foam in about 5 minutes, throw it out and start again with fresh yeast.

## Preparation time

The *Total Preparation Time* listed with each recipe has been calculated as honestly as possible, with time allowances made for measuring ingredients, peeling vegetables, cutting up meat, making the sauce or the pastry, and anything else that might be required. The *Total Preparation Time* indicates how many minutes will be needed from the time you take out the ingredients until the dish is ready to be served.

There are many ways to schedule preparation time so that the cooking can be done at your convenience. First, you can prepare almost any recipe to the point of final cooking or heating up to 1 day in advance and refrigerate it; because the food will be chilled, it may require additional minutes to heat through before serving. Second, you can accomplish part of the preparations, such as cooking the chicken or making the sauce, as long as 1 day ahead of time; then refrigerate the food and finish preparations before serving. (Any food that needs to be marinated or chilled can be prepared up to that step and refrigerated overnight.) And third, you can complete most dishes that don't involve micro-waving eggs or mayonnaise as long as 1 day in advance, refrigerate them, and reheat just before serving. You will find more detailed directions, when appropriate, in the tips following the recipes. Leftovers can be refrigerated and reheated in the cooking dish.

Soups, poultry entrées, meat casseroles and bread freeze well. As with all frozen foods, it is important that the freezer be maintained at no higher than −15°C (5°F), and preferably lower, for prolonged storage. If you wish to freeze foods for longer than 1 month, be sure that the packaging is airtight. Rigid plastic containers, freezer bags, freezer paper and heavy-duty aluminium foil are suitable packaging materials. You can store leftovers' TV-dinner style, in paper or metal trays or on paper plates; cover the trays or plates securely with aluminium foil. It's often convenient to freeze soups, stews and cas-seroles in casserole dishes lined with heavy-duty

aluminium foil. Once the food is frozen, remove it from the casserole, cover it with another sheet of foil, and put it back in the freezer. When you want to defrost and reheat it, the food can be unwrapped and fitted neatly into the casserole dish. Defrost foods in the microwave oven according to the manufac-turer's manual or the Defrosting chart on page 23.

## Microwave time

The *Microwave Time* that accompanies each recipe will allow you to tell at a glance whether it is possible to prepare more than one recipe within a certain time framework. You cannot save much time by microwaving more than one recipe at a time, since cooking time increases according to the volume of food in the oven.

If you want to prepare a dinner menu of a poultry entrée, a rice dish and a vegetable, for example, you might find that the recipes would require a total of about an hour of microwave time. So you couldn't possibly serve them together in less than an hour. You might then decide to change your menu plans or analyse the recipes for shortcuts.

You could cook the rice conventionally while the entrée was in the microwave oven. You could then let the entrée stand, covered with aluminium foil, while you microwaved the vegetable. Your total cooking time would be significantly reduced. You could also coordinate the recipes so that some ingredients for the rice dish could be cooking in the microwave oven while you were preparing entrée vegetable ingredients in the food processor. Or you might conclude that the microwave time for all these dishes would not impose on your schedule, since you could use that time for other jobs.

The microwave time is the 'bottom line' for each recipe. Total preparation time cannot be streamlined further than that, but you can use the microwave time to do other things, since the food will not require much attention.

Standing time is another factor to consider when you're scheduling microwave time. Many recipes finish cooking outside the microwave oven in 5 or 10 minutes of standing time. Often, it is convenient to microwave a vegetable or a dessert while the entrée is standing.

Remember that all foods can be slightly under-cooked and reheated in the microwave oven without reduction of quality. Therefore, you can microwave several dishes consecutively and reheat any of them that need it just before serving.

## Halving and doubling recipes

Most recipes serve 4–6 persons. You can cut the amount in half by cutting ingredient quantities in half; using a smaller casserole dish, if appropriate; and microwaving the food, as directed in the recipe, for about three-quarters of the recommended time. When cooking half-recipes of fish, vegetables or sauces, start checking to see if the dish is cooked after half the recommended microwave time has elapsed.

10–12 servings are about the maximum quantity of most foods that you can microwave efficiently. It is usually more time-efficient to cook larger quantities conventionally. To double recipes, double the amounts of ingredients and use a suitably larger cooking dish. Microwave as directed in the recipe, increasing the time by three-quarters. Be sure to keep stirring or rotating the dish throughout the cooking time. When preparing double quantities of ingredients in the food processor, be careful not to overload the workbowl. Check the manufacturer's manual for maximum quantities that can be processed with the Steel Knife. When using the Slicing or Shredding Disc, don't let food accumulate in the bowl to the point where it is pressing against the disc. Process only single batches of batters and doughs.

## The economy of convenience

The food processor and microwave oven can change the meaning of leftovers by giving them new identities. If you think about all the ways you can quickly transform the texture and taste of leftovers with the food processor and microwave oven—by chopping, puréeing, slicing, shredding, combining in a salad, melting, reheating or adding a sauce, just to name a few possibilities—you'll begin to recognise the potential for economy that is built into the appliances. The two stalks of broccoli, accumulated cheese scraps and boring chunks of ham that seem to take up almost permanent residence in many refrigerators need not be discarded. You'll find ways to use these foods, for example, in Three-vegetable terrine, French-style vegetable purée, Continuous cheese dip, and Ham salad rolls. Look at other recipes and you'll discover enough patterns of ingredient combinations and cooking procedures to ensure new life for virtually every single leftover.

# Defrosting chart

| FOOD | QUANTITY | APPROX TIME ON LOW SETTING | SPECIAL INSTRUCTIONS | APPROX STANDING TIME |
|---|---|---|---|---|
| **Fish/Seafood** | | | | |
| Crabmeat | 225g (8oz) | 3–5 min | turn into covered dish | 3–5 min |
| Salmon steaks | 4 × 150g (6oz) | 10–12 min | place in covered dish with thicker parts towards outside of dish | 5 min |
| Scallops | 225g (8oz) | 6–7 min | turn into covered dish; | 3–4 min |
| | 450g (1lb) | 9–10 min | stir during defrosting | 5–6 min |
| Shrimps | 450g (1lb) | 6–8 min | turn into covered dish; stir during defrosting | use as soon as possible |
| White fish fillets or steaks | 450g (1lb) | 6–8 min | place in covered dish with thicker parts towards outside of dish | 5 min |
| **Meat** | | | | |
| Bacon slices | 225g (8oz) pack | 2–3 min | slit pack; turn over during defrosting | 5 min |
| Beef, joints | per 450g (1lb) | 7–9 min | turn over during defrosting | 60 min |
| minced | per 450g (1lb) | 7–10 min | place in covered dish; break up with fork during defrosting | 5 min |
| cubed steak | per 450g (1lb) | 6–8 min | place in covered dish; stir during defrosting | 5 min |
| grilling steak | per 225g (8oz) | 4–5 min | place on covered dish | 5–10 min |
| Lamb/veal, joints | per 450g (1lb) | 6–8 min | turn over during defrosting | 45–60 min |
| chops | 2 × 100g–125g (4oz–5oz) | 4–5 min | place on covered plate; turn over during defrosting | 5 min |
| Liver, slices | per 450g (1lb) | 8–9 min | place in covered dish; separate during defrosting | 5 min |
| Pork, joints | per 450g (1lb) | 8–9 min | turn over during defrosting | 60 min |
| chops | 4 × 150g–175g (6oz–7oz) | 8–10 min | place on covered plate; turn over during defrosting | 10 min |
| Sausagemeat | per 450g (1lb) | 5–7 min | break up during defrosting | 10 min |
| **Poultry** | | | | |
| Chicken, whole | per 450g (1lb) | 6–7 min | place in covered dish; turn over during defrosting and remove giblets after defrosting | 30–40 min |
| portions | per 450g (1lb) | 7–8 min | place thicker parts towards outside of dish; cover | 15 min |
| livers | 225g (8oz) | 6–8 min | place in covered dish; separate during defrosting | use as soon as possible |
| Duckling | per 450g (1lb) | 6–8 min | place in covered dish; turn over during defrosting and remove giblets after defrosting | 30–40 min |
| **Miscellaneous** | | | | |
| Bread | large loaf | 6–8 min | unwrap; place on absorbent kitchen paper | 10–15 min |
| | small loaf | 4–6 min | | 10 min |
| 1 slice | 25g (1oz) | 10–15 sec | place on absorbent kitchen paper; DO NOT OVERHEAT | 1–2 min |
| pita | 4 | 2–3 min | place on absorbent kitchen paper; turn over during defrosting | 1–2 min |
| Butter, margarine | 225g (8oz) | 1½–2 min | remove foil wrapping; place on plate or in dish | 5 min |

| FOOD | QUANTITY | APPROX TIME ON LOW SETTING | SPECIAL INSTRUCTIONS | APPROX STANDING TIME |
|------|----------|---------------------------|---------------------|---------------------|
| Cranberries | 450g (1lb) | 6–7 min | place in covered dish; stir during defrosting | 5 min |
| Cream cheese | 75g (3oz) | 1–1½ min | remove foil wrapping; place on plate | 10–15 min |
| Fruit juice concentrate | 178ml (7fl oz) | 2–3 min | remove lid | 3–5 min |
| Puff pastry | 1 × 370g (14oz) pack | 2 min | leave in wrapping | 10 min |
| Rice, cooked (thaw/reheat) | 450g (1lb) cooked weight | 7–8 min on HIGH | turn into covered dish; stir with a fork during defrosting | 1–2 min |
| Scones | 4 | 1½–2½ min | place on absorbent kitchen paper | 1–2 min |
| Stock | 550ml (1pt) | 5–6 min on HIGH | place frozen block in bowl or jug; break down during defrosting | use as required |

# Appetisers

## Hot devilled eggs

Total Preparation Time: 12–13 min
Microwave Time: 2–3 min
Serves: 12

*Heat processed devilled eggs quickly to make them taste even creamier. All ingredients can be kept on hand for an impromptu appetiser, but these shrimp-topped eggs also can add interest to a lunch of cold meats and a salad.*

1 shallot or ¼ small onion, peeled
6 hard-boiled eggs, shelled, cut lengthwise into
　halves
50ml (2fl oz) mayonnaise or salad dressing
2 × 15ml tbsp (2tbsp) sour cream
½ × 5ml tsp (½tsp) Dijon mustard
pinch of dried dillweed
pinch of salt
1 × 15ml tbsp (1tbsp) drained capers
12 small cooked shrimps
fresh dill or parsley sprigs (optional)

With machine running (Steel Knife), drop shallot through feed tube; process until minced. Add egg yolks, mayonnaise, sour cream, mustard, dillweed and salt to bowl; process using on/off technique until smooth. Add capers to bowl; process using on/off technique until blended. Fill egg whites with yolk mixture; top eggs with shrimps. Place eggs around edge of 25cm (10in) glass quiche dish or pie dish. Microwave uncovered at 50% (Medium) just until warm, 2–3 minutes. Garnish with fresh parsley sprigs.

*Tips*
1 Microwave devilled eggs just until heated through; overcooking can make the yolks rubbery.
2 Do not attempt to boil eggs in the microwave oven; the build up of steam in the shell can cause an explosion. To hard-boil eggs conventionally, cover them with water and bring to a full boil. Remove from heat and let stand, covered, 10 minutes. Place eggs under cold running water to prevent further cooking and to make shelling easier.
3 If capers are very salty, place them in a strainer and rinse well under cold water.

4 Frozen or tinned salad shrimps may be used; rinse tinned shrimps and drain well. Substitute small pieces of smoked salmon for the shrimps, if you wish.

## Shrimp japonaise

Total Preparation Time: 10–10½ min
Microwave Time: 4½–5½ min
Serves: 6

*Simple to make, yet an extremely elegant appetiser—a delightful combination of delicate flavours and textures.*

450g (1lb) medium to large peeled, deveined,
　uncooked shrimps
1 egg yolk, room temperature
2 × 5ml tsp (2tsp) lemon juice
1 × 5ml tsp (1tsp) Dijon mustard
1 × 5ml tsp (1tsp) rice wine vinegar
pinch of salt
pinch of white pepper
50ml (2fl oz) vegetable oil
1 × 15ml tbsp (1tbsp) sesame oil
2 × 5ml tsp (2tsp) soy sauce

Arrange shrimps in single layer in baking dish; microwave covered at High until shrimps are pink, 4–5 minutes, stirring after 2 minutes. Drain well. Arrange on serving plate. Process (Steel Knife) egg yolk, lemon juice, mustard, vinegar, salt and pepper until smooth. With machine running, gradually add oils through feed tube, processing until very thick; add soy sauce through feed tube, processing until blended. Spoon dollop of sauce on each shrimp; microwave uncovered at 70% (Medium High) to heat sauce, 20–30 seconds (watch carefully as sauce can melt easily). Serve immediately.

*Tips*
1 Rice wine vinegar, sesame oil and soy sauce can be found in the Oriental sections of large supermarkets or in most delicatessens.
2 Because the mayonnaise-type sauce for the shrimps is made with only one egg yolk, you can process it more efficiently by tilting the food processor forward slightly. Use a book to prop up

25

the back of the machine. The sauce may be prepared in advance and refrigerated, covered, for up to 1 week.

3 Leave tails on shrimps, if desired, for most attractive serving. Shrimps may be cooked ahead of time and refrigerated. Heat shrimps with sauce on serving dish.

4 For a vegetable first course, substitute 450g (1lb) asparagus for the shrimps. Arrange asparagus in a spoke pattern, with tips in centre, on a glass plate; sprinkle with $2 \times 15ml$ tbsp (2tbsp) water. Microwave asparagus covered with clingfilm at High until crisp-tender, 5–6 minutes.

## Aubergine dip with pita triangles

Total Preparation Time: 14–17 min
(plus chilling time)
Microwave Time: 8–10 min
Makes: about 400ml (16fl oz)

*Prepared and cooked in the food processor bowl, this Aubergine dip is not only delicious but also incredibly convenient.*

8 sprigs parsley
2 cloves garlic, peeled
1 medium aubergine (about 450g [1lb]), pared cut
   into 2.5cm (1in) pieces
50ml (2fl oz) water
$1 \times 5ml$ (1tsp) fennel seeds, crushed (optional)
$1 \times 5ml$ tsp (1tsp) lemon juice
50ml (2fl oz) mayonnaise or salad dressing
50ml (2fl oz) sour cream
pita breads, cut into triangles

Process (Steel Knife) parsley using on/off technique until minced. With machine running, drop garlic through feed tube; process using on/off technique until minced. Add aubergine to bowl; process using on/off technique until finely chopped. Remove Steel Knife; add water to bowl. Microwave aubergine mixture and water in food processor bowl, covered with clingfilm, at High until aubergine is very tender, 5–7 minutes, stirring after 3 minutes; do not drain. Microwave fennel seeds on plate, uncovered, at High until toasted, about 3 minutes, stirring after $1\frac{1}{2}$ minutes.

Insert Steel Knife. Add fennel seeds, lemon juice, mayonnaise and sour cream to bowl; process until smooth. Spoon dip into serving bowl; refrigerate covered until chilled, about $1\frac{1}{2}$ hours. Serve with pita triangles for dipping.

*Tips*
1 Use a rubber scraper to push aubergine mixture away from the centre of the bowl when reinserting Steel Knife. Make sure that the Steel Knife is firmly in place.

2 To heat pita bread triangles, place them in a basket or serving dish lined with cloth or paper napkins and microwave on High just until warm, about 30 seconds. Be careful not to overheat or the bread will dry out and toughen.

## Hot beef and cheese dip

Total Preparation Time: 22–3 min
Microwave Time: 8–9 min
Makes: about 600ml ($1\frac{1}{4}$pt)

*There are plenty of practical reasons to serve this hot, substantial dip—as a warm welcome on a cold evening, an appetite-appeaser at cocktail parties, or a convenient after-theatre snack. Or simply enjoy the taste after a long day or on a lazy Sunday afternoon!*

2 carrots, peeled, cut to fit feed tube horizontally
1 medium courgette, cut to fit feed tube horizontally
100g (4oz) walnuts
1 small clove garlic, peeled
1 small onion, peeled, cut into quarters
65g ($2\frac{1}{2}$oz) cooked beef, sliced
50g (2oz) cheese, cut into 2.5cm (1in) cubes
75g (3oz) cream cheese, cut into 2.5cm (1in) cubes
225m (8fl oz) sour cream
50ml (2fl oz) mayonnaise or salad dressing
$\frac{1}{2} \times 5ml$ tsp ($\frac{1}{2}$tsp) Worcestershire sauce
pinch of dried chervil
$\frac{1}{2} \times 5ml$ tsp ($\frac{1}{2}$tsp) prepared horseradish
breadsticks/gristicks

Slice (Slicing Disc) carrots and courgette, positioning vegetables in feed tube horizontally; reserve both. Microwave walnuts on a plate, uncovered, at High until toasted, 3–4 minutes, stirring after 2 minutes. With machine running (Steel Knife), drop garlic through feed tube, processing until minced. Add onion to bowl; process until coarsely chopped. Add walnuts, beef and cheese to bowl; process until coarsely chopped. Add cream cheese, sour cream, mayonnaise, Worcestershire sauce, chervil and horseradish to bowl; process using on/off technique until blended. Transfer mixture to $1\frac{1}{2}$litre ($2\frac{1}{2}$pt) glass casserole. Microwave uncovered at 70% (Medium High) until hot through, about 5 minutes, stirring after 3 minutes. Serve dip hot with carrots, courgette and breadsticks for dipping.

*Tips*
1 Serve Hot beef and cheese dip as a fondue, if you wish. Transfer the dip to a fondue pot and serve it with cubes of French bread for dipping.
2 For buffet-style serving, microwave the dip in an attractive, heatproof bowl and place the bowl on a warming tray. Dip can be processed up to 1 day in advance; refrigerate covered and microwave just before serving.

# Liver pâté with cognac

Total Preparation Time: 18–20 min
(plus chilling time)
Microwave Time: 8–10 min
Makes: ½ litre (¾ pt)

*The food processor has made pâtés extremely popular by eliminating all the tedious chopping and grinding that used to be required. The microwave oven gets rid of the messy task of sautéing or simmering livers on top of the cooker as well. So few appetisers are easier to prepare than this elegant, subtly seasoned pâté.*

450g (1lb) chicken livers, cleaned, cut into halves
50ml (2floz) water
2 large sprigs parsley
¼ medium onion, peeled, cut into 2.5cm (1in) pieces
2 × 15ml tbsp (2tbsp) cognac or brandy
100g (4oz) butter or margarine, softened
pinch of salt
pinch of ground mixed spice
pinch of ground mace
pinch of ground ginger
Garlic-herb toast (optional; see Index)

Microwave livers and water in 1½ litre (2½ pt) casserole, covered, at High until livers lose pink colour, 8–10 minutes, stirring after 5 minutes. Drain. Process (Steel Knife) parsley using on/off technique until minced. Add onion to bowl; process using on/off technique until coarsely chopped. Add livers, cognac, 25g (1oz) of the butter, the salt, mixed spice, mace and ginger; process until smooth, adding 75g (3oz) butter, 15g (½ oz) at a time, through feed tube while machine is running. Spoon liver mixture into serving dish; refrigerate until ready to serve. Make Garlic-herb toast; serve with pâté.

*Tips*

1 Liver pâté with cognac can be prepared up to 4 days in advance and refrigerated covered; bring to room temperature before serving for spreading ease.
2 For smoothest texture, you can microwave the livers, process (Steel Knife) them with the parsley and onion until smooth, and then press the mixture through a fine sieve. Return the mixture to the food processor workbowl and proceed with the recipe. To soften butter, microwave at High just until softened, but not melted.

## Mixed nut pâté

Total Preparation Time: 22–6 min
Microwave Time: 7–8 min
Serves: 12

*A pâté without meat but with all the deep, rich flavour of ground walnuts and almonds bound with yogurt and wholewheat bread.*

3 large sprigs parsley
2 shallots or ½ small onion, peeled, cut into 2.5cm (1in) pieces
225g (8oz) shelled walnuts
25g (1oz) blanched almonds
4 slices wholewheat bread, torn into pieces
3 medium tomatoes, seeded, cut into 2.5cm (1in) pieces
2 eggs
2 × 15ml tbsp (2tbsp) plain yogurt
1 × 15ml tbsp (1tbsp) light brown sugar
pinch of salt
pinch of dried thyme
pinch of paprika
pinch of white pepper
150g (5.3oz) carton plain yogurt
½ × 5ml tsp (½tsp) dried dillweed

Process (Steel Knife) parsley using on/off technique until minced. With machine running, add shallots through feed tube, processing until minced. Add nuts and bread to bowl; process using on/off technique until very finely chopped. Add remaining ingredients except carton of yogurt and the dillweed to the bowl; process using on/off technique until throroughly mixed.

Spoon mixture into greased plastic ring mould. Microwave uncovered at High until set, 7–8 minutes, rotating mould ¼ turn every 2 minutes. Let stand on worktop, loosely covered, 5 minutes. Unmould onto serving plate. Serve warm or at room temperature; spoon yogurt over pâté and sprinkle with dillweed.

*Tips*

1 For a toasted nut flavour, microwave walnuts and almonds in glass pie dish, uncovered, at High 2 minutes. Stir to redistribute nuts; microwave at High until lightly toasted, 1–2 minutes. Cool and process as above.

2 A 1¼ litre (3pt) glass casserole, with a glass placed open end up in the centre, can be substituted for the plastic ring mould.

3 Mixed nut pâté can be prepared up to 3 days in advance. Unmould and refrigerate tightly covered with clingfilm; bring to room temperature and top with yogurt and dill before serving. This pâté makes excellent picnic fare. Carry it in the mould, with a separate container of yogurt and dill. Unmould before serving and spoon yogurt over.

## Three-vegetable terrine

Total Preparation Time: 65–72 min
Microwave Time: 30–7 min
Serves: 8

*Each slice of this beautiful terrine displays a tricolour of broccoli, cauliflower and carrots. French-inspired and fashionably light, the terrine is simpler and sturdier than it appears. Serve individual portions warm as a first course, framed by Fresh tomato or Butter sauce (see Index) or slice the whole terrine to set out on a buffet table at room temperature with sauce on the side.*

25g (1oz) Parmesan cheese, cut into 2.5cm (1in) pieces
50g (2oz) Cheddar cheese, chilled, cut to fit feed tube
225g (8oz) broccoli, cut to fit feed tube
225g (8oz) cauliflower, cut to fit feed tube
225g (8oz) carrots, cut to fit feed tube
6 × 15ml tbsp (6tbsp) water
115g (4½oz) butter or margarine
3 × 5ml tsp (3tsp) lemon juice
3 eggs
3 egg yolks
pinch of ground mace
¾ × 5ml tsp (¾tsp) white pepper
pinch of ground nutmeg
watercress or parsley sprigs

Process (Steel Knife) Parmesan cheese until finely grated. Shred (Shredding Disc) Cheddar cheese. Reserve cheeses. Slice (Slicing Disc) broccoli, cauliflower and carrots separately. Place each vegetable in small glass bowl; add 2 × 15ml tbsp (2tbsp) water to each and arrange in oven in triangular pattern. Microwave vegetables covered with clingfilm at High until very tender, 10–12 minutes; drain.

Process (Steel Knife) broccoli, 40g (1½oz) of the butter, the Cheddar cheese, 1 × 5ml tsp (1tsp) of the lemon juice, 1 egg, 1 egg yolk, the mace and ¼ × 5ml tsp (¼tsp) of the pepper until smooth; spread in bottom of ungreased 1 litre (1¾pt) glass loaf dish. Process (Steel Knife) cauliflower, 40g (1½oz) of the butter, the Parmesan cheese, 1 × 5ml tsp (1tsp) of the lemon juice, 1 egg, 1 egg yolk, the nutmeg and ¼ × 5ml tsp (¼tsp) of the pepper until smooth; spread over broccoli mixture. Process (Steel Knife) carrots, 40g (1½oz) butter, 1 × 5ml tsp (1tsp) lemon juice, 1 egg, 1 egg yolk and ¼ × 5ml tsp (¼tsp) pepper until smooth; spread over cauliflower mixture.

Place loaf dish in 30 × 20cm (12 × 8in) baking dish; fill baking dish with 1.25cm (½in) warm water. Microwave covered with clingfilm at 50% (Medium) until bottom of terrine appears set, 20–5 minutes. Let stand covered on worktop 10 minutes. Loosen edges of terrine with knife; unmould onto serving plate. Garnish with watercress or parsley sprigs.

*Tip*

Terrine can be made 1 day in advance. To reheat individual portions, place one slice on serving plate and microwave covered with greaseproof paper at 50% (Medium) until warm, 1½–2 minutes. Terrine can also be served cold.

## Hot cranberry punch

Total Preparation Time: 35–7 min
Microwave Time: 25–7 min
Serves: 12

*A delicious change of pace from ordinary cocktails and delightfully festive for the Christmas season. Keep a jugful on hand and reheat or serve cold. Add vodka or whisky, according to guests' preferences, at serving time.*

300g (12oz) fresh cranberries
1½ litres (2½pt) water
1 cinnamon stick
6 whole cloves
2 oranges, peeled, cut into quarters
1 lemon, peeled, cut into quarters
1 lime, peeled, cut into quarters
150–225g (6–8oz) sugar
freshly grated nutmeg

Process (Steel Knife) cranberries until very finely chopped. Microwave cranberries, water, cinnamon and cloves in 2 litre (3½pt) container, uncovered, at High until boiling, about 15 minutes. Strain through muslin or fine strainer; discard cranberries and spices. Process (Steel Knife) oranges, lemon and lime until all juice is extracted; strain and add juice to cranberry juice mixture. Discard pith and seeds. Stir in sugar according to taste and sweetness of fruit. Microwave uncovered at High until boiling, 10–12 minutes, stirring after 5 minutes. Serve hot in mugs or Irish coffee glasses; sprinkle with nutmeg.

*Tips*

1 Frozen cranberries can be used in this recipe. Microwave in 2 litre (3½pt) container at defrost setting until thawed, about 5 minutes. Proceed with recipe as above.
2 A dash of whisky or vodka can be stirred into each mug.
3 Hot cranberry punch is also delicious cold. Cool to room temperature; refrigerate until chilled. Serve over ice.

## Three-cheese quiche
Total Preparation Time: 33–4 min
Microwave Time: 19–20 min
Serves: 6

*A fluffy quiche without a crust starts a meal on a lighter note and doubles as a lunch or brunch entreé.*

6 slices bacon
1 medium onion, peeled, cut into 2.5cm (1in) pieces
2 spring onions and tops, cut into 2.5cm (1in) pieces
1–2 × 15ml tbsp (1–2tbsp) dry breadcrumbs
100g (4oz) Cheddar cheese, chilled, cut to fit feed tube
2 × 15ml tbsp (2tbsp) flour
25g (1oz) Parmesan cheese, cut into 2.5cm (1in) pieces
225g (8oz) cottage cheese
150ml ($\frac{1}{4}$pt) milk or single cream
3 eggs
pinch of ground nutmeg
salt and pepper

Microwave bacon in glass baking dish, covered with kitchen paper, at High until crisp, about 6 minutes, rotating dish $\frac{1}{4}$ turn after 3 minutes. Crumble bacon; drain all but 1 × 15ml tbsp (1tbsp) of the fat.

Process (Steel Knife) onions using on/off technique until chopped. Microwave onions in 1 × 15ml tbsp (1tbsp) fat in glass baking dish, uncovered, at High until tender, about 3 minutes.

Lightly grease 22.5cm (9in) glass quiche dish; coat with breadcrumbs. Shred (Shredding Disc) Cheddar cheese; sprinkle in bottom of quiche dish. Sprinkle with onion mixture, flour and bacon.

With machine running (Steel Knife), drop Parmesan cheese through feed tube; process until finely grated. Add remaining ingredients to bowl; process until smooth. Pour filling into quiche dish. Microwave uncovered at High until almost set, 10–11 minutes, rotating dish $\frac{1}{4}$ turn every 2 minutes; raise quiche dish on an inverted saucer after 8 minutes. Let stand uncovered on worktop 5 minutes. Cut into wedges to serve.

*Tip*
Raising the quiche dish on an inverted saucer or microwave meat rack for the last few minutes of cooking time will ensure that the centre cooks evenly.

## Hot buttered toddies
Total Preparation Time: 8–9 min
Microwave Time: 5–6 min
Serves: 8

*A deliciously warming drink to serve on a cold evening, either at a party or simply when relaxing in front of the TV. Prepare the ice cream mixture in advance for those unexpected guests!*

225ml (8fl oz) vanilla ice cream
100g (4oz) butter or margarine
125g (5oz) light brown sugar
50ml (2fl oz) honey
pinch of ground nutmeg
pinch of ground cloves
water, orange juice, pineapple juice or apple cider
dark rum, whisky or brandy
8 cinnamon sticks (optional)

Microwave ice cream in glass bowl, uncovered, at 10% (Low) until just softened, about 30 seconds. Microwave butter in glass bowl at High, uncovered, until softened. Process (Steel Knife) ice cream, butter, brown sugar, honey, nutmeg and cloves until blended. Store in covered container in freezer.

Fill mug with 150ml (6fl oz) water or desired juice; add 2 × 5ml tbsp (2tbsp) ice cream mixture. Microwave uncovered at High until water is boiling, about 2 minutes (about 5 minutes for 4 mugs). Stir 25ml (1fl oz) desired liquor into each mug; serve with cinnamon sticks for stirring.

# Soups

## Courgette soup

Total Preparation Time: 20–2 min
Microwave Time: 11–13 min
Serves: 4

*A lovely, light starter for a dinner party, as well as an easy, nutritious soup for everyday meals. You can adapt this recipe for all seasons by substituting other vegetables for courgettes.*

450g (1lb) courgettes, cut to fit feed tube
½ medium onion, peeled, cut to fit feed tube
225ml (8fl oz) chicken stock
2 × 15ml tbsp (2tbsp) Twice-as-fast sauce mix (see Index)
100ml (4fl oz) whipping cream
1 × 15ml tbsp (1tbsp) lemon juice
pinch of mixed spice
pinch of white pepper
1 × 15ml tbsp (1tbsp) port wine or 2 × 15ml tbsp (2tbsp) plum wine (optional)

Slice (Slicing Disc) courgettes and onion. Microwave courgettes, onion, stock and sauce mix in 1 litre (1¾pt) casserole, covered at High until courgettes are very tender, 5–7 minutes. Process (Steel Knife) mixture until smooth, about 2 minutes. Return mixture to casserole; stir in remaining ingredients. Microwave uncovered at 50% (Medium) until hot but not boiling, about 6 minutes.

*Tips*

1  Substitute 450g (1lb) of broccoli, asparagus or carrots for the courgettes and follow above directions. If soup is too thick, stir in equal amounts of water and cream. For broccoli or asparagus soup, you may wish to omit the wine and garnish each bowl with a thin slice of lemon; the juice can then be pressed into the soup to highlight the seasonings.

2  To prepare the soup in advance, microwave and purée the vegetable mixture. Refrigerate covered up to 2 days or freeze covered up to 2 months. Microwave frozen purée, covered, at 50% (Medium) until thawed, and proceed with recipe.

3  Garnish soup, if desired, according to the vegetable you use. Some suggestions: A thin ring of red pepper for Courgette soup; a sprig of fresh dill or parsley for carrot soup. You may wish to reserve a few uncooked slices of the vegetable you are using (or asparagus tips or broccoli florets) to garnish individual servings. If you wish, microwave slices in glass baking dish with 1 × 15ml tbsp (1tbsp) water, covered, at High until crisp-tender, 1–2 minutes.

## Hot gazpacho

Total Preparation Time: 20–4 min
Microwave Time: 12–14 min
Serves: 4

*A hot version of Spanish gazpacho enlivens winter tables with vegetable-garden flavour and a bright assortment of garnishes.*

2 carrots, peeled, cut into 1.25cm (½in) pieces
1 stick celery, cut into 1.25cm (½in) pieces
25g (1oz) fresh spinach leaves, stems discarded
¼ medium green pepper, seeded, cut into 2.5cm (1in) pieces
50ml (2fl oz) water
1 green pepper, seeded, cut into 2·5cm (1in) pieces
1 small onion peeled, cut into 2.5cm (1in) pieces
1 hard-boiled egg, cut into quarters
1 small avocado, peeled, cut into 2.5cm (1in) pieces
1 litre (1¾pt) tomato juice
2 × 5ml tsp (2tsp) Worcestershire sauce
½ × 5ml tsp (½tsp) dried chives
pinch of dried tarragon
pinch of cayenne pepper
a few drops of Tabasco

Microwave carrots, celery, spinach, ¼ green pepper and the water in 2 litre (3½pt) casserole, covered, at High until very tender, 6–8 minutes, stirring after 4 minutes.

Process (Steel Knife) 1 green pepper, the onion, egg and avocado separately, using on/off technique, until coarsely chopped. Place in small bowls; refrigerate.

Process (Steel Knife) carrot mixture, 300ml (12fl oz) of the tomato juice, the Worcestershire sauce, chives, tarragon, cayenne pepper and Tabasco until smooth, 30–60 seconds. Mix carrot mixture and remaining tomato juice in 1½ litre (2½pt) casserole. Microwave covered at High until very hot, about 6 minutes, stirring after 3 minutes. Serve in shallow bowls with selection of chopped vegetables and egg.

*Tips*

1 Hot gazpacho may be served in mugs, as a cocktail, without garnishes; stir a dash of vodka into each serving if desired. It makes an attractive starter for a cold-weather lunch.
2 Garlic or Herb croûtons (see Index) go well with Hot gazpacho.

## French onion soup

Total Preparation Time: 52–6 min
Microwave Time: 44–5 min
Serves: 4

*Microwave onions long enough to bring out fullest flavour in this classic soup and you still save hours of conventional preparation time. Serve as a starter for a French-style supper with a salad and an omelette or sliced cold meats to follow.*

Parmesan croûtons (see Index)
50g (2oz) Cheddar cheese, chilled, cut to fit feed tube
1kg (2lb) Spanish onions, peeled, cut to fit feed tube
2 cloves garlic, peeled
50g (2oz) butter or margarine
1 × 5ml tsp (1tsp) sugar
2 × 15ml tbsp (2tbsp) flour
¾ litre (1¼pt) beef stock
2 × 15ml tbsp (2tbsp) Worcestershire sauce
pinch of dried marjoram
pinch of dried thyme
50ml (2fl oz) dry sherry (optional)

Make Parmesan croûtons. Shred (Shredding Disc) cheese; reserve. Slice (Slicing Disc) onions and garlic. Microwave butter in 3 litre (5pt) casserole at High until melted. Stir in onions, garlic and sugar; microwave covered with clingfilm at High 20 minutes, stirring every 5 minutes. Stir in flour; microwave uncovered 2 minutes. Stir in stock, Worcestershire sauce, marjoram and thyme. Microwave covered at High 15 minutes. Stir in sherry; spoon soup into bowls. Sprinkle with croûtons; sprinkle with reserved cheese. Microwave uncovered at High until cheese is melted, about 45 seconds. Serve immediately.

*Tip*

French onion soup can be prepared 2 days in advance up to the addition of the sherry; refrigerate covered.

*Chicken with Curry Sauce (page 43); Coriander Rice (page 66); Fruit Salad with Pineapple-cream Dressing (page 83)*

# Chicken and vegetable chowder

Total Preparation Time: 40–4 min
Microwave Time: 26–30 min
Serves: 8

*Whipped cream gives a glorious, satiny chowder. Reduce the number of servings and enjoy it as a main course if you wish.*

675g (1½lb) boneless chicken breasts, skinned, cut into 2.5cm (1in) pieces
1 litre (1¾pt) stock
4 peppercorns
3 whole cloves
½ × 5ml tsp (½tsp) dried marjoram leaves
1 bay leaf
2 sprigs of parsley
1 clove garlic, peeled
1 medium onion, peeled, cut to fit feed tube
1 medium green pepper, seeded, cut to fit feed tube
2 carrots, peeled, cut to fit feed tube
2 medium courgettes, cut to fit feed tube
1 stick celery, cut to fit feed tube
4 × 15ml tbsp (4tbsp) Twice-as-fast sauce mix (see Index)
salt
pepper
225ml (8fl oz) whipping cream

Microwave chicken, stock, peppercorns, cloves, marjoram, bay leaf and parsley in 3 litre (5pt) glass casserole, covered, at High until chicken loses pink colour and is tender, 10–12 minutes. Remove chicken with slotted spoon; strain broth, discarding spices and herbs.

With machine running (Steel Knife), drop garlic through feed tube, processing until minced. Slice (Slicing Disc) onion, green pepper, carrots, courgettes and celery. Add to broth; microwave, covered, at High until tender, about 10 minutes. Stir in sauce mix; microwave uncovered at High until thickened, 4–5 minutes, stirring every 2 minutes.

Stir chicken back into broth; microwave, uncovered, at High until hot through, 2–3 minutes. Season to taste with salt and pepper. Process (Steel Knife) cream until thick; stir into soup just before serving.

*Tips*
1 Chowder can be prepared up to 2 days in advance; stir in whipped cream just before serving.
2 To slice green pepper easily, slit the cored, seeded pepper lengthwise down one side; roll up and place in feed tube, inserting from bottom of tube if necessary.

*Sloppy Joes (page 91); Hot and Cold Roquefort Salad (page 79); Wholewheat Cupcakes (page 110)*

# Double mushroom soup

Total Preparation Time: 34–8 min
Microwave Time: 14–18 min
Serves: 4

*Imported dried mushrooms deepen the flavour of fresh mushrooms just enough to add a note of intrigue to a favourite light soup.*

½ litre (1pt) water
25g (1oz) Chinese or European dried mushrooms
100g (4oz) fresh mushrooms
4 spring onions and tops, cut to fit feed tube
25g (1oz) butter or margarine
300ml (12fl oz) chicken stock
1 × 15ml tbsp (1tbsp) Worcestershire sauce
½ × 5ml tsp (½tsp) salt
pepper

Microwave ½ litre (1pt) water in ½ litre (1pt) measure at High until boiling. Pour over dried mushrooms in medium bowl; let stand until mushrooms are softened, about 20 minutes. Drain and reserve liquid; discard any tough mushroom centres.

Slice (Slicing Disc) fresh mushrooms and onions. Microwave fresh mushrooms and onions in butter in 1½ litre (2½pt) casserole, covered, at High 2 minutes. Process (Steel Knife) dried mushrooms using on/off technique until coarsely chopped; add to casserole with reserved liquid and remaining ingredients. Microwave uncovered at High until boiling, 8–12 minutes.

*Tip*
Any kind of imported dried mushroom can be used in Double mushroom soup. Dried morels have an especially delicate flavour.

# Cheese and corn chowder

Total Preparation Time: 26–8 min
Microwave Time: 21–3 min
Serves: 6

*A satisfying, main-course soup, rich with sausage, cheese and the flavour of corn. Add a tossed green salad for a complete lunch or supper.*

Savoury croûtons (optional; see Index)
1 clove garlic, peeled
½ medium onion, peeled, cut into 2.5cm (1in) pieces
1 medium green pepper, cut into 2.5cm (1in) pieces
1 medium potato, peeled, cut into 2.5cm (1in) pieces
50g (2oz) butter or margarine
¾ litre (1¼pt) milk
½ chicken stock cube
4 × 15ml tbsp (4tbsp) Twice-as-fast sauce mix (see Index)
450g (1lb) fully cooked smoked sausage, cut into scant 1.25cm (½in) chunks
450g (1lb) sweetcorn, drained
450g (1lb) creamed sweetcorn
225g (8oz) Cheddar cheese, chilled, cut to fit feed tube
2 medium tomatoes, cut into 2.5cm (1in) pieces

Make Savoury croûtons using chilli powder.

With machine running (Steel Knife), drop garlic through feed tube; process until minced. Add onion, green pepper and potato to bowl; process using on/off technique until chopped. Microwave butter in 3 litre (5pt) bowl at High until melted. Stir in garlic, onion, green pepper and potato; microwave uncovered at High until tender, about 4–6 minutes. Stir milk and crumbled stock cube into vegetables. Microwave uncovered at High until boiling, 8–10 minutes. Stir in sauce mix; microwave uncovered until thickened, 2–4 minutes, stirring every minute. Stir in sausage and corn; microwave covered at High until hot through, about 4 minutes.

Shred (Shredding Disc) cheese; remove. Process (Steel Knife) tomatoes until coarsely chopped. Stir cheese and tomatoes into soup until cheese is melted. Microwave uncovered at 50% (Medium) 2 minutes. Serve soup in bowls with croûtons.

*Tip*
Cheese and corn chowder can be prepared up to 2 days in advance; refrigerate covered.

# Shrimp bisque

Total Preparation Time: 29–36 min
Microwave Time: 21–6 min
Serves: 6

*The classic refinement of a smooth, pale pink bisque, with a hint of curry for excitement and little work for the cook.*

Garlic croûtons (optional; see Index)
250g (10oz) peeled, deveined, uncooked shrimps
1 medium onion, peeled, cut into 2.5cm (1in) pieces
25g (1oz) butter or margarine
2 × 15ml tbsp (2tbsp) flour
2 × 15ml tbsp (2tbsp) tomato paste
½ litre (1pt) chicken stock
2 × 5ml tsp (2tsp) curry powder
pinch of paprika
pinch of cayenne pepper
225ml (8fl oz) whipping cream
1 medium tomato, seeded, cut into 2.5cm (1in) pieces

Make Garlic croûtons. Arrange shrimps in single layer in glass baking dish; microwave covered with clingfilm at High until shrimps turn pink, 2–3 minutes, stirring after 1 minute.

Process (Steel Knife) onion using on/off technique until finely chopped. Microwave onion and butter in 1½ litre (2½pt) casserole, covered, at High until onion is tender, about 5 minutes. Stir in flour and tomato paste; microwave uncovered at High 1 minute. Stir in chicken stock, curry, paprika and pepper. Microwave uncovered at High until thickened, 10–12 minutes, stirring with whisk every 3 minutes.

Process (Steel Knife) shrimps using on/off technique until minced. Stir shrimps and cream into mixture; microwave uncovered at High just until boiling, 4–5 minutes. Process (Steel Knife) tomato until coarsely chopped. Spoon soup into small bowls; sprinkle with tomato and croûtons.

*Tips*
1 Any size shrimps may be used. If you wish to use cooked shrimps, omit the microwaving step. Rinse frozen cooked shrimps to separate them; arrange in a single layer in a glass baking dish and microwave at defrost setting until thawed.
2 Shrimp bisque can be prepared to the point of final heating 1 day in advance; refrigerate covered.

# Fish and Seafood

## Sole fillets with spinach sauce
Total Preparation Time: 29–31 min
Microwave Time: 10–12 min
Serves: 6

*Juicy sole fillets coated with a delicious spinach sauce make this a rich and colourful dish.*

225g (8oz) block frozen spinach
100g (4oz) mozzarella cheese, chilled, cut to fit feed tube
50g (2oz) Parmesan cheese, cut into 2.5cm (1in) pieces
1 small clove garlic, peeled
1 large shallot or ¼ small onion, peeled
2 × 15ml tbsp (2tbsp) walnuts
75ml (3fl oz) sour cream
1 × 15ml tbsp (1tbsp) dried basil
pinch of dried marjoram
salt
pepper
675g (1½lb) sole or other white fish fillets
2 × 15ml tbsp (2tbsp) dry vermouth or white wine

Remove paper wrappers from spinach box; make 1 or 2 cuts in box. Microwave in box at High until thawed, about 4 minutes. Drain spinach very well, pressing to remove as much moisture as possible.

Shred (Shredding Disc) mozzarella cheese; reserve. With machine running (Steel Knife), drop Parmesan cheese through feed tube; process until finely grated. Drop garlic and shallot through feed tube; process until minced. Add walnuts to bowl; process using on/off technique until coarsely chopped. Add spinach, sour cream, basil, marjoram, salt and pepper to bowl; process using on/off technique until blended.

Arrange fish in single layer in 30 × 20cm (12 × 8in) baking dish, folding thin ends of fillets under; sprinkle with vermouth. Spoon spinach sauce over. Microwave covered with clingfilm at High until fish is tender and flakes with a fork, 6–8 minutes, rotating dish ¼ turn and sprinkling with reserved mozzarella after 3 minutes.

*Tip*
Be careful not to overcook, as the fish should remain firm. Microwave most fish no longer than 4–5 minutes per 450g (1lb) covered, at High.

## Trout with hazelnut stuffing baked in parchment
Total Preparation Time: 29–35 min
Microwave Time: 13–17 min
Serves: 4

*Parchment paper wrappers promote even cooking of whole fish and keep the stuffing in place. Fishermen can appreciate this fast, respectful treatment of any mild-flavoured freshwater catch.*

basic Croûtons and variations (see Index)
50g (2oz) blanched hazelnuts or almonds
1 stick celery, cut into 2.5cm (1in) pieces
1 carrot, peeled, cut into 2.5cm (1in) pieces
100–150ml (4–6fl oz) chicken stock
2–4 × 15ml tbsp (2–4tbsp) dry white wine
4 whole dressed trout (about 225g [8oz] each)
lemon wedges

Make croûtons, using variations with garlic and chervil. Process (Steel Knife) nuts, celery and carrot using on/off technique until coarsely chopped. Combine croûtons, nuts, celery and carrot in medium bowl; add chicken stock and wine; toss. Stuff cavities of fish. Wrap each fish in piece of parchment paper; seal by folding edges of paper and crimping. Place fish packets in baking dish; microwave uncovered at High until fish is tender and flakes with a fork, 8–10 minutes, rotating baking dish ¼ turn every 4 minutes. Serve fish in parchment paper; garnish with lemon wedges.

*Tips*
1 Make croûtons up to 4 weeks in advance; see recipe for storage directions.
2 Parchment paper can be found in large supermarkets and hardware shops. Wrap fish efficiently to fit them into the baking dish, but not too tightly. If parchment paper is not available, fish can be cooked in a baking dish tightly covered with clingfilm.
3 Whole or boneless trout can be used. Recipe can be cut in half; microwave fish 4–5 minutes. Or stuffing can be divided between two 450g (1lb) fish; microwave as above.

# Salmon steaks with avocado butter

Total Preparation Time: 29–30 min
(plus marinating time)
Microwave Time: 10–12 min
Serves: 6

*Tempt even those who claim not to like fish with this superb balance of vinaigrette-seasoned salmon and pale green Avocado butter.*

2 × 15ml tbsp (2tbsp) olive or vegetable oil
2 × 15ml tbsp (2tbsp) water
2 × 15ml tbsp (2tbsp) white wine vinegar
1 × 15ml tbsp (1tbsp) lemon juice
pinch of paprika
pinch of ground cumin
salt
pepper
6 salmon steaks, 1.25–2cm ($\frac{1}{2}$–$\frac{3}{4}$in) thick, about
    1.25kg (2$\frac{1}{2}$lb)
Avocado butter (recipe follows)
coriander or parsley springs

Mix oil, water, vinegar, lemon juice, paprika, cumin, salt and pepper in 30 × 20cm (12 × 8) baking dish. Place salmon in baking dish, turning over to coat with vinaigrette. Let stand 20 minutes.

Make Avocado butter.

Microwave salmon, covered with clingfilm, at High until fish is tender and flakes with a fork, 4–5 minutes per 450g (1lb), rotating baking dish $\frac{1}{4}$ turn after 4 minutes. Arrange salmon steaks on serving plate; garnish with coriander and serve with Avocado butter.

*Tip*
Coriander rice (see Index) would go well with Salmon steaks with avocado butter. Fresh coriander, or Chinese parsley, can be found in large supermarkets and some market stalls.

## Avocado butter

3 large sprigs parsley
$\frac{1}{2}$ clove garlic, peeled
100g (4oz) butter or margarine, softened
1 large ripe avocado, peeled, stoned, cut into 2.5cm
    (1in) pieces
2 × 5ml tsp (2tsp) lime juice
pinch of chilli powder
dash of cayenne pepper

Process (Steel Knife) parsley using on/off technique until minced. With machine running, drop garlic through feed tube; process until minced. Add remaining ingredients to bowl; process until smooth, about 30 seconds, scraping side of bowl with spatula if necessary.

*Tips*
1 Avocado butter can be made 2 days in advance; refrigerate in covered container. Salmon steaks can be cooked, refrigerated covered, and served cold with Avocado butter for lunch, or a summer supper.
2 Halibut steaks can be substituted for the salmon.

# Crab-stuffed fillets of sole

Total Preparation Time: 22–5 min
Microwave Time: 8–11 min
Serves: 4

*Bright green asparagus and pink-flecked crab rolled in moist, white fillets—a very attractive choice for lunch or dinner.*

225g (8oz) fresh asparagus
50ml (2fl oz) water
75g (3oz) crab meat
1 egg
1 × 15ml tbsp (1tbsp) plain yogurt
1 × 15ml tbsp (1tbsp) dry breadcrumbs
1 × 5ml tsp (1tsp) drained capers
1 × 5ml tsp (1tsp) prepared mustard
salt
pepper
4 sole fillets (about 450g [1lb])
50ml (2fl oz) dry white wine
25g (1oz) Parmesan-garlic butter (see Index) or
    melted butter

Reserve 8 × 5cm (2in) asparagus spears; cut remaining asparagus into 2.5cm (1in) pieces. Microwave asparagus spears and water in 1 litre (1$\frac{3}{4}$pt) casserole, covered, at High until asparagus is crisp-tender, 3–4 minutes; drain. Process (Steel Knife) cut asparagus, the crab meat, egg, yogurt, breadcrumbs, capers, mustard, salt and pepper using on/off technique until finely chopped.

Spread crab mixture on fillets; place 2 asparagus spears on each fillet and roll up, enclosing spears. Place rolled fillets seam sides down in 20cm (8in) square baking dish; add wine. Microwave covered with greaseproof paper at High until fish is tender and flakes with a fork, 5–7 minutes, rotating dish $\frac{1}{4}$ turn after 3 minutes.

Make Parmesan-garlic butter; spoon over fish.

*Tips*
1 Use good-quality frozen or fresh crab meat for best results; if you use tinned crab meat, rinse well with cold water, drain, and remove any bits of shell.
2 If capers are very salty, place them in a strainer and rinse well under cold water.
3 Other mild-flavoured fish fillets, such as haddock, flounder, or turbot, can be substituted.

## Shrimps with feta cheese

Total Preparation Time: 26–30 min
Microwave Time: 16–20 min
Serves: 4

*The flavours of seafood, ripe olives, tomatoes, herbs and feta cheese combine to recall sunny Greek islands.*

3 sprigs parsley
1 medium onion, peeled, cut into 2.5cm (1in) pieces
1 × 15ml tbsp (1tbsp) olive oil or vegetable oil
1 medium carrot, cut into 2.5cm (1in) pieces
50g (2oz) ripe olives, stoned
3 medium tomatoes, seeded, cut into 2.5cm (1in) pieces
2 × 15ml tbsp (2tbsp) dry white wine
1 × 15ml tbsp (1tbsp) tomato paste
½ × 5ml tsp (½tsp) dried oregano
pinch of dried marjoram
100g (4oz) feta cheese, crumbled
450g (1lb) shelled, deveined shrimps

Process (Steel Knife) parsley using on/off technique until minced; remove half the parsley and reserve. Add onion to bowl; process using on/off technique until finely chopped. Microwave onion mixture and oil in 1½ litre (2½pt) casserole, covered, at High until tender, about 3 minutes.

Process (Steel Knife) carrot, olives and tomatoes separately, using on/off technique, until chopped; stir vegetables into onion mixture. Stir in wine, tomato paste, oregano and marjoram; microwave covered at High until mixture boils and carrots are tender, 8–10 minutes, stirring after 4 minutes.

Reserve 2 × 15ml tbsp (2tbsp) of the cheese; stir remaining cheese into vegetable mixture; microwave uncovered until cheese is melted, about 2 minutes. Stir in shrimps, microwave uncovered at High until shrimps turn pink, 3–5 minutes, stirring after 4 minutes. Spoon into serving dish; sprinkle with reserved parsley and cheese.

*Tips*

1 If feta cheese is very salty, soak it in cold water and squeeze it dry in several layers of muslin or a tea-cloth. Imported feta cheese, available in large supermarkets and delicatessens, is usually made from ewe's milk; it is stronger than domestic feta, which is made out of cow's milk. Both kinds of feta are preserved in brine, resulting in varying degrees of saltiness.
2 Plan a large party menu of Shrimps with feta cheese, Greek meatball kebabs, and Pastitsio, with Baklava for dessert, if you wish (see Index). Serve the entrées together, either buffet-style or sit-down and add a mixed salad with an oregano-seasoned vinaigrette and plenty of crusty bread.

3 Half portions of Shrimps with feta cheese can be served as an appetiser with an entrée of grilled chicken or roast lamb.

## Red snapper creole

Total Preparation Time: 37–41 min
Microwave Time: 24–8 min
Serves: 6

*This recipe features a robust sauce with just a hint of cayenne. Serve with plain rice, Onion rice, or Pimento rice (see Index). Haddock or halibut can be substituted for red snapper.*

3 cloves garlic, peeled
½ × 5ml tsp (½tsp) paprika
pinch of cayenne pepper
675g (1½lb) red snapper fillets
2 spring onions and tops, cut into 2.5cm (1in) pieces
1 medium onion, peeled, cut into 2.5cm (1in) pieces
1 stick celery, cut into 2.5cm (1in) pieces
1 medium green pepper, seeded, cut into 2.5cm (1in) pieces
25g (1oz) butter or margarine
1 × 397g (14oz) tin tomatoes, drained, cut into quarters
2 × 15ml tbsp (2tbsp) tomato paste
2 × 15ml tbsp (1tbsp) sugar
1 bay leaf

With machine running (Steel Knife), drop 2 of the garlic cloves through feed tube, processing until minced. Mix minced garlic, paprika and cayenne pepper; rub on snapper fillets. Arrange fillets in 30 × 20cm (12 × 8in) baking dish, with thickest portions towards outside of dish and thin ends folded under.

With machine running (Steel Knife), drop remaining clove of garlic through feed tube, processing until minced. Add onions, celery and green pepper; process using on/off technique until chopped. Microwave vegetable mixture and butter in 1 litre (1¾pt) casserole, covered, at High until tender, 6–8 minutes, stirring after 3 minutes. Process (Steel Knife) tomatoes using on/off technique until coarsely chopped. Add tomatoes, tomato paste, sugar and bay leaf to vegetable mixture; microwave covered with greaseproof paper at High until thick, about 9 minutes, stirring after 4 minutes.

Microwave fish covered with greaseproof paper at High until fish is tender and flakes with a fork, 6–8 minutes, rotating dish ¼ turn after 3 minutes; drain. Spoon sauce over fish; microwave uncovered at High until hot through, about 3 minutes.

# Pickled trout

Total Preparation time: 28–32 min
(plus cooling time)
Microwave Time: 18–22 min
Serves: 4

*The whole pickled fish makes a marvellous addition to a party buffet. Half-size portions, served chilled with Food processor mayonnaise (see Index), are a superb way to start a meal.*

1 medium onion, peeled, cut to fit feed tube
1 stick celery, cut to fit feed tube
1 carrot, cut to fit feed tube
400ml (16 fl oz) dry white wine
350ml (14 fl oz) water
250ml (½pt) white tarragon vinegar
50g (2oz) sugar
25g (1oz) whole pickling spice
1 × 15ml tbsp (1 tbsp) drained capers
1 whole dressed trout (¾–1kg [1¾–2lb])
1 lemon, cut to fit feed tube
watercress or parsley sprigs

Slice (Slicing Disc) onion, celery and carrot. Microwave vegetables and remaining ingredients except trout, lemon and watercress in 30 × 20cm (12 × 8in) baking dish, uncovered, at High until simmering, about 8 minutes.

Wrap trout in muslin; place in wine mixture. Microwave covered with clingfilm at High until fish is tender and flakes with a fork, 10–14 minutes, turning fish over every 5 minutes.

Let fish cool in wine mixture about 1½ hours, turning fish occasionally. Remove from wine mixture; drain and remove muslin. Place on serving plate. Slice (Slicing Disc) lemon; garnish trout with lemon and watercress.

*Tips*
1 If stronger pickled flavour is desired, refrigerate fish in wine mixture several hours or overnight.
2 You can purchase whole dressed trout, with bones intact, or boneless trout with head and tail attached. For buffet serving remove the top skin and make 2.5cm (1in) cuts along the fish to indicate servings but leave fish intact. You may wish to sprinkle the fish with chopped parsley. An equal weight of smaller trout can be substituted for the single, large trout.

## Mediterranean fish stew

Total Preparation Time: 45–7 min
Microwave Time: 21–2 min
Serves: 6

*An aromatic, colourful stew that's delicious when made with any saltwater fish fillets and exceptionally attractive when enriched with mussels. Serve with French bread and a dry white wine.*

4 sprigs parsley
2 cloves garlic, peeled
1 medium onion, peeled, cut into 2.5cm (1in) pieces
½ medium green pepper, seeded, cut to fit feed tube
50g (2oz) ripe olives, stoned
2 × 15ml tbsp (2tbsp) olive juice
1 × 15ml tbsp (1tbsp) olive or vegetable oil
1 × 5ml tsp (1tsp) dried basil
½ × 5ml tsp (½tsp) mixed herbs
a few fennel seeds, crushed
100g (4oz) mushrooms
2 large tomatoes, cored, cut into 2.5cm (1in) pieces
250ml (8fl oz) tomato sauce
100ml (4fl oz) dry white wine
100ml (4fl oz) fish or chicken stock
50ml (2fl oz) orange juice
½ × 5ml tsp (½tsp) grated orange rind
2 bay leaves
salt      .
pepper
450g (1lb) white fish fillets, cut into 5cm (2in)
   pieces
8–12 mussels, cleaned (optional)

Process (Steel Knife) parsley using on/off technique until minced. With machine running, drop garlic through feed tube, processing until minced. Add onion to bowl. Process using on/off technique until chopped; remove. Slice (Slicing Disc) green pepper and olives. Microwave onion mixture, pepper, olives, olive juice, olive oil, basil, mixed herbs and fennel in 3 litre (5pt) casserole, covered, at High, 6 minutes.

Slice (Slicing Disc) mushrooms; remove. Process (Steel Knife) tomatoes using on/off technique until chopped. Stir mushrooms, tomatoes, tomato sauce, wine, stock orange juice, orange rind, bay leaves, salt and pepper into casserole. Microwave uncovered at High 10 minutes, stirring after 5 minutes.

Using a slotted spoon, remove about 8 spoonfuls vegetables from casserole. Process (Steel Knife) vegetables until smooth; stir back into stew. Add fish and mussels; microwave uncovered until fish is tender and flakes with a fork, about 5 minutes, stirring after 3 minutes. Serve in shallow bowls.

*Tips*

1 For even cooking, place thinner or smaller pieces of seafood in the centre of the casserole. Make sure seafood is covered by the sauce to prevent dryness.
2 To clean mussels, scrub them with a stiff brush if they are very sandy or rub them together to remove traces of sand. If beards are attached, scrub with a stiff brush to remove them. Let mussels stand in cold, salted water 10 minutes; rinse well in cold water. Discard any mussels that are broken or opened.

## Baked scallop layer

Total Preparation Time: 22–4 min
Microwave Time: 7–9 min
Serves: 4

*Microwaves make it easy to control timing, both when toasting buttered breadcrumbs and 'baking' scallops. So the textures of both ingredients remain delicate, resulting in a simple but pleasing combination. Serve half portions as an elegant first course.*

Garlic-herb breadcrumbs (see Index)
100g (4oz) cold butter or margarine, cut into pieces
450g (1lb) sea scallops, cut into halves
3 × 15ml tbsp (3tbsp) dry white wine

Make Garlic-herb breadcrumbs; add butter to bowl and process using on/off technique until mixed. Microwave crumb mixture in glass pie dish, uncovered, at High until crisp, 3–4 minutes, stirring after 2 minutes.

Microwave scallops and wine in a casserole, covered with greaseproof paper, at High 2 minutes; drain well. Spoon half the crumbs into 4 shell dishes; spoon scallops over crumbs and top with remaining crumbs. Microwave uncovered at High until scallops are tender, 2–3 minutes. Serve immediately.

*Tips*

1 To serve as a first course, divide crumbs and scallops among 8 ramekins. Microwave 4 at a time for 1½–2 minutes; bring the first 4 to the table while the remainder are cooking. Set each ramekin on a plate garnished with sprigs of parsley or dill and a lemon wedge, if desired.
2 Shelled, deveined shrimps can be substituted for the scallops; proceed as above, microwaving until shrimps turn pink, 2–3 minutes.

# Poultry

## Chicken provençale

Total Preparation Time: 45–8 min
Microwave Time: 32–5 min
Serves: 4

*Moist, juicy chicken in a herb-flavoured tomato sauce. Spinach rice (see Index) would turn it into a feast; plain or Parmesan rice could complete a family meal.*

1 medium onion, peeled, cut into 2.5cm (1in) pieces
2 × 15ml tbsp (2tbsp) olive or vegetable oil
8 medium tomatoes, seeded, cut into 2.5cm (1in) pieces
150g (6oz) tomato paste
2 × 5ml tsp (2tsp) sugar
½ × 5ml tsp (½tsp) dried basil
½ × 5ml tsp (½tsp) dried tarragon
pinch of dried oregano
pinch of ground nutmeg
salt
pepper
100g (4oz) mushrooms
10 olives, stoned
1 chicken, cut up (about 1.5kg [3lb])
browning and seasoning sauce
2 medium courgettes, cut to fit feed tube
1 medium green pepper, seeded, cut to fit feed tube

Process (Steel Knife) onion using on/off technique until coarsely chopped. Microwave onion and oil in 2 litre (3½pt) casserole, covered, at High until tender, about 3 minutes. Process (Steel Knife) tomatoes using on/off technique until chopped. Stir tomatoes, tomato paste, sugar, basil, tarragon, oregano, nutmeg, salt and pepper into onion. Microwave covered at High 8 minutes, stirring every 3 minutes. Slice (Slicing Disc) mushrooms and olives; stir into tomato sauce. Microwave uncovered at High 4 minutes.

Arrange chicken pieces skin sides down in 30 × 20cm (12 × 8in) baking dish, placing meatier pieces towards edges of dish. Microwave uncovered at High 7 minutes. Turn pieces over; brush lightly with browning sauce. Spoon tomato sauce over chicken. Microwave covered with clingfilm at High until chicken is done, 10–13 minutes, rotating dish ¼ turn after 7 minutes. Slice (Slicing Disc) courgettes and green pepper; stir into sauce during last 5 minutes of cooking time. Let stand, covered, 5 minutes.

*Tips*

1 If you can obtain fresh herbs, substitute 1 × 5ml tsp (1tsp) each of fresh basil and tarragon and ½ × 5ml tsp (½tsp) fresh oregano leaves; chop them with the tomatoes. If fresh tomatoes are not available, 2 tins (397g [14oz] each) Italian-style plum tomatoes, seeded and drained, can be substituted.
2 To seed tomatoes, cut them horizontally into halves. Squeeze each half gently until seeds pop out.
3 Provençale dishes are often seasoned with garlic. You may wish to add 1 or 2 peeled cloves of garlic to this recipe. Process (Steel Knife) the garlic until minced before you process the onion; drop garlic cloves through the feed tube with the machine running.
4 Chicken provençale can be prepared 1 day in advance; refrigerate covered.

## Chicken with curry sauce

Total Preparation Time: 30–3 min
Microwave Time: 24–7 min
Serves: 6

*Curry powder, a seasoning shortcut blended from many spices, adds another dimension to speedy cooking. Serve with Minted or Coriander rice (see Index). Curry sauce is also good with green vegetables or lamb.*

6 chicken breast halves, skinned (about 1.5kg [3lb])
browning and seasoning sauce
50ml (2fl oz) chicken stock
Curry sauce (recipe follows)

Brush chicken with browning sauce; arrange pieces in 30 × 20cm (12 × 8in) baking dish with meatiest portions towards edges of dish. Add chicken stock; microwave covered with clingfilm at High until chicken is done and juices run clear when thickest pieces are pierced with a fork, 18–20 minutes, turning pieces over halfway through cooking time. Let stand, covered, 5 minutes.

Make Curry sauce; serve over chicken.

**Curry sauce**

2 × 15ml tbsp (2tbsp) Twice-as-fast sauce mix
  (see Index)
½ clove garlic, peeled
¼ medium onion, peeled, cut into 2.5cm (1in) pieces
225ml (8fl oz) chicken stock
pinch of curry powder
pinch of cayenne pepper
2 × 15ml tbsp (2tbsp) plain yogurt

Microwave sauce mix in 1 litre (1¾pt) measure, uncovered, at High 2 minutes. Process (Steel Knife) garlic and onion using on/off technique until minced; stir into sauce mix. Microwave uncovered at High 1 minute. Stir in chicken stock, curry powder and pepper; microwave uncovered at High until mixture boils and thickens, 3–3½ minutes, stirring with whisk every minute. Stir in yogurt.

## Indonesian chicken

Total Preparation Time: 40–5 min
Microwave Time: 20–3 min
Serves: 4

*An ideal recipe for the food processor and microwave oven. The rich flavour and colourful garnishes make it a good choice for entertaining. Easy to prepare, it also keeps well in the refrigerator and reheats beautifully.*

1 clove garlic, peeled
½ medium onion, peeled, cut into 2.5cm (1in) pieces
2 large spring onions and tops, cut into 2.5cm (1in)
  pieces
1 small cucumber, peeled, seeded, cut into 2.5cm
  (1in) pieces
1 large tomato, seeded, cut into 2.5cm (1in) pieces
25g (1oz) butter or margarine
1 × 15ml tbsp (1 tbsp) flour
150g (6oz) peanuts
300ml (12fl oz) chicken stock
½ × 5ml tsp (½tsp) paprika
1–1½kg (2–3lb) chicken pieces
coriander or parsley sprigs
1 lime or lemon, cut into wedges

With machine running (Steel Knife), drop garlic through feed tube, processing until minced. Add onions to bowl; process using on/off technique until finely chopped, and remove. Process (Steel Knife) cucumber and tomato separately, using on/off technique, until coarsely chopped; reserve. Microwave butter in 1 litre (1¾pt) casserole at High until melted; stir in onion mixture. Microwave uncovered at High 2 minutes; stir in flour. Microwave uncovered at High 1 minute.

Process (Steel Knife) peanuts using on/off technique until peanuts are coarsely chopped; remove

2 × 15ml tbsp (2tbsp) and reserve. Process remaining peanuts until a smooth peanut butter is formed; add stock through feed tube, processing until blended. Add onion mixture and paprika to bowl; blend into peanut mixture using on/off technique.

Arrange chicken pieces skin sides down in 30 × 20cm (12 × 8in) baking dish, placing meatier pieces towards edges of dish. Microwave loosely covered with greaseproof paper at High 7 minutes. Turn chicken pieces over; pour peanut mixture over chicken. Microwave loosely covered at High until chicken is tender, 10–13 minutes, rotating dish ¼ turn after 7 minutes. Let stand 5 minutes.

Arrange chicken on serving plate; garnish with reserved cucumber, tomato, chopped nuts, the coriander, and lime or lemon.

*Tips*

1 Turmeric rice (see Index) is excellent with this recipe. Make rice before cooking the chicken; let stand covered while chicken is cooking. Microwave covered at High until hot, about 2 minutes, while chicken is standing.
2 You can reduce some of the calories in this rich dish by making half the amount of sauce; cut quantities of ingredients other than cucumber, tomato, chicken and lime or lemon in half and proceed as above. The presentation will be much less lavish, but you will feel less guilty!
3 To seed cucumber, cut it lengthwise into halves and scrape out the seeds with a spoon or cut them out in strips with a small knife.

## Savoury chicken rolls

Total Preparation Time: 42–7 min
Microwave Time: 17–20 min
Serves: 4

*Two major advantages of food processor/microwave cooking—a stuffing made in seconds and moister chicken. Spoon Mushroom or Fresh tomato sauce (see Index) over the rolls for extra flavour.*

Garlic-herb breadcrumbs (see Index)
50g (2oz) mozzarella cheese, chilled, cut to fit feed
  tube
1 large carrot, cut to fit feed tube
6 medium mushrooms
½ small onion, peeled, cut into halves
50g (2oz) butter or margarine
salt
pepper
4 chicken breast halves, skinned, boned (about 1kg
  [2lb])
paprika

Make Garlic-herb breadcrumbs; dry crumbs. Shred (Shredding Disc) cheese and carrot separately;

remove. Process (Steel Knife) mushrooms and onion separately, using on/off technique, until finely chopped. Microwave butter in 1 litre (1¾pt) casserole at High until melted; reserve half the butter. Stir carrot, mushrooms and onion into remaining butter in casserole. Microwave covered at High until vegetables are tender, 3–4 minutes. Mix in crumbs, cheese, salt and pepper. Pound chicken breasts until even in thickness. Spread stuffing on chicken breasts; roll up tightly from narrow end and secure with wooden cocktail sticks. Place rolls in 30 × 20cm (12 × 8in) baking dish; brush with reserved butter and sprinkle with paprika. Microwave covered with clingfilm at High until chicken is done and juices run clear when chicken is pierced with a fork, about 10 minutes, rotating dish ¼ turn after 5 minutes. Let stand covered 5 minutes.

*Tip*

When guests surprise you, you can surprise them with this recipe. All ingredients can be kept on hand. Make the dried breadcrumbs whenever you have a supply of stale bread; they will keep for months. Freeze individually wrapped flattened chicken breast halves up to 2 months; thaw in microwave as needed. You can substitute tinned mushrooms for fresh ones or omit them. Keep Twice-as-fast sauce mix (see Index) in the refrigerator and turn it into any sauce that suits the supplies in your store-cupboard.

## Coq au vin in clay pot

Total Preparation Time: 46–7 min
Microwave Time: 24–5 min
Serves: 4

*A clay cooking pot achieves an almost miraculous blending of flavours in record time. The secret lies in the continuous release of steam from the lid and sides of the pot. For best flavour and appearance, however, you should brown chicken conventionally before combining it with other ingredients.*

1.5kg (3lb) chicken pieces
flour
3 × 15ml tbsp (3tbsp) vegetable oil
salt
pepper
3 large sprigs parsley
1 clove garlic, peeled
2 shallots or ½ small onion, peeled, cut into 2.5cm (1in) pieces
½ medium leek, cleaned, or 3 green onions and tops, cut into 2.5cm (1in) pieces
15g (½oz) butter or margarine
100ml (4fl oz) dry white wine
½ × 5ml tsp (½tsp) dried basil

pinch of dried marjoram
pinch of dried tarragon
1 × 250g (8oz) jar pearl onions, drained
100g (4oz) small mushrooms
2 × 15ml tbsp (2tbsp) cornflour
50ml (2fl oz) cold water

Soak clay pot in water 15 minutes. Coat chicken pieces with flour; sautée conventionally in oil in large skillet until browned on all sides. Sprinkle lightly with salt and pepper.

Process (Steel Knife) parsley using on/off technique until minced; reserve. With machine running (Steel Knife), drop garlic and shallots through feed tube; process until minced. Add leek to bowl; process using on/off technique until finely chopped. Remove Steel Knife; add butter to bowl. Microwave vegetables in food processor bowl covered with clingfilm at High until vegetables are tender, about 5 minutes.

Arrange chicken in clay pot with meatiest portions towards edges of pot. Stir wine, basil, marjoram and tarragon into vegetable mixture; spoon over chicken. Microwave covered at 70% (Medium High) until chicken is done and juices run clear when thickest pieces are pierced with a fork, about 15 minutes. Add pearl onions and mushrooms to clay pot during last 5 minutes of cooking time. Remove chicken to serving plate; let stand loosely covered with aluminium foil. Mix cornflour and water; stir into juices in clay pot. Microwave uncovered at High until thickened, 4–5 minutes, stirring every 2 minutes. Pour sauce mixture over chicken; sprinkle with reserved parsley.

*Tips*

1 You can use a clay pot designed for either conventional or microwave cooking; the latter is simply easier to clean. If you are using the pot for the first time, soak it at least 30 minutes. You can begin soaking any clay pot as far in advance as you wish; the longer it soaks, the better. There is no need to rotate a clay pot during cooking. If you do not have a clay pot, you can prepare this recipe in an oven roasting bag set in a 30 × 20cm (12 × 8in) baking dish; coat the inside of the bag with 1 × 15ml tbsp (1tbsp) flour to prevent it from splitting. Close the bag with a non-metallic twist tie or string and turn it over halfway through the cooking time. You can also prepare the recipe in a 30 × 20cm (12 × 8in) baking dish tightly covered with clingfilm.

2 To make beef bourguignon, substitute 1kg (2lb) lean, cubed beef (chuck or sirloin) for the chicken and use red wine instead of white. You may not need to thicken the juices in the pot at the end of the cooking time; if you wish to, stir the cornflour and water mixture directly into the stew and heat until thickened.

## Chicken and shrimps in fillo shells

Total Preparation Time: 53–8 min
Microwave Time: 16–18 min
Serves: 6

*A spectacular entrée for a formal lunch. Make the Fillo pastry shells days in advance, if you wish.*

Fillo pastry shells (see Index)
40g (1½oz) Parmesan cheese, cut into 2.5cm (1in) pieces
75g (3oz) Gruyère cheese, chilled, cut to fit tube
150g (6oz) mushrooms
1 large clove garlic, peeled
3 medium spring onions and tops, cut into 2.5cm (1in) pieces
3 × 15ml tbsp (3tbsp) Twice-as-fast sauce mix (see Index)
300ml (12fl oz) single cream
salt
pepper
300g (¾lb) cooked chicken, cut into 2.5cm (1in) pieces
300g (¾lb) cooked, shelled, deveined shrimps
25g (1oz) flaked almonds

Make Fillo pastry shells. Process (Steel Knife) Parmesan cheese until finely grated; remove. Shred (Shredding Disc) cheese; remove. Slice (Slicing Disc) mushrooms; remove. With machine running (Steel Knife), drop garlic through feed tube, processing until minced. Add onions to bowl; process using on/off technique until chopped. Microwave onion mixture, mushrooms and sauce mix in 1 litre (¾pt) casserole, covered, at High 4 minutes, stirring after 2 minutes. Stir in cream, salt and pepper. Microwave uncovered at High until thickened, 5–6 minutes, stirring every 1½ minutes with whisk. Stir in cheeses, chicken and shrimps; microwave uncovered at High until hot through, about 3 minutes. Spoon mixture into shells; sprinkle with almonds.

*Tips*
1 One whole, large chicken breast will give about 300g (¾lb) cooked chicken. Microwave skinned chicken breast in glass baking dish, covered with clingfilm, at High just until tender and juices run clear, about 7 minutes; remove meat from bones and cut into 2.5cm (1in) pieces.
2 450g (1lb) medium shrimps in shells will give just under 300g (¾lb) cooked, shelled shrimps. Microwave shelled, deveined, uncooked shrimps in glass measure, covered with clingfilm, at High 3–4 minutes.
3 Chicken and shrimp mixture can be topped with seasoned breadcrumbs (see Index) and heated in ramekins or shell dishes as above, omitting Fillo pastry shells and almonds.

## Roast poussins with fruit pilaf

Total Preparation Time: 54–6 min
Microwave Time: 47–53 min
Serves: 4

*Those who dislike the dryness of conventionally roasted poussins (baby chickens) will be delighted by the taste of these. A fruit glaze and a crunchy, brown rice stuffing flatter the meat perfectly. This is a good festive alternative to turkey for a small gathering.*

400ml (16fl oz) hot water
1½ × 15ml tbsp (1½tbsp) orange juice
salt
100g (4oz) uncooked brown rice
1 small cucumber, peeled, seeded, cut into 2.5cm (1in) pieces
1 small onion, peeled, cut into quarters
75g (3oz) walnuts
25g (1oz) raisins
40g (1½oz) dried apricots, cut into halves
2 × 15ml tbsp (2tbsp) orange marmalade
4 poussins (about 450g [1lb] each)
100g (4oz) orange marmalade
1 × 5ml tsp (1tsp) made mustard
1 × 5ml tsp (1tsp) distilled white vinegar
1 × 5ml tsp (1tsp) soy sauce
a few drops browning and seasoning sauce

Microwave hot water, orange juice and salt in 2 litre (2¾pt) casserole, covered, at High until boiling; stir in rice. Microwave covered at High 5 minutes; stir after 3 minutes. Microwave covered at 50% (Medium) 20 minutes, or until rice is tender and water is absorbed.

Process (Steel Knife) cucumber, onion, walnuts, raisins and apricots using on/off technique until chopped. Stir cucumber mixture into rice; stir in 2 × 15ml tbsp (2tbsp) marmalade. Stuff cavities of poussins with rice mixture. Place breast sides down on microwave roasting rack in 30 × 20cm (12 × 8in) baking dish. Mix 100g (4oz) marmalade and remaining ingredients; brush poussins with half the mixture. Microwave uncovered at High 10 minutes. Turn birds breast sides up; brush with remaining glaze. Microwave uncovered 10–15 minutes, or until juices run clear when pierced with fork at inside thigh. Remove from oven; cover loosely with aluminium foil. Let stand 6–8 minutes before serving.

*Tip*
To thaw the 4 frozen poussins, microwave in wrapping at 30% (Medium Low) 20 minutes; then place birds, without unwrapping, in bowl of cold water for 30 minutes. Check manufacturer's manual for special defrosting features of your oven or see the Defrosting chart.

# Chicken livers stroganoff

Total Preparation Time: 27–31 min
Microwave Time: 13–14 min
Serves: 4

*Microwaves retain the tenderness of liver, producing a texture to match the fine flavour of this brandy-laced stroganoff. The recipe can easily be doubled for a buffet and set out, with noodles, on a warming tray.*

4 sprigs parsley
1 medium onion, peeled, cut into 2.5cm (1in) pieces
25g (1oz) butter or margarine
300g (12oz) chicken livers, cut into halves
100g (4oz) mushrooms
2 × 15ml tbsp (2tbsp) brandy
100ml (4fl oz) sour cream
2 × 15ml tbsp (2tbsp) flour
chicken stock cube
1 × 5ml tsp (1tsp) Worcestershire sauce
$\frac{1}{2}$ × 5ml tsp ($\frac{1}{2}$tsp) Dijon mustard
few drops browning and seasoning sauce
cooked noodles

Process (Steel Knife) parsley using on/off technique until minced; reserve. Process (Steel Knife) onion using on/off technique until coarsely chopped. Microwave onion and butter in 1$\frac{1}{2}$ litre (2$\frac{1}{2}$pt) casserole, covered, at High 3 minutes. Stir in livers; microwave covered at High until livers lose pink colour, 4–5 minutes, stirring after 2 minutes. Slice (Slicing Disc) mushrooms; stir into liver mixture. Microwave uncovered at High 2 minutes. Microwave brandy in a cup at High 15–20 seconds; ignite and pour over liver mixture. Mix sour cream and flour; stir into liver mixture. Stir in crumbled stock cube, Worcestershire sauce, mustard and browning sauce.

Microwave covered at High until hot through, about 3 minutes, stirring after 1$\frac{1}{2}$ minutes. Serve over noodles; garnish by sprinkling with reserved parsley.

## Roast duckling with sweet and sour cabbage

Total Preparation Time: 64–75 min
Microwave Time: 54–65 min
Serves: 4

*Duck skin will not crisp in the microwave oven, but the bonus is uniformly moist meat. The succulent texture of duck is complemented by an eastern European-style accompaniment of sausage, cabbage, apples and caraway.*

225g ($\frac{1}{2}$lb) sausagemeat
450g (1lb) cabbage (about $\frac{1}{2}$ medium head), cut into wedges to fit feed tube
2 medium apples, unpeeled, cored, cut into 2.5cm (1in) pieces
$\frac{1}{2}$ small onion, peeled, cut into 2.5cm (1in) pieces
50ml (2fl oz) water
50ml (2fl oz) cider vinegar
2 × 15ml tbsp (2tbsp) apricot jam
2 × 5ml tsp (2tsp) caraway seeds
1 duckling (2–2$\frac{1}{2}$kg [4–5lb])
50ml (2fl oz) orange juice
1 × 15ml tbsp (1tbsp) apricot jam
1 × 15ml tbsp (1tbsp) browning and seasoning sauce
1 small apple, cored, cut into halves (optional)
watercress or parsley sprigs

Crumble sausage into 3 litre (5pt) casserole; microwave covered with greaseproof paper at High until meat loses pink colour, about 3 minutes. Drain well. Slice (Slicing Disc) cabbage; add to casserole. Process (Steel Knife) 2 apples and the onion using on/off technique until coarsely chopped; stir into cabbage mixture. Stir water, vinegar, 2 × 15ml tbsp (2tbsp) jam and the caraway seeds into cabbage mixture. Microwave covered at High 8 minutes. Stir cabbage mixture; let stand covered while duckling is cooking.

Split duckling lengthwise through breastbone. Turn duckling skin side up and press down to crack bones so that duckling will lie flat. Pierce duckling skin liberally with fork. Place duckling on microwave rack in 30 × 20cm (12 × 8in) baking dish. Mix orange juice, 1 × 15ml tbsp (1tbsp) jam, and the browning sauce; reserve.

Microwave duckling uncovered at 70% (Medium High) about 9 minutes per 450g (1lb); when duckling is done, meat near bone will not be pink and juices will run clear when duckling is pierced with fork at inside thigh. During cooking time, rotate baking dish $\frac{1}{4}$ turn every 10 minutes, basting duckling with reserved orange juice mixture and shielding wing tips and legs with small pieces of aluminium foil if necessary to prevent overcooking. Remove duckling from oven; cover loosely with aluminium foil and let stand 10 minutes.

Microwave cabbage mixture covered at High until cabbage is tender, 8–10 minutes. Slice (Slicing Disc) the small apple. Spoon cabbage mixture onto serving plate; arrange duckling on cabbage. Garnish with sliced apple and watercress. Cut duckling into quarters to serve.

*Tip*
To crisp skin, transfer duckling to grill pan after microwaving and grill until crisp about 10 minutes.

# Turkey breast with honey-mustard sauce

Total Preparation Time: 63–7 min
Microwave Time: 43–5 min
Serves: 6–8

*Enjoy economical, low-cholesterol turkey breast regularly by cutting back the cooking time. If you are counting calories, resist adding the sauce and just enjoy the moist, piquant-glazed meat.*

4 sprigs watercress or parsley
1 small clove garlic, peeled
3–4 × 15ml tbsp (3–4tbsp) Dijon mustard
3–4 × 15ml tbsp (3–4tbsp) butter or margarine
1 × 15ml tbsp (1tbsp) honey
½ × 5ml tsp (½tsp) dried rosemary
pinch of dried thyme
1 turkey breast (about 1½–2kg [3–4lb])
paprika
2 × 15ml tbsp (2tbsp) flour
milk
watercress or parsley sprigs

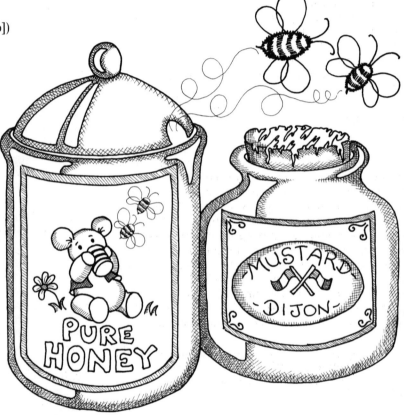

Process (Steel Knife) 4 sprigs watercress until minced. With machine running (Steel Knife), drop garlic through feed tube; process using on/off technique until minced. Add mustard, butter, honey, rosemary and thyme; process until smooth.

Place turkey breast upside down on microwave meat rack in 30 × 20cm (12 × 8in) baking dish; brush with half the mustard mixture. Microwave uncovered at High 5 minutes. Microwave at 50% (Medium) 15 minutes, rotating dish ¼ turn after 7 minutes. Turn breast right side up on rack; brush with mustard sauce. Microwave at 50% (Medium)

until meat thermometer inserted in thickest part of meat registers 82°C (180°F), 18–22 minutes, rotating baking dish ¼ turn and basting with sauce after 10 minutes. Sprinkle turkey with paprika. Let stand loosely covered with aluminium foil 10 minutes.

Pour meat juices into 500ml (1pt) glass measure; stir in remaining mustard mixture and the flour. Stir in enough milk to measure 300ml (12fl oz). Microwave uncovered at High until boiling and thickened, 5–7 minutes, stirring with whisk every 2 minutes. Arrange turkey on serving plate; garnish with watercress. Slice and serve with sauce.

*Tips*

1 If turkey breast is frozen, thaw according to directions in manufacturer's manual. Or remove from wrapping, place in 30 × 20cm (12 × 8in) baking dish and microwave covered with grease-proof paper at High 3 minutes; then microwave at 70% (Medium High) 6 minutes and let stand until thawed, 20–30 minutes.

2 Leftover turkey breast can be used in Turkey tetrazzini (following recipe) or cut up and turned into a delicious salad with sliced celery and Walnut mayonnaise (see Index). The turkey can also be substituted for the chicken in Chicken and shrimps in fillo shells or Double-dressed chicken salad (see Index).

3 An inverted plate can be substituted for the microwave meat rack. Do not use a conventional meat thermometer in the microwave oven; use a microwave meat thermometer or remove turkey from the oven to check temperature with a conventional meat thermometer.

## Turkey tetrazzini

Total Preparation Time: 32–6 min
Microwave Time: 11–14 min
Serves: 4–6

*A favourite recipe for leftover turkey. This version differs from the classic in that the spaghetti is cooked separately. There are also several advantages: the spaghetti stays firm, the dish takes less time to prepare, and the turkey mixture can be prepared ahead of time.*

50g (2oz) Cheddar cheese, chilled, cut to fit feed tube
1 medium green pepper, seeded, cut to fit feed tube
100g (4oz) mushrooms
1 medium onion, peeled, cut into 2.5cm (1in) pieces
1 stick celery, cut into 2.5cm (1in) pieces
50g (2oz) pimento
15g ($\frac{1}{2}$oz) butter or margarine
300g (12oz) cooked turkey, cut into 2.5cm (1in) pieces
4 × 15tbsp (4tbsp) Twice-as-fast sauce mix (see Index)
400ml (16fl oz) single cream
1 × 15ml tbsp (1tbsp) dry sherry
$\frac{1}{2}$ × 5ml tsp ($\frac{1}{2}$tsp) dry mustard
pepper
hot cooked spaghetti or noodles

Shred (Shredding Disc) cheese; reserve. Slice (Slicing Disc) green pepper and mushrooms separately. Process (Steel Knife) onion and celery using on/off, technique until chopped. Add pimento to bowl; process using on/off technique until chopped.
Microwave vegetables and butter in 2 litre (3$\frac{1}{2}$pt)

casserole, covered, at High until vegetables are tender, 4–5 minutes. Process (Steel Knife) turkey using on/off technique until coarsely chopped; stir into vegetable mixture. Let stand covered while preparing sauce.
Microwave sauce mix in 500ml (1pt) glass measure, uncovered, at High 2–3 minutes, stirring after 1 minute. Stir in cream, sherry, mustard and white pepper with whisk. Microwave uncovered at High until mixture boils and thickens, 5–6 minutes, whisking every minute. Stir in turkey-vegetable mixture and reserved cheese. Serve over spaghetti or noodles.

*Tip*
Turkey tetrazzini, without spaghetti, can be refrigerated covered 2 days; it can be frozen, in a sealed container, up to 1 month.

## Lemon chicken with mangetout peas

Total Preparation Time: 43–9 min
Microwave Time: 18–22 min
Serves: 4–6

*This attractive Oriental stir-fry recipe combines a delicate blend of seasonings, textures and colours.*

3 large lemons, cut to fit feed tube
450g (1lb) boneless chicken breasts, skinned, cut into 2cm ($\frac{3}{4}$in) pieces
3 × 15ml tbsp (3tbsp) soy sauce
1 × 5ml tsp (1tsp) granulated sugar
2 × 5ml tsp (2tsp) sesame seeds
1 spring onion and top, cut into 2.5cm (1in) pieces
225g (8oz) fresh or frozen mangetout peas, ends trimmed
1 × 15ml tbsp (1tbsp) peanut or vegetable oil
225ml (8fl oz) chicken stock
50g (2oz) light brown sugar
2 × 15ml tbsp (2tbsp) cornflour
$\frac{1}{2}$ × 5ml tsp ($\frac{1}{2}$tsp) dry mustard
hot cooked rice

Slice (Slicing Disc) 1 lemon; reserve. Grate rind from 1 lemon; reserve. Peel 2 whole lemons and cut into quarters. Process (Steel Knife) lemon pulp until all juice is extracted; strain and discard pith and seeds. Mix chicken, 2 × 15ml tbsp (2tbsp) of the lemon juice, the soy sauce and granulated sugar in bowl; let stand 15 minutes.
Microwave sesame seeds in glass pie dish, uncovered, at High until toasted, about 3 minutes, stirring after 1$\frac{1}{2}$ minutes. Process (Steel Knife) onion until coarsely chopped; remove. Slice (Slicing Disc) mangetout peas, placing peas in feed tube horizontally. Remove Slicing Disc; microwave peas in food processor bowl, covered with clingfilm, at High until crisp-tender, about 2 minutes.

Microwave oil in $30 \times 20$cm $(12 \times 8$in) baking dish at High until hot. Drain excess liquid from chicken and reserve; microwave chicken in hot oil in baking dish, uncovered, at High until chicken loses pink colour, 5–7 minutes, stirring every 2 minutes. Drain oil; let chicken stand loosely covered while preparing sauce.

Mix stock, remaining lemon juice, reserved liquid from chicken, brown sugar, cornflour, dry mustard and reserved lemon rind in 1 litre (1¾pt) measure; microwave uncovered at High until thickened, 5–6 minutes, stirring every 2 minutes. Stir sauce and mangetout peas into chicken; microwave uncovered at High until hot through, about 2 minutes. Spoon onto serving plate. Sprinkle with sesame seeds and onion; garnish with sliced lemon. Serve with rice.

*Tip*
To slice mangetout peas horizontally, you may find it easier to pack them into the bottom of the feed tube, which is slightly wider than the top. If any of the peas are too long, cut in half to fit.

## Mock-fried chicken breasts
Total Preparation Time: 28–32 min
Microwave Time: 18–20 min
Serves: 6

*Much lighter than true-fried, and much more convenient to prepare. Remove the skin from the chicken if you wish to reduce calories and cholesterol.*

Wheat and walnut breadcrumbs (see Index)
25g (1oz) butter or margarine
1 egg
6 boneless chicken breast halves (about 1kg [2lb])

Make Wheat and walnut breadcrumbs; dry crumbs. Microwave butter in glass pie dish at High until melted; whisk in egg until smooth. Dip chicken breasts in egg mixture to coat; dip into crumb mixture, pressing crumbs firmly onto chicken. Arrange chicken on microwave meat rack in $30 \times 20$cm $(12 \times 8$in) glass baking dish with meatiest portions towards the edges of dish. Microwave uncovered at High until chicken is tender and juices run clear when thickest portions are pierced with a fork, about 14 minutes.

*Tips*
1 Any of the seasoned breadcrumb variations can be used in this recipe. Crumbs can be made in advance; see recipe for storage instructions.
2 1kg (2lb) cut-up chicken pieces can be substituted for the boneless breast halves.

*Ham Salad Rolls (page 94); Date and Walnut Loaf (page 107); Orange Spiced Coffee (page 122)*

# Meat

## Whisky pot roast

Total Preparation Time: 86–92 min
Microwave Time: 76–81 min
Serves: 6

*This pot roast is transformed into something special in its relatively brief cooking time—the vegeatables pick up the distinctive flavour of the whisky-sauced meat and the juices thicken into a natural gravy.*

2 cloves garlic, peeled
50ml (2fl oz) whisky
1 boneless beef pot roast (about 1½kg [3½lb])
225ml (8fl oz) stock
25g (1oz) plain flour
225ml (8fl oz) tomato juice
1 × 5ml tsp (1tsp) dry mustard
salt
pepper
3 medium potatoes, unpeeled, cut to fit feed tube
2 carrots, peeled, cut to fit feed tube
2 medium onions, peeled, cut to fit feed tube

With machine running (Steel Knife), drop garlic through feed tube; process until minced. Add 1 × 15ml tbsp (1tbsp) of the whisky to bowl; process 2 seconds. Rub garlic mixture into pot roast. Microwave remaining whisky in small cup, uncovered, at High until hot, 20–30 seconds. Ignite and pour over pot roast. Mix stock and flour in small bowl; stir in tomato juice, dry mustard, salt and pepper; pour over roast in 30 × 20cm (12 × 8in) baking dish. Microwave covered with clingfilm at High 15 minutes; turn roast over. Microwave covered at 50% (Medium) until roast is tender, about 1 hour.

Slice (Slicing Disc) potatoes, carrots and onions separately; add vegetables to roast during the last 30 minutes of cooking time.

*Tips*

1 Use any cut of pot roast, such as boneless chuck, topside or brisket. If using a roast thicker than 5cm (2in), turn it over when you add the vegetables.

2 Igniting the whisky burns off the alcohol, eliminating its harsh taste.

*Shrimp Bisque (page 37); Crab-stuffed Fillets of Sole (page 39); Trout with Hazelnut Stuffing (page 38)*

# Chinese pepper beef

Total Preparation Time: 26–9 min
(plus 30 min marinating time and freezing time)
Microwave Time: 15–18 min
Serves: 6

*The precision provided by the food processor and microwave oven is the key to the ease of this Oriental 'stir-fry.' No laborious slicing and chopping, no need to stand over a wok! Yet the taste is authentically fresh.*

450g (1lb) beef flank steak, cut to fit feed tube
1 sprig fresh coriander or $\frac{1}{2}$ × 5ml tsp ($\frac{1}{2}$tsp) dried coriander
1 clove garlic, peeled
100ml (4fl oz) dry sherry
50ml (2fl oz) soy sauce
pinch of ground ginger
2 × 5ml tsp (2tsp) light brown sugar
2 spring onions and tops, cut into 2.5cm (1in) pieces
2 medium green peppers, seeded, cut to fit feed tube
225g (8oz) mushrooms
2 × 15ml tbsp (2tbsp) peanut or vegetable oil
225g (8oz) mangetout peas
225g (8oz) fresh or tinned bean sprouts, rinsed, drained
1 × 15ml tbsp (1tbsp) cornflour
225ml (8fl oz) beef stock
hot cooked rice

Freeze meat until slightly frozen (meat will feel frozen but you can pierce meat with tip of sharp knife); slice (Slicing Disc) and place in 30 × 20cm (12 × 8in) baking dish. Process (Steel Knife) coriander using on/off technique until minced. With machine running, drop garlic through feed tube, processing until minced. Add sherry, soy sauce, ginger and sugar to bowl; process using on/off technique until blended. Pour mixture over meat; let stand 30 minutes. Drain, reserving marinade.

Process (Steel Knife) onions using on/off technique until chopped; remove. Slice (Slicing Disc) peppers and mushrooms. Microwave oil in 2 litre (3$\frac{1}{2}$pt) baking dish, uncovered, at High until hot, about 2 minutes. Stir in meat, onions, peppers, mushrooms, mangetout peas and bean sprouts. Microwave uncovered at High until vegetables are crisp-tender, 10–12 minutes, stirring every 4 minutes. Combine reserved marinade, the cornflour and beef stock; stir into meat mixture. Microwave uncovered at High until sauce has thickened, 3–4 minutes, stirring after 2 minutes. Serve with rice.

*Tips*
1 Beef can be prepared and refrigerated in the marinade hours in advance.
2 If you are using tinned bean sprouts, crisp them in iced water. If time allows, leave them in the water refrigerated for several hours.
3 Steam rice conventionally according to packet directions while preparing Chinese pepper beef for greatest time advantage. To improve fluffiness of rice without rinsing it, which removes nutrients, remove pan from heat 5 minutes before end of recommended cooking time and place several layers of kitchen paper between the pan and the lid. Let stand 10 minutes or until ready to serve.

# Curry beef stew with chive dumplings

Total Preparation Time: 82–94 min
Microwave Time: 72–84 min
Serves: 8

*This meaty curry-seasoned stew is guaranteed to keep out the cold! Light dumplings complete the meal.*

2 medium onions, peeled, cut into 2.5cm (1in) pieces
1$\frac{1}{4}$kg (2$\frac{1}{2}$lb) lean beef cubes for stew (2.5cm [1in] cubes)
2 × 15ml tbsp (2tbsp) flour
400ml (16fl oz) stock
1$\frac{1}{2}$ × 5ml tsp (1$\frac{1}{2}$tsp) curry powder
salt
pepper
100g (4oz) frozen peas
25g (1oz) plain flour
75ml (3fl oz) cold water
Chive dumplings (recipe follows)

Process (Steel Knife) onions using on/off technique until chopped; remove. Process (Steel Knife) 300g ($\frac{3}{4}$lb) of the beef using on/off technique until finely chopped. Microwave chopped beef in 3.75 litre (6$\frac{3}{4}$pt) casserole, covered, at High until meat loses pink colour, 3–5 minutes, stirring after 2 minutes; drain. Toss remaining beef cubes with 2 × 15ml tbsp (2tbsp) flour. Stir beef cubes, onions, stock, curry powder, salt and pepper into chopped beef. Microwave covered at High 10 minutes; stir. Microwave uncovered at 50% (Medium) until meat is tender, 50–60 minutes, stirring every 20 minutes and adding peas during last 10 minutes of cooking time.

Mix flour and the water; stir into stew. Microwave covered at High until boiling, about 4 minutes; boil until thickened, about 1 minute.

Make dumpling mixture. Drop dumpling mixture by spoonfuls onto hot stew. Microwave covered at High until dumplings are cooked, 5–7 minutes.

## Chive dumplings

225g (8oz) Baking mix (see Index)
225ml (8fl oz) milk
1 × 15ml tbsp (1tbsp) dried chives
pinch of curry powder

Process (Steel Knife) all ingredients until smooth.

*Tips*
1 Unless you have a large-model food processor, chop no more than 225g (8oz) beef at a time. A larger quantity will result in uneven texture.
2 Curry beef stew, without peas and dumplings, can be frozen, in a covered container, up to 3 months. Add peas when reheating; add dumplings to hot stew.
3 Substitute different seasonings for the chives to vary the dumplings, if you wish. Dried dillweed or toasted sesame seeds would be good choices. To toast sesame seeds, spread them in a glass baking dish and microwave uncovered at High 2 minutes.

## Sirloin steak with mushrooms
Total Preparation Time: 32–3 min
Microwave Time: 17–18 min
Serves: 4

*Steak, mushrooms, and a rich sauce—a popular combination and a favourite when entertaining.*

25g (1oz) Parmesan cheese, cut into 2.5cm (1in) pieces
675g (1½lb) lean, boneless sirloin steak, cut into 4 serving pieces
salt
pepper
225g (8oz) mushrooms
12 olives, stoned
1 clove garlic, peeled
½ medium onion, peeled, cut into 2.5cm (1in) pieces
40g (1½oz) butter or margarine
2 × 15ml tbsp (2tbsp) flour
125ml (¼pt) whipping cream
2 × 15ml tbsp (2tbsp) dry white wine
½ × 5ml tsp (½tsp) Worcestershire sauce
½ × 5ml tsp (½tsp) Dijon mustard
2 × 15ml tbsp (2tbsp) vegetable oil

With machine running (Steel Knife), drop cheese through feed tube, processing until finely grated; reserve.

Pound steak with mallet to scant 1.25cm (½in) thickness; sprinkle lightly with salt and pepper. Slice (Slicing Disc) mushrooms and olives separately; remove. With machine running (Steel Knife), drop garlic through feed tube, processing until minced. Add onion to bowl; process using on/off technique until chopped. Microwave onion mixture and butter in 500ml (1pt) glass measure, uncovered, at High 2 minutes. Stir in flour; microwave at High 1 minute. Stir in cream, wine, Worcestershire sauce, mustard

and olives; microwave uncovered at High until thick, 4–5 minutes, stirring with whisk every 2 minutes.

Microwave oil in 30 × 20cm (12 × 8in) baking dish, uncovered, at High 2 minutes. Add steak; microwave uncovered at High 3 minutes. Turn steak pieces over and top with mushrooms; microwave uncovered at High 2 minutes. Spoon sauce over mushrooms; sprinkle with reserved cheese. Microwave uncovered at 50% (Medium) until steak is cooked as required, about 3 minutes for medium.

## Crumb-crusted roast beef
Total Preparation Time: 56–60 min
Microwave Time: 36–9 min
Serves: 6–8

*Microwaves retain the juiciness of a naturally tender cut. The roast cooks evenly, without drying out, and the herbed crumbs seal in the juices as they season the meat. Because there is no dry heat in the microwave oven, however, the crumb crust will not become crisp.*

1 beef tenderloin or fillet (about 2kg [4lb])
Garlic-herb breadcrumbs (see Index)
50g (2oz) butter or margarine

Place tenderloin on microwave roasting rack in 30 × 20cm (12 × 8in) baking dish; fold tip end of meat under so that meat is as uniform in thickness as possible. Make Garlic-herb breadcrumbs, using wholewheat or French bread. Microwave butter in a small bowl at High until melted; add to crumb mixture in food processor bowl. Process (Steel Knife) using on/off technique until butter is mixed into crumb mixture; pat mixture on top and sides of tenderloin. Microwave uncovered at High 5 minutes; rotate baking dish ¼ turn. Microwave uncovered at 50% (Medium) until meat thermometer registers 65°C (150°F) (for medium cooking), about 30 minutes, rotating baking dish ¼ turn every 10 minutes. Let stand loosely covered with aluminium foil until meat thermometer registers 70°C (160°F), about 10 minutes. Place on serving plate and carve.

*Tips*
1 You can prop up the meat on an overturned heatproof plate if you don't have a microwave roasting rack; remove the plate as soon as you remove the meat from the oven.
2 Do not use a conventional meat thermometer in the microwave oven. If you don't have a microwave meat thermometer, remove the roast from the oven and check to see if it is done with a regular meat thermometer.

# Basic meat loaf with variations

Total Preparation Time: 25–30 min
Microwave Time: 9–11 min
Serves: 4–6

*Processor chopping ensures desired leanness for meat loaf and microwave cooking prevents dryness—results will be even better if you add savoury seasonings and a sauce or glaze. Choose from these exciting variations— Lemon meat loaf with Egg lemon sauce, Italian meat loaf, and Sweet and sour ham loaf. Or select a sauce, such as Mushroom or Fresh tomato (see Index), to serve with Basic meat loaf. Make an extra meat loaf to slice cold for sandwiches—it's delicious and inexpensive.*

1 sprig parsley
2 slices firm white bread, torn into pieces
½ medium onion, peeled, cut into 2.5cm (1in) pieces
1 green pepper, seeded, cut into 2.5cm (1in) pieces
1 egg
¼ × 5ml tsp (½tsp) Dijon mustard
salt
pepper
450g (1lb) boneless beef (topside or silverside), cut into 2.5cm (1in) pieces
2 × 15ml tbsp (2tbsp) beef stock

Process (Steel Knife) parsley using on/off technique until minced. Add bread to bowl; process using on/off technique until fine crumbs are formed. Add onion and green pepper to bowl; process using on/off technique until chopped. Add egg, mustard, salt and pepper to bowl; process until blended; remove breadcrumb mixture.

Process (Steel Knife) beef using on/off technique until finely chopped. Microwave stock in glass measure at High until boiling. Add stock mixture to bowl; process using on/off technique until blended.

Combine meat and breadcrumb mixture; pat into 1½ litre (2½pt) plastic or glass ring mould. Microwave uncovered at High until meat loses pink colour, 8–10 minutes, rotating mould ¼ turn after 5 minutes. Let stand loosely covered with aluminium foil 5 minutes. Invert onto serving plate.

*Tips*
1 Unless you have a large-model food processor, chop no more than 225g (8oz) beef at a time.
2 Although you can process beef without any fat, meat loaf, burgers and meatballs will be juicier, yet not greasy, if you leave some fat on the meat; 10% fat is the preferred ratio of fat to lean.
3 Lean, boneless pork and veal can be substituted for part of the beef; one-third each of beef, pork and veal is the traditional meat loaf mix.
4 A 2 litre (3½pt) glass casserole, with a glass placed open end up in the centre, can be substituted for the ring mould.

5 Meat loaves can be frozen, raw or cooked, tightly wrapped, up to 1 month. To thaw, microwave according to manufacturer's instructions or the Defrosting chart. Toppings for Italian meat loaf and Sweet and sour ham loaf can be added prior to freezing or after thawing.

## Variations

**Lemon meat loaf:** Make Basic meat loaf as above, processing 1 × 15ml tbsp (1tbsp) lemon juice, 1 × 15ml tbsp (1tbsp) grated lemon rind, and ¼ × 5ml tsp (¼tsp) dried savory with the egg and mustard. Complete as in Basic meat loaf recipe.

Make Egg lemon sauce (recipe follows); serve with meat loaf.

### Egg lemon sauce

25g (1oz) butter or margarine
2 × 15ml tbsp (2tbsp) flour
100ml (4fl oz) chicken stock
100ml (4fl oz) milk
1 egg yolk
50ml (2fl oz) whipping cream
3–4 × 15ml tbsp (3–4tbsp) lemon juice
1 × 5ml tsp (1tsp) grated lemon rind
salt
pepper

Microwave butter in ½ litre (1pt) glass measure at High until melted; stir in flour. Microwave uncovered at High 30 seconds. Stir in stock and milk; microwave uncovered at High until sauce boils and thickens, about 4 minutes, stirring with whisk every 2 minutes.

Mix egg yolk and cream in small bowl; stir part of sauce mixture into egg mixture. Stir egg mixture into sauce mixture. Microwave uncovered at High until mixture boils and thickens, 1½–2 minutes, stirring with whisk after 1 minute. Stir in remaining ingredients.

**Italian meat loaf:** With machine running (Steel Knife), drop 15g (½oz) Parmesan cheese through feed tube; process until finely grated. Shred (Shredding Disc) 75g (3oz) chilled mozzarella cheese, cut to fit feet tube.

Make Basic meat loaf, processing (Steel Knife) 1 peeled garlic clove with the parsley and 4 stoned olives with the onion and green pepper. Stir three-quarters of the cheeses and 50ml (2fl oz) tomato sauce into meat loaf mixture; stir in pinch of dried basil and pinch of dried oregano. Complete as in Basic meat loaf recipe above.

Invert cooked meat loaf onto serving plate; top with 2 × 15ml tbsp (2tbsp) tomato sauce and remaining cheeses; let stand loosely covered with aluminium foil 5 minutes.

**Sweet and sour ham loaf:** Make Basic meat loaf, processing 75g (3oz) blanched almonds and 75g (3oz) mixed dried fruit with the onion and green pepper. Substitute 100g (4oz) cooked ham (cut into 2.5cm [1in] pieces) for 100g (4oz) of the beef.

Combine 4 × 15ml tbsp (4tbsp) jam, 1 × 15ml tbsp (1 tbsp) cider vinegar, 2 × 15ml tbsp (2tbsp) ketchup and 2 × 5ml tsp (2tsp) soy sauce; stir all but 1 × 15ml tbsp (1tbsp) of the mixture into the stock mixture. Complete meat loaf as in Basic meat loaf recipe above.

Invert cooked meat loaf onto serving plate; top with 1 × 15ml tbsp (1tbsp) jam mixture; let stand loosely covered with aluminium foil 5 minutes.

## Three-meat goulash

Total Preparation Time: 88–93 min
Microwave Time: 83–5 min
Serves: 8

*The combined juices of three kinds of meat give this dish an excellent flavour. Remember this recipe when you have a crowd to feed—it is easy to prepare and makes a large quantity.*

225g (8oz) mushrooms
3 medium onions, peeled, cut to fit feed tube
4 spring onions and tops, cut to fit feed tube
25g (1oz) butter or margarine
4 medium tomatoes, seeded, cut into 2.5cm (1in) pieces
450g (1lb) beef cubes for stew
450g (1lb) pork cubes for stew
450g (1lb) veal cubes for stew
150g (6oz) tomato paste
½ × 5ml tsp (½tsp) caraway seeds
pinch of dried dillweed
225ml (8fl oz) beef stock
1 × 15ml tbsp (1tbsp) paprika
2 × 5ml tsp (2tsp) salt
½ × 5ml tsp (½tsp) pepper
225ml (8fl oz) sour cream
25g (1oz) plain flour
hot cooked noodles (optional)

Slice (Slicing Disc) mushrooms, onions and spring onions. Microwave vegetable mixture and butter in 3¾ litre (6¼pt) casserole, covered, at High until vegetables are tender, 8–10 minutes, stirring every 4 minutes. Process (Steel Knife) tomatoes using on/off technique until coarsely chopped; stir into mushroom mixture. Stir in meats, tomato paste, caraway seeds, dillweed, stock, paprika, salt and pepper. Microwave covered with clingfilm at High 10 minutes; microwave covered with clingfilm at 50% (Medium) until meat is tender, about 1 hour, stirring after 30 minutes. Mix sour cream and flour;

stir into stew. Microwave covered at 50% (Medium) until thickened, about 5 minutes, stirring after 3 minutes. Serve over noodles.

*Tips*

1 Cook noodles conventionally, while the goulash is cooking, to save maximum time. Serve the goulash with thick slices of rye, pumpernickel or French bread, instead of noodles, if you wish.
2 100ml (4fl oz) dry white or red wine or beer can be substituted for 100ml (4fl oz) of the water specified in the recipe.
3 Three-meat goulash can be prepared up to the addition of sour cream and flour and frozen up to 2 months. You may wish to remove and freeze half the goulash before adding the sour cream and proceed as above, using half the sour cream and flour to complete the remaining portion.
4 To store leftover tomato paste, pour a thin layer of vegetable oil over the paste and refrigerate; pour off the oil when you're ready to use the paste. Leftover paste can also be frozen. Place teaspoons of paste on a sheet of greaseproof paper, freeze until firm, and transfer to a plastic bag; remove portions as needed.

## Veal rolls with prosciutto

Total Preparation Time: 30–5 min
Microwave Time: 12–15 min
Serves: 4

*An elegant but economical entrée that makes the most of veal. One great advantage when you're entertaining is not having to watch and turn the veal continuously, as you would if you sautéed the rolls conventionally.*

6 sprigs parsley
25g (1oz) Parmesan cheese, cut into 2.5cm (1in) pieces
1 clove garlic, peeled
½ medium onion, peeled, cut into 2.5cm (1in) pieces
100g (4oz) mozzarella cheese, chilled, cut into 2.5cm (1in) pieces
100g (4oz) prosciutto, cut into 2.5cm (1in) pieces
pinch of dried savory leaves
8 veal scallops, pounded paper-thin (about 450g [1lb])
100m (4fl oz) dry white wine
1 × 15ml tbsp (1tbsp) cornflour
50ml (2fl oz) cold water

Process (Steel Knife) parsley using on/off technique until minced. With machine running, drop Parmesan cheese and garlic through feed tube; process until finely grated. Add onion, mozzarella, prosciutto and savory to bowl; process using on/off technique until mixture is chopped and thoroughly mixed.

Divide cheese mixture on veal scallops; roll up and

secure with wooden cocktail sticks. Microwave veal rolls and wine in $30 \times 20$cm ($12 \times 8$in) baking dish covered with clingfilm at High until veal is cooked and juices run clear when veal is pierced with a fork, 10–12 minutes, rotating dish $\frac{1}{4}$ turn every 4 minutes. Arrange veal rolls on serving plate; cover loosely with aluminium foil. Pour pan juices into measure. Mix cornflour and cold water; stir into pan juices. Microwave sauce uncovered at High until thickened, 2–3 minutes, stirring with whisk every minute. Spoon sauce over veal rolls.

*Tips*

1 Use good-quality veal scallops, preferably cut from the loin, for meat that can be pounded to most attractive thinness. Other cuts of boneless veal will cook to tenderness in this recipe, but it is much harder to flatten them.
2 Prosciutto can be found in the delicatessen section of large supermarkets or in specialist delicatessens. Smoked ham can be substituted.

## Hot chilli casserole
Total Preparation Time: 45–8 min
Microwave Time: 23–4 min
Serves: 6

*Add extra spice to this dish with hot Italian sausage. The texture of processor-chopped beef shows up especially well in chilli. Be careful not to overprocess the meat—it should be slightly chunky.*

225g (8oz) hot or mild Italian sausage, cut into 1.25cm ($\frac{1}{2}$in) pieces
225ml (8fl oz) water
1 clove garlic, peeled
1 medium onion, peeled, cut into 2.5cm (1in) pieces
1 medium green pepper, seeded, cut into 2.5cm (1in) pieces
$1 \times 15$ml tbsp (1tbsp) vegetable oil
300g (12oz) boneless beef (topside or silverside), excess fat trimmed, cut into 2.5cm (1in) pieces
$2 \times 397$g (14oz) tins tomatoes, undrained
$2 \times 439$g (15oz) tins red kidney beans, drained
$2 \times 15$ml tbsp (2tbsp) tomato paste
$2 \times 15$ml tbsp (2tbsp) Worcestershire sauce
$1 \times 15$ml tbsp (1tbsp) sugar
$1–2 \times 5$ml tsp (1–2tsp) crushed dried red pepper
$\frac{1}{2}–1 \times 5$ml tsp ($\frac{1}{2}$–1tsp) chilli powder
1 or 2 dashes Tabasco

Microwave sausage in water in 1 litre ($1\frac{1}{4}$pt) casserole, uncovered, at High until sausage loses pink colour, about 5 minutes; drain well. With machine running (Steel Knife), drop garlic through feed tube, processing until minced. Add onion and green pepper to bowl; process using on/off technique until coarsely chopped. Microwave onion mixture and oil in a 3 litre ($5\frac{1}{2}$pt) casserole, uncovered, at High 4 minutes.

Process (Steel Knife) beef using on/off technique until coarsely chopped; stir into onion mixture. Microwave uncovered at High until beef loses pink colour, about 4 minutes, stirring after 2 minutes. Process (Steel Knife) tomatoes using on/off technique until coarsely chopped. Stir tomatoes, sausage and remaining ingredients into casserole; microwave uncovered at High until boiling, about 10 minutes, stirring after 5 minutes.

*Tips*

1 Unless you have a large-model food processor, chop no more than 225g (8oz) beef at a time.
2 Hot chilli casserole can be frozen up to 1 month. Freeze individual portions for quick lunches, suppers, or snacks, or freeze in a single container.

## Braised liver and onions
Total Preparation Time: 28–32 min
Microwave Time: 16–19 min
Serves: 4

*Exceedingly tender calf's liver with the addition of fresh, crisp, sliced leek and the traditional topping of bacon.*

1 medium leek, cleaned, or 6 spring onions and tops, cut to fit feed tube
1 stick celery, cut to fit feed tube
$2 \times 15$ml tbsp (2tbsp) dry white wine
4 slices bacon
450g (1lb) calf's liver
25g (1oz) plain flour
pinch of dried chervil
pinch of cayenne pepper
1 small tomato, cut into 2.5cm (1in) pieces

Slice (Slicing Disc) leek and celery; microwave leek, celery and wine in 1 litre ($1\frac{1}{4}$pt) casserole, covered, at High until vegetables are tender, 4–5 minutes. Microwave bacon in glass baking dish, uncovered, at High until crisp, 5–6 minutes. Drain bacon and crumble; reserve fat.

Cut liver, if necessary, so that pieces are similar in size. Coat liver with combined flour, chervil and cayenne pepper. Microwave liver in bacon fat in $30 \times 20$cm ($12 \times 8$in) baking dish, covered with greaseproof paper, at High 3 minutes, turning liver after $1\frac{1}{2}$ minutes. Process (Steel Knife) tomato using on/off technique until chopped. Sprinkle leek mixture and tomato over liver. Microwave, covered with greaseproof paper, at High 4–5 minutes, or until liver loses pink colour; let stand 5 minutes. Arrange on serving plate; sprinkle with bacon.

# Mustard roast beef

Total Preparation Time: 48–53 min
Microwave Time: 30–5 min
Serves: 6

*An easy trick with a sirloin roast: rub the meat with a spicy beef suet mixture to guarantee juiciness and flavour in every slice. The suet melts away during cooking, while the seasonings are absorbed by the meat. The leftovers make great sandwiches!*

100g (4oz) beef suet, room temperature, cut into
   2.5cm (1in) pieces
1 × 15ml tbsp (1tbsp) mustard
1 × 15ml tbsp (1tbsp) light brown sugar
1 × 5ml tsp (1tsp) caraway seeds, crushed
½ × 5ml tsp (½tsp) prepared horseradish
¼ × 5ml tsp (¼tsp) ground allspice
1 boneless beef sirloin roast (about 1¼kg [3lb]), all
   fat trimmed

Process (Steel Knife) suet, mustard, sugar, caraway seeds, horseradish and allspice until smooth; spread on all surfaces of meat. Place meat on microwave meat rack in 30 × 20cm (12 × 8in) baking dish. Microwave uncovered at 70% (Medium High) 15 minutes. Turn meat over; microwave uncovered at 50% (Medium) until meat thermometer registers 65°C (150°F) (for medium roasting), 15–20 minutes. Let stand loosely covered with aluminium foil 10 minutes. Place on serving plate; slice to serve.

*Tips*
1 Mustard roast beef can be refrigerated, wrapped in aluminium foil, and served cold or at room temperature.
2 See Crumb-crusted roast beef, p55, for microwave tips.

# Spinach-stuffed ham

Total Preparation Time: 65–70 min
Microwave Time: 50–2 min
Serves: 14–16

*An extremely attractive and generous ham that's equally appropriate for a sit-down dinner or a buffet.*

2 cloves garlic, peeled
½ medium onion peeled, cut into 2.5cm (1in) pieces
150g (6oz) mushrooms
25g (1oz) butter or margarine
75g (3oz) walnut pieces
2 blocks (250g [10oz] each) frozen chopped
   spinach, thawed, well drained
2 × 15ml tbsp (2tbsp) Twice-as-fast sauce mix (see
   Index)
pinch of ground mace
75g (3oz) Swiss cheese, chilled, cut to fit feed tube
1 × 2½kg (5lb) packaged or tinned cooked ham

With machine running (Steel Knife), drop garlic through feed tube, processing until minced. Add onion to bowl; process using on/off technique until finely chopped. Process (Steel Knife) mushrooms until finely chopped. Microwave butter in 1½ litre (2½pt) casserole at High until melted. Stir in onion mixture and mushrooms; microwave covered at High until onion is tender, about 3 minutes.

Process (Steel Knife) walnuts until finely chopped; stir into onion mixture with spinach, sauce mix and mace. Microwave covered at High 3 minutes. Shred (Shredding Disc) cheese. Reserve 25g (1oz) cheese; stir remaining cheese into spinach mixture.

Cut ham lengthwise into slices 2.5cm (1in) apart, cutting to, but not through, bottom of ham. Spoon spinach mixture into cuts; place ham in 30 × 20cm (12 × 8in) baking dish. Microwave covered with greaseproof paper at 50% (Medium) until hot through, about 8 minutes per 450g (1lb); rotate baking dish ¼ turn every 10 minutes. Sprinkle spinach mixture with reserved 25g (1oz) cheese; microwave uncovered at High until cheese is melted, about 2 minutes.

*Tip*
The ham is cut lengthwise to create pockets for the spinach-walnut mixture so that each serving will feature 'stripes' of the meat and stuffing.

# Roast loin of pork with apples

Total Preparation Time: 72–5 min
Microwave Time: 42–5 min
Serves: 8

*Microwave potato-stuffed pork in a clay pot to save more than two-thirds of the time it would take to achieve an equally moist roast in a conventional oven. Then serve the roast with spiced apples 'baked' with the pork. This is a perfect Sunday dinner for cooks who would like to take the day off!*

1 medium potato, peeled, cut to fit feed tube
50g (2oz) butter or margarine
40g (1½oz) light brown sugar
50g (2oz) walnuts
50g (2oz) raisins
2 × 15ml tbsp (2tbsp) light rum
pinch ground nutmeg
pinch ground cardamom
4 medium tart apples, peeled, cored
1 boned, rolled, tied pork loin roast (about 1½kg [3lb])

Soak clay pot in water 15 minutes. Slice (Slicing Disc) potato; remove. Process (Steel Knife) butter and sugar until smooth; add walnuts, raisins, rum, nutmeg and cardamom. Process (Steel Knife) using on/off technique until coarsely chopped. Stuff apples with 25g (1oz) of the butter mixture. Add potato to bowl with remaining butter mixture; process (Steel Knife) using on/off technique until finely chopped.

Cut 4–6 slices in pork roast, making cuts 5cm (2in) deep and 5cm (2in) apart; spoon potato mixture into cuts. Place roast in clay pot; microwave covered at 50% (Medium) 30 minutes. Microwave covered at High 5 minutes. Add apples to pot; microwave covered at High until apples are crisp-tender and roast registers 70°C (160°F) on meat thermometer, 7–10 minutes. Let stand loosely covered with aluminium foil until roast registers 75°C (170°F) on meat thermometer, about 15 minutes. Arrange meat on serving plate; cut apples into halves and arrange around roast.

*Tip*
You can use a clay pot designed for either conventional or microwave cooking. If you are using the pot for the first time, soak it at least 30 minutes. There is no need to rotate a clay pot during cooking. If you do not have a clay pot, you can prepare this recipe in an oven roasting bag set in a 30 × 20cm (12 × 8in) baking dish; coat the inside of the bag with 1 × 15ml tbsp (1tbsp) flour to prevent it from splitting. Close the bag with a non-metallic twist tie or string and turn it over halfway through the first 30 minutes of cooking. Let roast stand in the bag instead of covered with aluminium foil. The recipe can also be prepared in a 30 × 20cm (12 × 8in) baking dish tightly covered with clingfilm.

# Courgette-ham loaf

Total Preparation Time: 50–5 min
Microwave Time: 24–7 min
Serves: 8

*Fill the centre of this glazed, courgette-flecked ring with steamed carrots, Brussels sprouts, cauliflower or broccoli—a fresh look for a refreshingly moist loaf for lunch or supper.*

Dill sauce (see Index)
fresh Breadcrumbs (see Index)
1 medium courgette, cut to fit feed tube
1 small onion, peeled, cut into 2.5cm (1in) pieces
675g (1½lb) smoked ham, cut into 2.5cm (1in) pieces
450g (1lb) uncooked pork, excess fat trimmed, cut into 2.5cm (1in) pieces
2 eggs
2 × 15ml tbsp (2tbsp) single cream or milk
1 × 5ml tsp (1tsp) made mustard
pinch of ground mace
pinch of ground cloves
25g (1oz) butter or margarine
2 × 15ml tbsp (2tbsp) light brown sugar

Make Dill sauce. Make Breadcrumbs; do not dry crumbs.

Shred (Shredding Disc) courgette; drain well between layers of kitchen paper. Process (Steel Knife) onion using on/off technique until finely chopped; remove. Process (Steel Knife) ham using on/off technique until finely chopped; remove. Process (Steel Knife) pork using on/off technique until finely chopped. Mix courgette, onion, ham, pork, breadcrumbs, eggs, single cream, mustard, mace and cloves.

Press mixture into 1½ litre (2½pt) microwave ring mould (or into 2 litre [3½pt] glass casserole, with glass tumbler placed open end up in centre). Microwave uncovered at High 15 minutes, rotating mould ¼ turn every 5 minutes. Let stand loosely covered with aluminium foil 5 minutes.

Microwave butter and sugar in small glass bowl at High until butter is melted and sugar is dissolved. Turn out ham loaf onto serving plate; spoon butter glaze over. Microwave Dill sauce at High until hot through; serve with ham loaf.

*Tips*
1 Unless you have a large-model food processor, chop no more than 225g (8oz) meat at a time for best results.
2 Courgette-ham loaf can be frozen without the glaze, tightly wrapped, up to 1 month. Add glaze after reheating.

# Pork chops gruyère

Total Preparation Time: 29–35 min
Microwave Time: 14–20 min
Serves: 4

*The nutty flavour of Gruyère, blended with a strong mustard, turns pork chops into something special.*

4–6 loin pork chops (1.25cm [½in] thick each)
browning sauce
salt
pepper
4 sprigs parsley
100g (4oz) Gruyère or Swiss cheese, chilled, cut to fit feed tube
2 × 15ml tbsp (2tbsp) whipping cream
1½ × 15ml tbsp (1½tbsp) Dijon mustard

Brush chops lightly on both sides with browning sauce. Arrange chops in 30 × 20cm (12 × 8in) baking dish, with meatiest portions towards edges of dish. Microwave covered with greaseproof paper at 70% (Medium High) until chops lose their pink colour, 12–18 minutes, draining chops and rotating dish ¼ turn halfway through cooking time. Sprinkle chops lightly with salt and pepper. Let stand loosely covered with aluminium foil 10 minutes.

Process (Steel Knife) parsley using on/off technique until minced; remove. Shred (Shredding Disc) cheese; mix cheese, cream and mustard. Sprinkle cheese mixture over chops. Microwave uncovered at 70% (Medium High) until cheese is melted, about 2 minutes. Sprinkle with parsley.

# Sweet mustard glazed ribs

Total Preparation Time: 45–52 min
Microwave Time: 35–42 min
Serves: 4

*Pork spare ribs in a thick, sweet-tangy sauce taste extremely good.*

1kg (2lb) pork spare ribs, cut into serving-size pieces
½ × 5ml (½tsp) salt
pepper
50ml (2fl oz) water
1 large spring onion and top, cut into 2.5cm (1in) pieces
2 large dill pickles, cut into 2.5cm (1in) pieces
1 clove garlic, peeled
2–3 × 15ml tbsp (2–3tbsp) sugar
1 × 15ml tbsp (1tbsp) flour
1 × 15ml tbsp (1tbsp) dry mustard
1 egg yolk
225ml (8fl oz) whipping cream
1–2 × 5ml tsp (1–2tsp) soy sauce
2 × 15ml tbsp (2tbsp) cider vinegar

Sprinkle both sides of ribs with salt and pepper. Arrange in 30 × 20cm (12 × 8in) baking dish with meatiest portions of ribs towards edges of dish; add water. Microwave covered with greaseproof paper at 70% (Medium High) for 5 minutes; drain ribs and turn over. Microwave covered with greaseproof paper at 50% (Medium) until ribs are fork tender and juices run clear, 20–25 minutes; turn ribs over after 10 minutes. Drain well. Process (Steel Knife) onion and pickles using on/off technique until chopped; sprinkle over ribs. Microwave covered with greaseproof paper at 70% (Medium High) 10 minutes; drain ribs and rearrange.

With machine running (Steel Knife), process garlic until minced. Add remaining ingredients except vinegar to bowl; process until smooth. Microwave in 1 litre (1¾pt) measure uncovered at High until thick, 3–4 minutes, stirring with whisk every minute. Stir in vinegar. Spoon sauce over ribs; microwave uncovered at High until hot through, 2–3 minutes.

*Tip*
1kg (2lb) loin pork chops can be substituted for the spare ribs.

## Fruit-stuffed leg of lamb
Total Preparation Time: 65–70 min
Microwave Time: 44–52 min
Serves: 8

*Sample the mouth-watering combination of lamb and spiced fruit in this delicious entrée, suitable for all occasions. The food processor quickly turns part of the fruit into a natural sauce for the rolled lamb.*

125g (5oz) dried apples
125g (5oz) dried apricots
2 × 15ml tbsp (2tbsp) flour
300g (12oz) apricot purée
225ml (8fl oz) apple juice
pinch of ground allspice
pinch of ground cloves
1 boned, rolled, leg of lamb (about 1½kg [3lb])
½ × 5ml tsp (½tsp) ground cinnamon
2 × 15ml tbsp (2tbsp) brandy
mint or watercress sprigs

Process (Steel Knife) apples, apricots and flour using on/off technique until fruit is finely chopped. Microwave fruit mixture, apricot purée, apple juice, allspice and cloves in 1½ litre (2½pt) casserole, uncovered, at High 10 minutes, or until fruit is tender, stirring every 3 minutes. Lay lamb flat on worktop; spoon half the fruit mixture on lamb. Roll lamb up and tie with string in several places; place in 30 × 20cm (12 × 8in) baking dish. Rub cinnamon

on to lamb; spoon remaining fruit mixture around lamb. Microwave uncovered at 50% (Medium) 11–13 minutes per 450g (1lb) until meat thermometer registers 75°C (170°F), rotating baking dish ¼ turn every 15 minutes. Let roast stand loosely covered with aluminium foil for 10 minutes.

Process (Steel Knife) fruit, pan juices and brandy until smooth. Microwave in 1 litre (1¾pt) glass measure, uncovered, at High until hot through, about 45 seconds. Place roast on serving plate and carve; garnish with mint. Serve with fruit sauce.

*Tip*
The microwave time specified in the recipe will produce a tender, well-done roast. Do not use a conventional meat thermometer in the microwave oven; if you do not have a microwave meat thermometer, remove roast from the oven and check to see if joint is done with a regular thermometer.

## Country sausage skillet
Total Preparation Time: 48–51 min
Microwave Time: 26–9 min
Serves: 6

*The superior flavour of homemade sausage raises a country-kitchen skillet dish to gourmet status. Prepare the sausage mixture separately for fried breakfast patties or a poultry stuffing.*

Sour-cream onion sauce (see Index)
50ml (2fl oz) milk
50ml (2fl oz) sour cream
100g (4oz) Cheddar cheese, chilled, cut to fit feed tube
½ medium onion, peeled, cut into 2.5cm (1in) pieces
1 stick celery, cut into 2.5cm (1in) pieces
50ml (2fl oz) water
1 × 5ml tsp (1tsp) dried marjoram
1 × 5ml tsp (1tsp) dried sage
½ × 5ml tsp (½tsp) dried thyme
pinch of dried mixed herbs
1 bay leaf
dash of nutmeg
1 × 5ml tsp (1tsp) salt
1 × 5ml tsp (1tsp) pepper
300g (¾lb) lean boneless pork, cut into 2.5cm (1in) pieces
100g (4oz) pork fat, cut into 2.5cm (1in) pieces
675g (1½lb) frozen hash-brown potatoes or grated, fried potatoes

Make Sour-cream onion sauce; stir in milk and sour cream. Shred (Shredding Disc) cheese; remove. Process (Steel Knife) onion and celery using on/off technique until finely chopped.

Microwave water, marjoram, sage, thyme, mixed

herbs, bay leaf, nutmeg, salt and pepper in small glass bowl, uncovered, at High 1 minute; remove bay leaf and discard. Process (Steel Knife) pork using on/off technique until finely chopped; process (Steel Knife) pork fat using on/off technique until finely chopped. Mix meat, fat and herb mixture in 30 × 20cm (12 × 8in) baking dish. Microwave covered with greaseproof paper at High until meat loses pink colour, 4–5 minutes, stirring after 2 minutes. Drain excess fat. Let stand covered with greaseproof paper 2 minutes. Spread sausage evenly in baking dish.

Microwave potatoes in 1 litre (1¾pt) casserole, uncovered, at 10% (Low) until potatoes are thawed, about 6 minutes, stirring after 3 minutes. Stir Sourcream onion sauce, 50g (2oz) of the cheese, the onion and celery into potatoes; spoon potato mixture over sausage in baking dish. Microwave uncovered at 70% (Medium High) until hot through, 13–15 minutes, rotating baking dish ¼ turn after 6 minutes. Sprinkle with remaining cheese; microwave uncovered at High 2 minutes. Let stand covered with aluminium foil 5 minutes.

*Tips*

1 Unless you have a large-model food processor, chop no more than 225g (8oz) meat at a time. The ratio of 100g (4oz) fat to 300g (¾lb) pork results in juicy sausages.

2 To make sausage for other uses, follow second paragraph as above, but do not microwave meat. Sausage mixture can be prepared, shaped into a roll, and sliced for convenient freezer storage; separate slices with greaseproof paper, wrap in freezer film, and freeze up to 2 months.

# Greek meatball kebabs

Total Preparation Time: 51–9 min
Microwave Time: 25–8 min
Serves: 4

*A novel way to present a classic Greek menu. Wrap herbed lamb meatballs in microwave-softened grapevine leaves and cook the packets on skewers for convenient serving.*

16 grapevine leaves, rinsed, drained
600ml (24fl oz) water
75g (3oz) dry Breadcrumbs (see Index)
1 clove garlic, peeled
1 small onion, peeled, cut into 2.5cm (1in) pieces
650g (1¼lb) boneless lamb, cut into 2.5cm (1in) pieces
pinch of dried oregano
pinch of dried mint
½ × 5ml tsp (½tsp) salt

1 egg
2 × 15ml tbsp (2tbsp) plain yogurt
1 small tomato, cut into quarters
4 medium mushrooms
50g (2oz) butter or margarine
Yogurt sauce (recipe follows)

Microwave grapevine leaves and water in 2 litre (3½pt) casserole, uncovered, at High until boiling, about 8 minutes; let boil 2 minutes. Rinse with cold water and drain well.

Make Breadcrumbs; dry crumbs and reserve. With machine running (Steel Knife), drop garlic through feed tube, processing until minced. Add onion to bowl; process using on/off technique until finely chopped. Process (Steel Knife) lamb using on/off technique until finely chopped. Mix meat, onion mixture, breadcrumbs, oregano, mint, salt, egg and yogurt; form into 16 meatballs. Wrap meatballs in grapevine leaves; place 2 meatballs each on 8 bamboo skewers. Place a tomato quarter or mushroom on the end of each skewer.

Lay skewers across 30 × 20cm (12 × 8in) glass baking dish. Microwave butter in a cup uncovered at High until melted; brush over meatballs. Microwave meatballs covered with greaseproof paper at High until meatballs are cooked, about 10 minutes, rearranging skewers and basting with remaining butter after 5 minutes. Let stand loosely covered 5 minutes.

Make Yogurt sauce; serve with meatballs.

## Yogurt sauce

Makes: about 225ml (8fl oz)

½ small onion, peeled, cut into 2.5cm (1in) pieces
225ml (8fl oz) plain yogurt
1 × 5ml tsp (1tsp) dried mint

Process (Steel Knife) onion using on/off technique until chopped; mix with yogurt and mint. Refrigerate until serving time.

*Tips*

1 Grapevine leaves can be found in large supermarkets and some delicatessens. They are usually packed in brine and must be rinsed with cold water before using.

2 Unless you have a large-model food processor, chop no more than 225g (8oz) meat at a time.

3 The meatball packets can be cooked without skewers; arrange in a circle on a plate and proceed as above, rotating dish ¼ turn halfway through cooking time.

4 Greek meatball kebabs can be served as an appetiser; allow 1 kebab per person.

## Moroccan lamb stew

Total Preparation Time: 50–5 min
Microwave Time: 38–43 min
Serves: 4

*An extraordinary lamb stew, with the addition of fragrant spices and garnished with almonds and sultanas. Feature it on a Middle Eastern-style dinner menu with an appetiser of Aubergine dip with pita triangles and Baklava for dessert (see Index).*

1 clove garlic, peeled
1 medium onion, peeled, cut into 2.5cm (1in)
 pieces
2 × 15ml tbsp (2tbsp) vegetable oil
pinch of ground cinnamon
pinch of ground ginger
pinch of ground turmeric
pinch of ground cloves
4 medium tomatoes, seeded, cut into 2.5cm (1in)
 pieces
675g (1½lb) boneless lamb cubes, excess fat trimmed
2 × 15ml tbsp (2tbsp) flour
50ml (2fl oz) beef stock
salt
pepper
Turmeric rice (see Index)
40g (1½oz) flaked almonds
2 × 15ml tbsp (2tbsp) sultanas
parsley sprigs

With machine running (Steel Knife), drop garlic through feed tube, processing until minced. Add onion to bowl; process using on/off technique until chopped. Microwave onion mixture and oil in 2½ litre (4½pt) casserole, covered, at High 3–4 minutes. Stir in cinnamon, ginger, turmeric and cloves; microwave uncovered at High 2 minutes.

Process (Steel Knife) tomatoes using on/off technique until coarsely chopped; stir tomatoes and lamb into casserole. Microwave covered at High 10 minutes; microwave uncovered at 50% (Medium) 10 minutes, stirring every 5 minutes. Mix flour and stock; stir into lamb mixture. Microwave covered at 50% (Medium) until lamb is tender, about 10–15 minutes. Season to taste with salt and pepper. Let stand 5 minutes.

Make Turmeric rice conventionally while microwaving lamb mixture.

Microwave almonds in glass pie dish, uncovered, at High until toasted, about 3 minutes, stirring after 1½ minutes. Spoon lamb mixture onto serving dish; garnish with almonds, sultanas and parsley. Serve with Turmeric rice.

*Tip*
Moroccan lamb stew can be cooked 1 day in advance without garnishes or Turmeric rice; refrigerate covered. Add garnishes and make rice before serving. The stew can be frozen, tightly covered, up to 1 month.

# Rice and Pasta

## Spinach rice

Total Preparation Time: 35–40 min
Microwave Time: 15–19 min
Serves: 6

*You may wish to double the recipe for this creamy green rice dish since the leftovers will disappear quickly—especially at lunch the next day.*

15g ($\frac{1}{2}$oz) Parmesan cheese, cut into 2.5cm (1in) pieces
250g (10oz) fresh spinach, stems removed
1 × 15ml tbsp (1tbsp) water
$\frac{1}{2}$ medium onion, peeled, cut into 2.5cm (1in) pieces
50g (2oz) mushrooms
2 slices bacon
50g (2oz) Cheddar cheese, chilled, cut to fit feed tube
450g (1lb) cooked rice
75ml (3fl oz) single cream
2 eggs, beaten
pinch of ground nutmeg
salt
pepper

With machine running (Steel Knife), drop Parmesan cheese through feed tube, processing until finely grated; reserve. Slice (Slicing Disc) spinach; microwave spinach and water in 3 litre (5$\frac{1}{2}$pt) casserole, covered, at High until cooked, 4–5 minutes. Drain thoroughly in a strainer, pressing to remove excess moisture.

Process (Steel Knife) onion using on/off technique until coarsely chopped; add mushrooms to bowl; process using on/off technique until coarsely chopped. Microwave bacon in 1$\frac{1}{2}$ litre (2$\frac{1}{2}$pt) casserole, uncovered, at High until crisp, about 3 minutes. Crumble bacon; reserve 1 × 15ml tbsp (1tbsp) fat in casserole. Microwave onion mixture in fat, covered, at High until onion is tender, 2–3 minutes.

Shred (Shredding Disc) Cheddar cheese. Stir cheese, spinach and remaining ingredients except Parmesan cheese into onion mixture. Microwave covered at 70% (Medium High) until all liquid is absorbed, 6–8 minutes, stirring after 4 minutes. Stir in Parmesan cheese; let stand covered 5 minutes.

*Tips*

1 Cook rice conventionally or in the microwave oven, as directed in Rice and seasoned variations (following recipe), using 150g (6oz) rice and 300ml (12fl oz) water. Reduce salt proportionately, or omit, if desired.

2 One 250g (10oz) block frozen chopped spinach can be substituted for the sliced fresh spinach; remove paper wrapper, cut slits in box and microwave at High 4–5 minutes. Drain as above.

## Rice and seasoned variations

Total Preparation Time: 26–9 min
Microwave Time: 19–22 min
Serves: 4

*Combine the convenience of microwave rice with the infinite versatility of processor-chopped seasonings. All variations can be made with conventionally cooked rice, too, and doubled or tripled when you're preparing larger quantities of rice. Rice reheats well in the microwave, so you may wish to renew plain leftovers with any of the seasoning blends.*

*Just a few of the serving possibilities: Turmeric rice or Minted rice with curries; Coriander rice with lamb dishes; Cardamom rice with meat loaf or pot roast; Peanut rice with barbecued spare ribs or roast pork; Pimento rice with goulash or stroganoff.*

500ml (1pt) hot water, chicken or beef stock
1 × 5ml tsp (1tsp) salt (optional; omit if using stock)
150g (6oz) uncooked long-grain rice

Microwave water and salt or stock in 2 litre (3$\frac{1}{2}$pt) casserole, uncovered, at High until boiling; stir in rice. Microwave covered at High until rice is tender and water is absorbed, 16–18 minutes, stirring after 8 minutes. Let stand covered 5 minutes.

### Variations

**Onion rice:** Process (Steel Knife) 1 small onion, peeled and cut into 2.5cm (1in) pieces, using on/off technique until chopped. Microwave with 15g ($\frac{1}{2}$oz) butter or margarine in small glass bowl, covered, at High until onion is tender, about 4 minutes. Make rice as above, stirring onion into cooked rice.

**Turmeric rice**: Make rice as above, stirring pinch of ground turmeric into boiling water with rice. Stir $\frac{1}{4}$–$\frac{1}{2}$ × 5ml tsp ($\frac{1}{4}$–$\frac{1}{2}$tsp) ground ginger into cooked rice.

**Coriander rice**: Process (Steel Knife) 2 sprigs coriander using on/off technique until minced. Make rice as above, stirring coriander and 2 × 5ml tsp (2tsp) dried chives into cooked rice.

**Tomato rice**: Make rice as above, stirring 1 × 5ml tsp (1 tsp) dried basil and $\frac{1}{2}$ × 5ml tsp ($\frac{1}{2}$tsp) dried rosemary into cooked rice; stir in 2 × 15ml tbsp (2tbsp) tomato paste and 50ml (2fl oz) sour cream.

**Cardamom rice**: Make rice as above, stirring a pinch of ground cardamom into cooked rice.

**Minted rice**: Process (Steel Knife) 3 sprigs mint and 2 sprigs parsley using on/off technique until minced. Make rice as above, stirring mint and parsley into cooked rice.

**Peanut rice**: Process (Steel Knife) 75g (3oz) peanuts using on/off technique until chopped. Process (Steel Knife) $\frac{1}{4}$ large red pepper (cut into 2.5cm [1in] pieces and 1 spring onion and top (cut into 2.5cm [1in] pieces) using on/off technique until chopped. Micro-wave pepper, onion and 15g ($\frac{1}{2}$oz) butter in small glass bowl, covered, at High until tender, about 3 minutes. Make rice as above, stirring onion mixture, peanuts and a pinch of curry powder into cooked rice.

**Parmesan rice**: Process (Steel Knife) 25–50g (1–2oz) Parmesan cheese (cut into 2.5cm [1in] pieces) using on/off technique until finely grated. Make rice as above, stirring cheese into cooked rice.

**Pimento rice**: Process (Steel Knife) 2 whole pimentos (cut into 2.5cm [1in] pieces) using on/off technique until coarsely chopped. Make rice as above, stirring pimento and $\frac{1}{2}$ × 5ml tsp ($\frac{1}{2}$tsp) paprika into cooked rice.

## Pastitsio

Total Preparation Time: 58–9 min
Microwave Time: 28–9 min
Serves: 8

*Mediterranean spices highlight this layered casserole topped with a custard-like sauce. The classic version calls for macaroni; this rice variation is lighter and more versatile. Serve small squares with chicken, fish or lamb. Or increase the portion size for a one-dish entrée.*

25g (1oz) Parmesan cheese, cut into 2.5cm (1in) pieces
40g (1½oz) blanched almonds
1 medium onion, peeled, cut into 2.5cm (1in) pieces
50g (2oz) mushrooms
225g (8oz) boneless beef, cut into 2.5cm (1in) pieces
225g (8oz) boneless lean lamb, cut into 2.5cm (1in) pieces
40g (1½oz) sultanas
50ml (2fl oz) tomato sauce
pinch of dried marjoram
pinch of ground cinnamon
pinch of ground allspice
pinch of ground cloves
1 × 5ml tsp (1tsp) salt
pepper
¾kg (1¾lb) cooked rice
2 eggs, beaten
½ × 5ml tsp (½tsp) salt
100ml (4fl oz) Twice-as-fast sauce mix (see Index)
500ml (1pt) single cream
½ × 5ml tsp (½tsp) salt
2 eggs, beaten

With machine running (Steel Knife), drop Parmesan cheese through feed tube, processing until finely grated; remove. Process (Steel Knife) almonds using on/off technique until finely chopped; remove. Process (Steel Knife) onion and mushrooms using on/off technique until finely chopped; remove. Process (Steel Knife) beef and lamb using on/off technique until finely chopped. Microwave beef, lamb and onion mixture in 1½ litre (2½pt) casserole, covered, at High until meat loses pink colour, 3–4 minutes, stirring after 2 minutes. Drain. Stir in almonds, sultanas, tomato sauce, marjoram, cinnamon, allspice, cloves, 1 × 5ml tsp (1tsp) salt and the pepper.

Combine rice, 2 eggs and ½ × 5ml tsp (½tsp) salt. Combine sauce mix, single cream and ½ × 5ml tsp (½tsp) salt in 1 litre (1¾pt) measure. Microwave uncovered at High until thickened, about 5 minutes, stirring with whisk every 1½ minutes. Stir about 50ml (2fl oz) sauce mixture into 2 eggs; stir egg mixture into sauce mixture.

Spoon half the rice mixture in bottom of greased 30 × 20cm (12 × 8in) baking dish; sprinkle with half the Parmesan cheese. Spoon meat mixture over rice mixture; spoon remaining rice mixture over meat mixture. Pour sauce over rice mixture; microwave uncovered at 70% (Medium High) until sauce is just set in the centre, about 20 minutes, rotating dish ¼ turn every 5 minutes. Sprinkle with remaining Parmesan cheese; let stand loosely covered with aluminium foil 5 minutes. Cut into squares to serve.

*Tips*
1 Unless you have a large-model food processor, chop no more than 225g (8oz) meat at a time.
2 Meat mixture can be made 1 day in advance; refrigerate covered.
3 Cook rice conventionally or as directed in Rice and seasoned variations (see previous recipe).

## Sherried brown rice with mushrooms and pork

Total Preparation Time: 60–3 min
Microwave Time: 48–55 min
Serves: 10–12

*A most cosmopolitan accompaniment for grilled or roasted meats, fish or poultry. Dried mushrooms, almonds, sherry and orange rind complement the delicious nutty flavour of brown rice. In larger portions, serve as a nutritious first course.*

225ml (8fl oz) hot water
12 Chinese dried mushrooms
600ml (24fl oz) hot water
1 × 5ml tsp (1tsp) salt
1 × 225g (8oz) uncooked brown rice
65g (2½oz) blanched almonds
2 sticks celery, cut to fit feed tube
½ medium onion, peeled, cut into 2.5cm (1in) pieces
450g (1lb) lean boneless pork, cut into 2.5cm (1in) pieces
50ml (2fl oz) sherry
100ml (4fl oz) sour cream
1 × 5ml tsp (1tsp) grated orange rind

Pour 225ml (8fl oz) hot water over mushrooms; let stand until mushrooms are soft, 10–20 minutes.

Microwave 600ml (24fl oz) water and the salt in 3 litre (5½pt) casserole, uncovered, at High until boiling, about 4 minutes. Stir in rice; microwave uncovered at High until rice is tender and liquid is absorbed, 30–35 minutes, stirring after 15 minutes. Let stand covered 5 minutes.

Process (Steel Knife) almonds until coarsely chopped; remove. Drain mushrooms; cut out tough stems. Slice (Slicing Disc) celery and mushrooms. Process (Steel Knife) onion using on/off technique until chopped. Microwave pork and 50ml (2fl oz) sherry in 1 litre (1¾pt) casserole, covered, at High until meat loses pink colour, 7–9 minutes. Drain, reserving 2 × 5ml tbsp (2tbsp) cooking liquid.

Microwave celery, mushrooms and onion in reserved cooking liquid in 1 litre (1¾pt) casserole, covered, at High until onion is tender, about 4 minutes. Stir pork mixture, vegetable mixture, almonds, sour cream and rind into rice; microwave covered at High until hot through, about 3 minutes.

*Tip*
To microwave plain brown rice for other uses, follow the second paragraph as above. This will give about 675g (1½lb).

## Oriental fried rice
Total Preparation Time: 20–4 min
Microwave Time: 11–12 min
Serves: 4

*An exciting alternative to plain rice with Chinese pepper beef (see Index). However, the Chinese eat this as a snack on its own using leftover rice, and you may wish to also.*

2 sprigs fresh coriander or parsley
225g (8oz) fresh green beans, trimmed
3 × 15ml tbsp (3tbsp) water
675g (1½lb) cooked rice
1 × 15ml tbsp (1tbsp) peanut or vegetable oil
100g (4oz) cooked ham, cut into 2.5cm (1in) pieces
50g (2oz) mushrooms
1 spring onion and top, cut into 2.5cm (1in) pieces
2 eggs, beaten
2 × 15ml tbsp (2tbsp) soy sauce
1 × 5ml tsp (1tsp) sugar
soy sauce

Process (Steel Knife) coriander using on/off technique until minced; remove. Slice (Slicing Disc) beans, placing them in feed tube vertically. Microwave beans and water in 1 litre (1¾pt) casserole dish, covered, at High until crisp-tender, about 4 minutes; drain. Microwave rice and oil in 2 litre (3½pt) casserole, uncovered, at High until hot through, about 3 minutes, stirring after 1½ minutes.

Process (Steel Knife) ham using on/off technique until coarsely chopped. Process (Steel Knife) mushrooms and onion using on/off technique until coarsely chopped. Mix eggs, 2 × 15ml tbsp (2tbsp) soy sauce and the sugar. Stir beans, ham, mushroom mixture and egg mixture into hot rice. Microwave uncovered at High until eggs are set, 4–5 minutes, stirring every 2 minutes. Sprinkle with coriander; serve with additional soy sauce.

*Tips*
1 For a quick variation, substitute one 250g (10oz) packet frozen peas for the green beans and do not slice. Remove paper wrapper, cut several slits in box or bag and microwave at High 5 minutes; drain.
2 Cook rice conventionally or as directed in Rice and seasoned variations (see Index).
3 Cooked chicken or beef, cut into 2.5cm (1in) pieces, can be substituted for the ham. 100g (4oz) shrimps can also be substituted; small shrimps need not be chopped.

## Green noodles with yogurt-dill sauce
Total Preparation Time: 17–18 min
Microwave Time: 7–8 min
Serves: 4–6

*The slightly tangy flavour of green noodles and a creamy sauce turns grilled fish or chicken into something special.*

2 large sprigs parsley
1 clove garlic, peeled
½ small onion, peeled, cut into 2.5cm (1in) pieces
1 spring onion and top, cut into 2.5cm (1in) pieces
225ml (8fl oz) plain yogurt
50g (2oz) cottage cheese
75g (3oz) cream cheese, softened
1 × 15ml tbsp (1tbsp) Twice-as-fast sauce mix (see Index)
15g (1oz) butter or margarine, softened
1 × 5ml tsp (1tsp) dried dillweed or 4 sprigs fresh dill
1 × 5ml tsp (1tsp) dried marjoram
salt
pepper
300g (12oz) green noodles, cooked

Process (Steel Knife) parsley using on/off technique until minced; with machine running, add garlic through feed tube, processing until minced. Add onions to bowl; process (Steel Knife) using on/off technique until chopped. Add onion mixture, yogurt, cottage cheese, cream cheese, sauce mix, butter, dill, marjoram, salt and pepper to bowl; process (Steel Knife) until mixture is smooth. Transfer mixture to 2 litre (3½pt) casserole; microwave uncovered at High until slightly thickened, 5–6 minutes, stirring every 2 minutes. Stir in noodles; microwave uncovered at High until hot through, about 2 minutes.

*Tips*
1 Cook noodles conventionally, since there is no time saved in the microwave with more than 225g (8oz) pasta.
2 If using dill, process it with the parsley.
3 Sauce can be refrigerated covered up to 2 days.

# Aubergine spaghetti

Total Preparation Time: 25–8 min
Microwave Time: 16–18 min
Serves: 6–8

*A marvellous first course or a side dish with baked chicken or grilled meats. But if you love aubergines, you'll want to make a whole meal of this tasty dish.*

2 sprigs parsley
1 clove garlic, peeled
1 medium aubergine (about 450g [1lb]), peeled, cut to fit feed tube
100g (4oz) mushrooms
4 spring onions and tops, cut to fit feed tube
2 × 15ml tbsp (2tbsp) olive or vegetable oil
2 × 397g (14oz) tins Italian-style plum tomatoes, undrained, cut into quarters
150g (6oz) tomato paste
2 × 15ml tbsp (2tbsp) dry white wine
2 × 5ml tsp (2tsp) dried oregano
$\frac{1}{2}$ × 5ml tsp ($\frac{1}{2}$tsp) dried basil
$\frac{1}{2}$ × 5ml tsp ($\frac{1}{2}$tsp) sugar
1 × 5ml tsp (1tsp) salt
pepper
450g (1lb) spaghetti, cooked

Process (Steel Knife) parsley using on/off technique until minced. With machine running, drop garlic through feed tube, processing until minced; remove. Slice (Slicing Disc) aubergine, mushrooms and onions. Microwave garlic mixture, aubergine, mushrooms, onions and oil in 3 litre (5$\frac{1}{2}$pt) casserole, covered, at High until vegetables are tender, about 6 minutes, stirring after 3 minutes.

Process (Steel Knife) tomatoes and liquid using on/off technique until chopped. Stir tomatoes and remaining ingredients except spaghetti into aubergine mixture; microwave uncovered at High 10 minutes, stirring after 5 minutes. Serve sauce over hot spaghetti.

*Tips*
1 If you can obtain fresh basil, substitute 2 large leaves for the $\frac{1}{2}$ × 5ml tsp ($\frac{1}{2}$tsp) dried and mince them with the parsley.
2 Cook spaghetti conventionally since no time will be saved in the microwave with more than 225g (8oz) pasta.

## Spaghetti carbonara

Total Preparation Time: 28–34 min
Microwave Time: 20–6 min
Serves: 4–6

*Spaghetti is so versatile—as this recipe with bacon, ham and eggs proves. Somewhat lighter than spaghetti bolognese, yet it needs only a large tossed salad to complete a supper menu.*

1 litre (1¾pt) water
225g (8oz) uncooked spaghetti
1 × 15ml tbsp (1 tbsp) olive or vegetable oil
1 × 5ml tsp (1 tsp) salt
4 slices bacon
50g (2oz) Parmesan cheese, cut into 2.5cm (1in)
    pieces
150g (6oz) bacon or ham, cut into 2.5cm (1in)
    pieces
2 × 15ml tbsp (2 tbsp) butter or margarine
1 × 15ml tbsp (1 tbsp) olive or vegetable oil
3 eggs
pepper

Microwave water at High until boiling. Arrange spaghetti in 30 × 20cm (12 × 8in) baking dish; sprinkle with 1 × 15ml tbsp (1 tbsp) oil and the salt. Pour boiling water over spaghetti; microwave covered with clingfilm at High until spaghetti is *al dente*, 8–10 minutes, stirring twice. Drain.

Microwave bacon in baking dish, covered with kitchen paper, at High until bacon is crisp, 3–4 minutes. Drain and crumble.

With machine running (Steel Knife), drop cheese through feed tube, processing until finely grated. Process (Steel Knife) bacon or ham using on/off technique until chopped.

Microwave butter and 1 × 15ml tbsp (1 tbsp) oil in casserole at High until butter is melted; whisk in eggs until smooth. Stir in spaghetti, grated cheese, bacon or ham, crumbled bacon and pepper. Microwave uncovered at High until eggs are set, 3–4 minutes, stirring every minute.

*Tip*
Spaghetti can be cooked conventionally, if desired.

## Chicken lasagne

Total Preparation Time: 90–7 min
Microwave Time: 72–8 min
Serves: 8

*This Mediterranean-style dish has an unusually rich flavour and creamy texture. Ideal for casual entertaining or family dinners.*

1½ litres (2½pt) water
1 × 15ml tbsp (1 tbsp) vegetable oil
½ × 5ml tsp (½tsp) salt
12 lasagne noodles
50g (2oz) Parmesan cheese, cut into 2.5cm (1in)
    pieces
300g (12oz) mozzarella cheese, chilled, cut to fit
    feed tube
1 medium carrot, peeled, cut into 2.5cm (1in)
    pieces
1 stick celery, cut into 2.5cm (1in) pieces
1 medium onion, peeled, cut into 2.5cm (1in)
    pieces
1 medium green pepper, seeded, cut into 2.5cm
    (1in) pieces
1 × 15ml tbsp (1 tbsp) olive or vegetable oil
6 medium tomatoes, seeded, cut into 2.5cm (1in)
    pieces
2 × 397g (14oz) tins tomato sauce
1 × 5ml tsp (1 tsp) sugar
1 × 5ml tsp (1 tsp) dried basil
½ × 5ml tsp (½tsp) dried oregano
pinch of dried marjoram
2 large sprigs parsley
1 clove garlic, peeled
300g (12oz) cooked, skinned, boned chicken cut
    into 2.5cm (1in) pieces
450g (1lb) ricotta cheese
3 eggs, beaten
salt
pepper

Microwave water, 1 × 15ml tbsp (1 tbsp) oil and ½ × 5ml tsp (½tsp) salt in 30 × 20cm (12 × 8in) baking dish at High until boiling; add noodles. Microwave covered with clingfilm at High until noodles are *al dente*, about 10 minutes. Drain; rinse with cold water.

With machine running (Steel Knife), drop Parmesan cheese through feed tube, processing until finely grated; remove. Shred (Shredding Disc) mozzarella cheese; remove. Process (Steel Knife) carrot, celery, onion and green pepper using on/off technique until finely chopped. Microwave vegetable mixture and 1 × 15ml tbsp (1 tbsp) oil in 2 litre (3½pt) casserole, covered, at High until tender, about 4 minutes.

Process (Steel Knife) tomatoes using on/off technique until coarsely chopped. Stir tomatoes, tomato sauce, sugar, basil, oregano and marjoram into vegetable mixture in casserole. Microwave uncovered at High 25 minutes, or until thickened, stirring every 5 minutes.

Process (Steel Knife) parsley using on/off technique until minced. With machine running, drop garlic through feed tube, processing until minced. Add chicken to bowl; process using on/off technique until coarsely chopped. Mix chicken mixture, 150g (6oz) of the mozzarella, 2 × 15ml tbsp (2 tbsp) of the

Parmesan, the ricotta cheese, eggs, salt and the pepper.

Layer 4 lasagne noodles in bottom of 30 × 20cm (12 × 8in) baking dish. Spread half the chicken mixture over noodles; spoon a third of the sauce mixture over chicken mixture. Repeat layers, ending with remaining sauce. Microwave uncovered at 50% (Medium) 20 minutes, rotating dish ¼ turn every 5 minutes. Microwave uncovered at High until bubbly, about 5 minutes. Sprinkle remaining mozzarella and Parmesan cheese over top. Let stand loosely covered 10 minutes. Cut into squares to serve.

*Tips*

1 Noodles can be cooked conventionally, according to packet directions.
2 To microwave chicken, arrange skinned chicken pieces in a 30 × 20cm (12 × 8in) baking dish with meatiest portions towards edges of dish. Microwave covered with clingfilm at High, about 7 minutes per 450g (1lb). Let stand until cool enough to remove meat from bones; cut meat into 2.5cm (1in) pieces. 1kg (2lb) chicken pieces will give about 300g (12oz) cooked chicken.
3 Chicken and sauce mixtures can be made 1 day in advance: refrigerate separately, covered. Chicken lasagne can be prepared 1 hour before cooking.

## Cheese canneloni with meat sauce
Total Preparation Time: 47–55 min
Microwave Time: 24–9 min
Serves: 6

*This pasta dish has the addition of a delicious spicy meat sauce which goes extremely well with the cheese stuffing.*

Meat sauce (recipe follows)
100g (4oz) mozzarella cheese, chilled, cut to fit feed tube
4 sprigs parsley
25g (1oz) Parmesan cheese, cut into 2.5cm (1in) pieces
1 clove garlic, peeled
1 small onion, peeled, cut into 2.5cm (1in) pieces
450g (1lb) ricotta cheese
2 eggs
½ × 5ml tsp (½tsp) dried basil
12 cooked canneloni

Make Meat sauce.

Shred (Shredding Disc) mozzarella cheese; remove. Process (Steel Knife) parsley using on/off technique until minced. With machine running, drop Parmesan cheese through feed tube, processing until finely grated. With machine running, drop garlic through feed tube, processing until minced. Add onion to bowl; process using on/off technique until finely chopped. Add ricotta cheese, half the mozzarella cheese, the eggs and basil to bowl; process using on/off technique just until blended (do not overprocess or consistency of filling will be too thin).

Spoon half the Meat sauce in bottom of 30 × 20cm (12 × 8in) baking dish. Fill canneloni with cheese mixture; arrange in baking dish. Spoon remaining Meat sauce over canneloni. Microwave uncovered at High 13–15 minutes, or until hot through, rotating dish ¼ turn every 5 minutes. Sprinkle with remaining mozzarella cheese; let stand loosely covered 5 minutes.

**Meat sauce**
Makes: about 1½ litres (2½pt)

300g (12oz) Italian sausage, casing removed, crumbled
100g (4oz) pepperoni sausage, cut into 2.5cm (1in) pieces
¼ large green pepper, seeded, cut into 2.5cm (1in) pieces
6 medium tomatoes, seeded, cut into 2.5cm (1in) pieces
300g (12oz) tomato paste
100ml (4floz) water
50ml (2floz) dry white wine
2 × 15ml tbsp (2tbsp) light brown sugar
½ × 5ml tsp (½tsp) dried oregano
pinch of dried marjoram
pinch of dried thyme
½ × 5ml tsp (½tsp) salt
pepper

Microwave Italian sausage in 3 litre (5½pt) casserole, uncovered, at High until meat loses pink colour, 5–6 minutes, stirring after 3 minutes; drain well. Process (Steel Knife) pepperoni using on/off technique until finely chopped; remove. Process (Steel Knife) green pepper using on/off technique until chopped. Add tomatoes to bowl; process using on/off technique until chopped. Stir pepperoni, tomato mixture and remaining ingredients into Italian sausage; microwave loosely covered with greaseproof paper at High until sauce is slightly thickened, about 8 minutes, stirring after 4 minutes.

*Tips*

1 Microwave canneloni according to first paragraph of Chicken lasagne (previous recipe) or cook conventionally.
2 Cheese mixture can be made 1 day in advance; refrigerate covered. Meat sauce can be made and refrigerated covered 2 days in advance, or frozen in a covered container up to 1 month.

# Barley casserole

Total Preparation Time: 45–50 min
Microwave Time: 38–43 min
Serves: 6–8

*The marvellous flavour and combined textures of this casserole will justify the cooking time required by the barley. An extremely economical family dish—and full of goodness too.*

150g (6oz) uncooked pearl barley
10 sprigs parsley
1 medium onion, peeled, cut into 2.5cm (1in)
    pieces
1 medium carrot, peeled, cut to fit feed tube
100g (4oz) mushrooms
1 stick celery, cut to fit feed tube
1 litre (1¾pt) beef stock
½ × 5ml tsp (1tsp) dried marjoram
a few caraway seeds
pepper
75g (3oz) salted cashew nuts

Microwave barley in 2 litre (3½pt) casserole, uncovered, at High 3 minutes, stirring after 1½ minutes. Process (Steel Knife) parsley using on/off technique until minced. Add onion to bowl; process using on/off technique until chopped, and remove. Slice (Slicing Disc) carrot, mushrooms and celery separately. Stir beef stock, onion mixture, carrot, celery, marjoram, caraway seeds and pepper into barley. Microwave uncovered at High until barley is tender, 35–40 minutes, stirring every 10 minutes.

Stir mushrooms and cashew nuts into barley mixture during last 10 minutes of cooking time.

*Tip*
To microwave plain barley, follow the first paragraph above, omitting vegetables, herbs and pepper. Substitute chicken stock for the beef stock, if you wish.

# Vegetables

## Ratatouille

Total Preparation Time: 35–40 min
Microwave Time: 20–5 min
Serves: 6

*A versatile French classic. Serve it hot or at room temperature with beef, lamb, chicken or sliced sausages, or chill it and arrange on lettuce as a first course.*

1 small aubergine, peeled, cut to fit feed tube
1 medium green pepper, seeded, cut to fit feed tube
12 olives, stoned
2 cloves garlic, peeled
2 small onions, peeled, cut into quarters
1 × 397g (14oz) tin Italian-style plum tomatoes, undrained, cut into quarters
2 × 15ml tbsp (2tbsp) olive or vegetable oil
50ml (2fl oz) red wine vinegar
2 × 15ml tbsp (2tbsp) light brown sugar
2 × 15ml tbsp (2tbsp) tomato paste
1 × 15ml tbsp (1tbsp) drained capers
pinch of dried basil
pinch of dried tarragon
pinch of dried oregano
salt
pepper
25g (1oz) flaked almonds

Slice (Slicing Disc) aubergine, green pepper and olives; remove. With machine running (Steel Knife), drop garlic through the feed tube, processing until minced. Add onions to bowl; process using on/off technique until coarsley chopped, remove. Process (Steel Knife) tomatoes and liquid using on/off technique until coarsely chopped. Microwave onion mixture, aubergine, green pepper, olives, tomatoes and oil in 2 litre (3½pt) casserole, covered, at High until aubergine is tender, 12–15 minutes, stirring every 5 minutes. Stir in remaining ingredients except nuts; microwave covered at 50% (Medium) 8–10 minutes. Stir in nuts.

*Tip*
Substitute 3 large fresh tomatoes, cored and cut into 2.5cm (1in) pieces, for the tinned tomatoes, if wished. Substitute fresh herbs, using twice the amounts of dried or more, according to taste; chop them with the onions.

## French-style vegetable purée

Total Preparation Time: 44–52 min
Microwave Time: 28–34 min
Serves: 4

*Update a refined French accompaniment for roast meats. The shredded potato thickener for puréed peas is classic, but microwave cooking allows you to achieve optimum consistency without the hours of simmering on top of the cooker that used to be required.*

300g (12oz) potatoes
2 × 225g (8oz) frozen peas
50-75ml (2-3fl oz) whipping cream
50g (2oz) butter or margarine, softened
salt
pepper
freshly ground nutmeg

Prick potatoes with fork. Microwave on kitchen paper at High until tender, 6–7 minutes; wrap in aluminium foil and let stand 5 minutes. Peel potatoes. Shred (Shredding Disc) potatoes; spoon into 1½ litre (2½pt) casserole.

Remove wrapper and make 1 or 2 slashes in box or packet of peas; microwave in box or packet at High until tender, 10–12 minutes. Process (Steel Knife) until smooth; stir into potato. Microwave uncovered at High until very thick, 10–12 minutes, stirring every 2 minutes. Stir in cream, 1 × 15ml tbsp (1tbsp) at a time; stir in butter, 1 × 15ml tbsp (1tbsp) at a time, until blended. Season to taste with salt, pepper and nutmeg. Microwave covered at High until hot through, about 2–4 minutes.

*Tip*
French-style vegetable purée can be made with various fresh or frozen vegetables, including carrots, broccoli and asparagus. Substitute 675g (1½lb) fresh vegetables for the frozen peas; slice (Slicing Disc) vegetables or cut into 2.5cm (1in) pieces. Microwave fresh vegetables with 2 × 15ml tbsp (2tbsp) water in 1½ litre (2½pt) casserole, covered, at High until vegetables are tender, 10–12 minutes. Proceed with recipe as above. Or you may substitute 2 packets (8oz each) frozen vegetables for the peas such as carrots, broccoli, asparagus, cauliflower or beans; cook as above.

# Cauliflower with avocado and almonds

Total Preparation Time: 20–2 min
Microwave Time: 9–11 min
Serves: 6

*This may well become your favourite way of serving cauliflower. The whole cauliflower, covered with lime-flavoured avocado sauce, looks attractive and tastes delicious.*

2 × 15ml tbsp (2tbsp) blanched almonds
½ head iceberg lettuce, cut into wedges to fit feed tube
1 spring onion and top, cut into 2.5cm (1in) pieces
1 medium avocado, peeled, stoned, cut into 2.5cm (1in) pieces
1 × 15ml tbsp (1tbsp) lime juice
pinch of ground nutmeg
1 medium head cauliflower, core removed
100ml (4fl oz) chicken stock
1 × 15ml tbsp (1tbsp) pimento pieces

Process (Steel Knife) almonds until coarsely chopped. Microwave almonds in glass pie dish uncovered, at High until toasted, about 2 minutes, stirring after 1 minute.

Slice (Slicing Disc) lettuce; arrange in layer on serving plate and refrigerate. Process (Steel Knife) onion using on/off technique until finely chopped; add avocado, lime juice and nutmeg to bowl, and process using on/off technique until almost smooth. Refrigerate.

Microwave cauliflower and stock, covered with clingfilm, at High until crisp-tender, 7–9 minutes, rotating casserole ¼ turn after 4 minutes.

Serve cauliflower warm or refrigerate and serve cold. Place cauliflower on lettuce on serving plate; spoon avocado mixture over cauliflower. Sprinkle with almonds; garnish with pimento.

# Stir-fried broccoli and walnuts

Total Preparation Time: 19–22 min
Microwave Time: 9–12 min
Serves: 4

*Food processor slicing turns broccoli stalks into slim, attractive disc-shapes, and quick cooking retains the crisp-tender texture. This is a good way of preserving the high vitamin C content of broccoli, which can be destroyed by prolonged heat.*

50g (2oz) walnuts
1 small onion, peeled, cut into quarters
300g (12oz) fresh broccoli, cut to fit feed tube
1 × 15ml tbsp (1tbsp) olive or vegetable oil
50ml (2fl oz) chicken stock
2 × 5ml tsp (2tsp) soy sauce
1 × 5ml tsp (1tsp) sugar

Process (Steel Knife) walnuts using on/off technique until coarsely chopped. Microwave in glass pie dish uncovered at High until toasted, 2–3 minutes, stirring every minute.

Process (Steel Knife) onion using on/off technique until chopped; remove. Slice (Slicing Disc) broccoli. Microwave oil in 1 litre (1¾pt) casserole, uncovered, until hot, 1 minute. Stir in onion; microwave uncovered at High until tender, 2–3 minutes. Stir in broccoli, chicken stock, soy sauce and sugar. Microwave covered at High until broccoli is crisp-tender, 4–5 minutes. Sprinkle with walnuts.

*Tip*
Substitute asparagus for the broccoli, if you wish. With either broccoli or asparagus, you can cut off and reserve small florets or tips prior to slicing and microwave them with the sliced vegetable as above.

# Corn soufflé

Total Preparation Time: 40–6 min
Microwave Time: 28–34 min
Serves: 6–8

*Because all ingredients can be kept on hand, this is a good recipe to remember for winter suppers and unexpected guests.*

50ml (2fl oz) Twice-as-fast sauce mix (see Index)
1 chicken stock cube
½ × 5ml tsp (½tsp) dried savory
pinch of dried marjoram
pepper
300ml (12fl oz) milk
100g (4oz) Cheddar cheese, chilled, cut to fit feed tube
1 large tin sweetcorn, drained
6 egg yolks
6 egg whites
2 × 15ml tbsp (2tbsp) sugar
1 × 15ml tbsp (1tbsp) flour
2 × 15ml tbsp (2tbsp) water
1 × 5ml tsp (1tsp) lemon juice

Microwave sauce mix in 1½ litre (2½pt) cassserole at High, uncovered, 2 minutes, stirring after 1 minute. Stir in crumbled stock cube, savory, marjoram and pepper; stir in milk. Microwave uncovered at High until sauce boils and thickens, 3–4 minutes, stirring with whisk every minute.

Shred (Shredding Disc) cheese. Stir cheese into sauce mixture; microwave covered at High just until boiling, about 3 minutes, stirring after 2 minutes. Process (Steel Knife) half the corn using on/off technique until minced. Add egg yolks to bowl; process using on/off technique until blended. Stir corn mixture and remaining corn into sauce mixture.

Insert Steel Knife in clean processor bowl. Add egg whites, sugar and flour; with machine running, pour combined water and lemon juice through feed tube. Process until egg whites are stiff, about 2 minutes. Fold egg whites into corn mixture. Pour mixture into ungreased 2 litre (3½pt) soufflé dish. Microwave uncovered at 50% (Medium) until centre is almost set, 20–25 minutes, rotating soufflé dish ¼ turn every 5 minutes. Serve immediately.

*Tip*

This is one occasion when you will need to wash and dry the food processor workbowl before processing the egg whites in this recipe.

## Braised kale

Total Preparation Time: 28–9 min
Microwave Time: 17–18 min
Serves: 4

*The appearance of kale in the market is one of the first, and best, signs of spring. The ruffled leaves have both a wonderful flavour and extremely high vitamin A content.*

4 slices of bacon
1 medium leek or 6 spring onions and tops,
    cleaned, cut to fit feed tube
450g (1lb) kale, stems removed
100ml (4fl oz) chicken stock
75ml (3fl oz) sour cream
1 × 5ml tsp (1tsp) Dijon mustard
pepper

Microwave bacon in 2 litre (3½pt) casserole, uncovered, at High until crisp, about 4 minutes. Drain bacon and crumble; reserve fat.
    Slice (Slicing Disc) leek; microwave in bacon fat in casserole, covered, at High until tender, 3–4 minutes, stirring after 2 minutes. Slice (Slicing Disc) kale. Stir kale and stock into casserole. Microwave covered at High until kale is tender, about 10 minutes, stirring after 5 minutes. Drain well. Stir in sour cream, mustard and pepper; sprinkle with bacon.

*Tips*

To slice kale, stack the leaves neatly, roll up and insert the roll vertically in the food processor feed tube, through the bottom of the tube if necessary. Slice with light pressure.
2 Use this recipe to enjoy the taste and goodness of all the deep-green, leafy vegetables that usually require long simmering on top of the cooker. You can also substitute spinach; because it is much more tender than kale, spinach will require only about 5 minutes of microwave cooking.

## Potatoes au gratin

Total Preparation Time: 22–4 min
Microwave Time: 16–20 min
Serves: 6

*If you are looking for a fast, flavoursome potato casserole, this recipe is the answer!*

550g (1¼lb) potatoes (about 4 medium), peeled, cut
    to fit feed tube
2 × 15ml tbsp (2tbsp) water
50g (2oz) Cheddar cheese, chilled, cut to fit feed
    tube
1 small onion, peeled, cut into quarters
1 small stick celery, cut into 2.5cm (1in) pieces
2 × 15ml tbsp (2tbsp) Twice-as-fast sauce mix (see
    Index)
225ml (8fl oz) milk
100ml (4fl oz) sour cream
1 × 15ml tbsp (1tbsp) dried chives
salt
pepper
paprika

Slice (Slicing Disc) potatoes; microwave with water in 1½ litre (2½pt) casserole, covered, at High until tender, 4–5 minutes, rotating casserole ¼ turn after 2 minutes. Drain any excess liquid.
    Shred (Shredding Disc) cheese; remove. Process (Steel Knife) onion and celery, using on/off technique, until finely chopped. Microwave sauce mix in 1 litre (1¾pt) measure at High, uncovered, 2 minutes, stirring after 1 minute. Stir in onion, celery and milk; microwave at High, uncovered, until sauce boils and thickens, about 3 minutes, stirring with whisk every minute. Stir in cheese until melted; stir in sour cream and chives. Season to taste.
    Stir sauce mixture into potatoes. Microwave uncovered at 70% (Medium High) until hot through, 7–9 minutes. Sprinkle with paprika.

## Baked sweet potatoes with seasoned butter

Total Preparation Time: 9–11 min
Microwave Time: 7–9 min
Serves: 4

*When Columbus arrived in America, he discovered sweet potatoes, among other things. But he could not have realised what a rich source of vitamin A he had found!*

4 medium sweet potatoes
Strawberry or Chutney butter (see Index)

Pierce potatoes with fork. Microwave on kitchen paper at High until tender, 7–9 minutes. Make desired butter. Pierce tops of potatoes and press to open; spoon butter in potatoes.

# Tomato timbales

Total Preparation Time: 39–43 min
Microwave Time: 29–33 min
Serves: 6

*In French cuisine, a timbale is a savoury custard baked
in a small drum-shaped mould. This tomato version
resembles the classic dish in texture and appearance but
does not require the usual, slow water-bath baking, since
microwaves cook with remarkable evenness and without
dry heat. The result is an impressive first course or an
unusual vegetable accompaniment for roast meats,
steaks, chops or poultry.*

Fresh tomato sauce (see Index)
25g (1oz) Parmesan cheese, cut into 2.5cm (1in)
    pieces
2 × 15ml tbsp (2tbsp) Twice-as-fast sauce mix (see
    Index)
100ml (4fl oz) milk
2 eggs, beaten
watercress or parsley sprigs

Make Fresh tomato sauce.

Process (Steel Knife) cheese until finely grated.
Microwave sauce mix in 1 litre (1¾pt) measure,
uncovered, at High 2 minutes, stirring with whisk
every minute. Stir in milk; microwave uncovered at
High until mixture boils and thickens, 2–3 minutes,
stirring every minute (mixture will be extremely
thick).

Stir Fresh tomato sauce into sauce mix; stir in
eggs and grated cheese. Spoon mixture into 6
ungreased 150ml (6fl oz) cups. Arrange cups in
circle in oven. Microwave uncovered at High until
set, 5–7 minutes, rotating cups ¼ turn after 3
minutes. Let stand 5 minutes.

Loosen edges of cups with knife; unmould onto
serving plate. Garnish each timbale with sprig of
watercress.

*Tips*
1 To impress your guests unmould individual timbales onto large dinner plates after you have
arranged the meat portions; then spoon a serving of
steamed green vegetables onto the plate for maximum colour contrast.
2 To serve timbales as a first course, unmould them
onto salad-size plates, garnish with watercress and
spoon Butter sauce (see Index) around, not over,
each serving.

# Green beans and tomatoes

Total Preparation Time: 40–2 min
Microwave Time: 30–2 min
Serves: 4

*An irresistible adaptation of a Greek speciality—green beans braised until tender with fresh tomatoes, garlic and herbs.*

Fresh tomato sauce (see Index)
1 clove garlic, peeled
300g (¾lb) green beans, trimmed
½ × 5ml tsp (½tsp) dried basil
pinch of dried oregano

Make Fresh tomato sauce, adding 1 additional clove garlic and using 1½ litre (2½pt) casserole. Stir beans, basil and oregano into sauce; microwave covered at High until beans are tender, about 10 minutes, stirring after 5 minutes.

*Tips*

1 Green beans vary greatly in texture according to age and size. Very small green beans may require less cooking time; check to see if cooked when you stir them. If beans are thick and not very fresh, you may want to French-cut them prior to cooking; if so, place beans horizontally in the feed tube and slice (Slicing Disc).
2 Courgettes can be substituted for the green beans. Cut 300g (¾lb) courgettes to fit feed tube and slice; microwave at High as above until tender, about 5 minutes.

# Courgette and potato pancake

Total Preparation Time: 28–31 min
Microwave Time: 6½–7 min
Serves: 4

*This tasty dish fits all kinds of menus, for it can accompany anything from scrambled eggs to chicken.*

½ slice day-old bread, torn into pieces
25g (1oz) Parmesan cheese, cut into 2.5cm (1in) pieces
1 medium courgette, cut to fit feed tube
1 medium potato, peeled, cut to fit feed tube
1 clove garlic, peeled
½ medium onion, peeled, cut into 2.5cm (1in) pieces
1 egg
1 × 15ml tbsp (1tbsp) mayonnaise or salad dressing
pinch of dried marjoram
pinch of dried dillweed
salt
pepper
paprika

Process (Steel Knife) bread to form fine crumbs; reserve. With machine running (Steel Knife), drop cheese through feed tube; process until finely ground and reserve. Shred (Shredding Disc) courgette; reserve. Shred potato; soak potato in iced water to cover for 15 minutes. Drain; pat dry between layers of kitchen paper. Microwave potato in lightly greased 22.5cm (9in) glass pie dish, covered with clingfilm, at High 2 minutes.

With machine running (Steel Knife), drop garlic through feed tube, processing until minced. Add onion to bowl; process using on/off technique until finely chopped. Stir onion mixture, courgette, breadcrumbs, egg, mayonnaise, marjoram, dillweed, salt and pepper into potato in pie dish. Press mixture evenly on bottom and one-third up side of pie dish. Microwave covered with clingfilm at High 2½ minutes. Sprinkle with reserved cheese; microwave uncovered at High 2 minutes, or until cheese is melted. Sprinkle with paprika. Slide onto serving plate; cut into wedges to serve.

*Tip*
The shredded potato must be soaked to remove excess starch.

# Sweet potato pudding

Total Preparation Time: 22–4 min
Microwave Time: 12–14 min
Serves: 6

*Shredded sweet potatoes lighten this version of an all-American tradition. Use firm pressure on the food processor pusher to shred raw potatoes most efficiently.*

50g (2oz) walnuts
450g (1lb) sweet potatoes, peeled, cut to fit feed tube
50g (2oz) light brown sugar
2 × 15ml tbsp (2tbsp) flour
2 × 15ml tbsp (2tbsp) granulated sugar
50ml (2fl oz) milk
1 × 15ml tbsp (1tbsp) orange-flavoured liqueur
grated rind of 1 orange
pinch of ground mace
pinch of ground allspice
25g (1oz) butter or margarine
2 × 15ml tbsp (2tbsp) light brown sugar

Process (Steel Knife) walnuts using on/off technique until finely chopped; remove. Shred (Shredding Disc) sweet potatoes. Combine potatoes, 50g (2oz) brown sugar, the flour, granulated sugar, milk, liqueur, orange rind, mace and allspice in a greased 1 litre (1¾pt) casserole. Dot with butter; sprinkle with 2 × 15ml tbsp (2tbsp) brown sugar and the walnuts. Microwave covered at High until potatoes are set, about 12 minutes, rotating dish ¼ turn every 4 minutes.

## Shredded carrot casserole

Total Preparation Time: 45–50 min
Microwave Time: 36–41 min
Serves: 4–6

*An unusual and appetising way to serve carrots—especially in winter when they are in plentiful supply. Excellent with cold meats and sausages.*

125g (5oz) blanched almonds
450g (1lb) carrots, peeled, cut to fit feed tube
400ml (16fl oz) milk
225ml (8fl oz) whipping cream
100g (4oz) sultanas
50g (2oz) light brown sugar
½ stick cinnamon
2 cloves
2–4 × 15ml tbsp (2–4tbsp) plain yogurt

Process (Steel Knife) almonds using on/off technique until coarsely chopped; remove. Shred (Shredding Disc) carrots. Combine carrots, half the almonds and the remaining ingredients except yogurt in 2 litre (3½pt) casserole. Microwave covered at High 6 minutes. Microwave uncovered until carrots have absorbed almost all the liquid, 30–35 minutes, stirring every 10 minutes. Remove cinnamon stick. Stir in yogurt; top with remaining almonds.

## Onion and apple bake

Total Preparation Time: 20–3 min
Microwave Time: 10–13 min
Serves: 6–8

*An excellent accompaniment for pork or poultry, and a tasty relish for leftover turkey or ham.*

40g (1½oz) butter or margarine
50g (2oz) light brown sugar
pinch of dry mustard
pinch of ground mace
450g (1lb) onions, peeled, cut to fit feed tube
3 medium apples, peeled, cored into halves

Microwave butter in 2 litre (3½pt) casserole at High until melted; stir in sugar, mustard and mace.

Slice (Slicing Disc) onions and apples; add to casserole, stirring to coat with butter mixture. Microwave covered at High until tender, 8–10 minutes, stirring every 4 minutes.

# Salads

## Layered vegetable salad with garlic dressing

Total Preparation Time: 25–8 min
(plus overnight refrigeration)
Microwave Time: 11–14 min
Serves: 8

*This extremely attractive salad benefits from overnight refrigeration. Add a layer or two of sliced or chopped ham, turkey or roast beef and you'll have a ready-prepared entrée.*

Garlic dressing (recipe follows)
1 small head cauliflower, cut into florets
50ml (2fl oz) water
150g (6oz) fresh mangetout peas
4 sprigs parsley
100g (4oz) mushrooms
150g (6oz) fresh spinach, stems discarded
1 small onion, cut into halves
2 large carrots, peeled, cut to fit feed tube
150g (6oz) fresh bean sprouts, rinsed, well drained

Make Garlic dressing.

Microwave cauliflower and water in 1½ litre (2½pt) casserole, covered, at High until cauliflower is crisp-tender, 6–8 minutes. Add mangetout peas to casserole for last 3 minutes of cooking time. Rinse vegetables with cold water; drain well.

Process (Steel Knife) parsley using on/off technique until minced; remove. Slice (Slicing Disc) mushrooms, spinach and onion separately. Shred (Shredding Disc) carrots. Layer vegetables in a salad bowl. Pour Garlic dressing over top; sprinkle with parsley. Refrigerate loosely covered overnight. Toss before serving.

### Garlic dressing

Makes: about 400ml (¾pt)
50g (2oz) plain flour
2 × 15ml tbsp (2tbsp) sugar
½ × 5ml tsp (½tsp) dry mustard
½ × 5ml tsp (½tsp) salt
pinch cayenne pepper
150ml (6fl oz) water
2 egg yolks
50ml (2fl oz) white wine vinegar

1 small clove garlic
2.5cm (1in) piece onion
2 × 15ml tbsp (2tbsp) vegetable oil
100ml (4fl oz) sour cream
1 × 5ml tsp (1tsp) prepared horseradish

Combine flour, sugar, mustard, salt and cayenne pepper in 1 litre (1¾pt) measure; stir in water. Mix egg yolks and vinegar; stir into flour mixture. Microwave uncovered at 50% (Medium) until thickened, 5–6 minutes, stirring with whisk every 2 minutes.

With machine running (Steel Knife), drop garlic and onion through feed tube, processing until minced. Add cooked dressing to bowl; with machine running, add oil through feed tube, 1 × 15ml tbsp (1tbsp) at a time. Add sour cream and horseradish to bowl; process using on/off technique until blended. Refrigerate covered until ready to use.

*Tips*
1 Vegetables can be layered any way you wish. But do place at least some of the mangetout peas or carrots on top to provide colour contrast for the pale dressing.
2 With the addition of 450g (1lb) sliced or cubed cooked meat or poultry, the salad will serve 8.

## Hot and cold Roquefort salad

Total Preparation Time: 7–10 min
Microwave Time: 2–3 min
Serves: 6

*A hot, tangy dressing and cool, crisp lettuce complement each other in this tasty salad.*

50g (2oz) Parmesan cheese, cut into 2.5cm (1in) pieces
½ spring onion and top, cut into 2.5cm (1in) pieces
225ml (8fl oz) Food processor mayonnaise (see Index)
½ × 5ml level tsp (½ level tsp) prepared horseradish
pinch of dried basil
75g (3oz) Roquefort or blue cheese
6 wedges iceberg lettuce (1.25cm [½in] thick), well chilled
paprika

With machine running (Steel Knife), drop Parmesan cheese through feed tube, processing until finely grated. Add onion to bowl; process using on/off technique until finely chopped.

Make Food processor mayonnaise; add Parmesan cheese mixture, horseradish and basil to bowl; process until smooth. Add Roquefort cheese; process using on/off technique just until blended.

Microwave mayonnaise mixture in ½ litre (1pt) glass measure, covered, at 50% (Medium) just until hot, about 2 minutes, stirring after 1 minute (do not overcook, as mixture will separate). Spread mixture over lettuce wedges; sprinkle with paprika. Serve immediately.

*Tip*

Prepare mayonnaise mixture 1 day in advance; refrigerate covered and heat just before serving.

## Artichokes with vegetables vinaigrette

Total Preparation Time: 35–40 min
(plus chilling time)
Microwave Time: 12–14 min
Serves: 4

*A versatile combination, fancy enough for a dinner-party first course, yet perfectly convenient for a picnic.*

50ml (2fl oz) red wine vinegar
50ml (2fl oz) water
2 × 15ml tbsp (2tbsp) lemon juice
2 × 15ml tbsp (2tbsp) sugar
1 × 15ml tbsp (1tbsp) dried chives
pinch of crumbled dried bay leaves
salt
pepper
100g (4oz) mushrooms
1 small red or green pepper, seeded, cut to fit feed tube
1 small courgette, cut to fit feed tube
1 stick celery, cut to fit feed tube
6 olives, stoned
2 medium artichokes, cut lengthwise into halves
4 × 5ml tsp (4tsp) lemon juice
100ml (4fl oz) water

Microwave vinegar, 50ml (2fl oz) water, 2 × 15ml tbsp (2tbsp) lemon juice, the sugar, chives, bay leaves, salt and ground pepper in ½ litre (1pt) measure at High for 2 minutes, or until boiling. Let stand until room temperature.

Slice (Slicing Disc) mushrooms, red pepper, courgette, celery and olives; arrange in bowl and pour vinegar mixture over. Refrigerate covered at least 1 hour for flavours to blend.

Sprinkle cut edges of artichokes with 4 × 5ml tsp (4tsp) lemon juice; arrange, cut sides up, in glass baking dish. Add 100ml (4fl oz) water; microwave covered with clingfilm at High until tender, 10–12 minutes, rotating dish ¼ turn every 4 minutes. Cool artichokes until warm; remove chokes with spoon. Cool to room temperature; refrigerate until serving time. Spoon vegetable mixture into artichoke halves.

*Tips*

1 Artichokes with vegetables vinaigrette can be served hot as a first course or side dish. Remove chokes from artichokes before cooking; microwave as above. Microwave vegetables in vinegar mixture uncovered at 70% (Medium High) until hot through, about 3 minutes; spoon into hot artichoke halves.
2 To prepare fresh artichokes for cooking, cut off stems, remove tough bottom leaves and trim leaf tips with kitchen scissors or a knife.

## Creamy potato salad

Total Preparation Time: 19–20 min
(plus chilling time)
Microwave Time: 9–10 min
Serves: 6

*Grated cheese makes potato salad creamier than ever, and microwave cooking ensures perfect potato texture.*

450g (1lb) potatoes, peeled, cut to fit feed tube
50ml (2fl oz) water
150g (6oz) Cheddar cheese, chilled, cut to fit feed tube
1 green pepper, seeded, cut into 2.5cm (1in) pieces
1 small onion, peeled, cut into 2.5cm (1in) pieces
50ml (2fl oz) mayonnaise or salad dressing
50ml (2fl oz) sour cream
1½ × 5ml tsp (1½tsp) Dijon mustard
½ × 5ml tsp (½tsp) salt
pepper
4 slices bacon

Slice (Slicing Disc) potatoes; microwave potatoes and water in 1½ litre (2½pt) casserole, covered, at High until just tender, 5–6 minutes. Drain; let stand covered 5 minutes. Cool to room temperature.

Shred (Shredding Disc) cheese; remove. Process (Steel Knife) green pepper and onion using on/off technique until chopped. Combine potatoes, cheese, green pepper and onion in large bowl. Mix mayonnaise, sour cream, mustard, salt and pepper; pour over potato mixture and stir. Refrigerate several hours or overnight (texture of salad is creamiest if refrigerated overnight).

Microwave bacon in glass baking dish, covered with kitchen paper, at High until crisp, about 4 minutes. Drain bacon and crumble; sprinkle over salad.

# Asparagus and cucumber vinaigrette

Total Preparation Time: 16–18 min
(plus chilling time)
Microwave Time: 7–9 min
Serves: 4–6

*A superb marinated salad for a picnic or outdoor lunch.*
*The dressing goes well with all Oriental-style dishes, too.*

1 × 15 ml tbsp (1 tbsp) sesame seeds
225 g (8 oz) fresh asparagus
1 medium cucumber, peeled, seeded, cut to fit feed
   tube
½ medium onion, peeled, cut to fit feed tube
50 ml (2 fl oz) water
50 ml (2 fl oz) cider vinegar
2 × 15 ml tbsp (2 tbsp) soy sauce
1 × 15 ml tbsp (1 tbsp) vegetable oil
2 × 15 ml tbsp (2 tbsp) sugar
pinch of dry mustard
pinch of ground ginger

Spread sesame seeds on bottom of glass pie dish; microwave uncovered at High until golden, 2–3 minutes, stirring every minute. Cut tips off asparagus and reserve; cut stalks to fit feed tube. Slice (Slicing Disc) asparagus stalks, cucumber and onion separately. Microwave asparagus stalks, reserved tips, and water in 1 litre (1¾pt) casserole, covered, at High until asparagus is crisp-tender, 4–5 minutes. Rinse with cold water and drain.

Add cucumber and onion to casserole. Microwave vinegar and remaining ingredients in a small bowl, uncovered, at High 1 minute. Stir with whisk; pour over vegetables and toss. Refrigerate covered at least 1 hour for flavours to blend. Sprinkle with sesame seeds before serving.

*Tip*
To seed cucumber, cut it lengthwise into halves. Cut around centre with a knife and remove seeds in a strip, or scoop out seeds with a spoon.

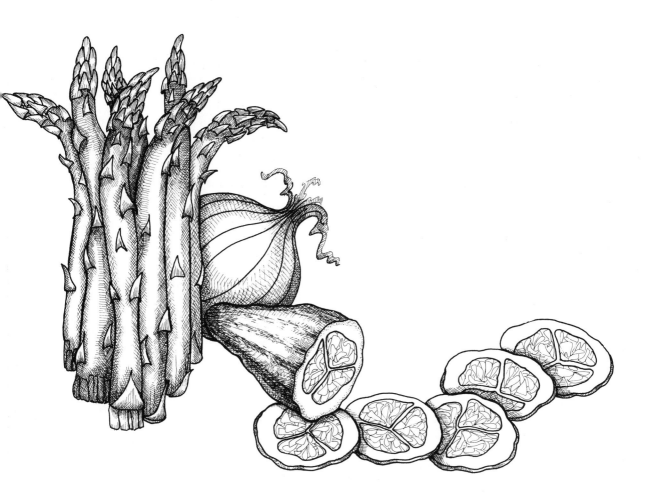

## Double-dressed chicken salad

Total Preparation Time: 22–5 min
(plus chilling time)
Microwave Time: 9–11 min
Serves: 4–6

*The food processor and microwave oven make it easy to achieve the most important features of this salad—moist chicken and delicate mayonnaise.*

450g (1lb) boneless chicken breast halves, skinned
100ml (4fl oz) chicken stock
50g (2oz) walnuts
1 × 150g (6oz) water chestnuts, drained
2 sprigs parsley
2 × 15ml tbsp (2tbsp) cider vinegar
salt
pepper
50ml (2fl oz) vegetable oil
50ml (2fl oz) Cucumber mayonnaise (see Index)
50ml (2fl oz) sour cream
1 × 5ml tsp (1tsp) dried dillweed
½ × 5ml tsp (½tsp) Dijon mustard
2 hard-boiled eggs, shelled, cut into quarters

Microwave chicken and stock in 1½ litre (2½pt) casserole, covered, at High until chicken is done and juices run clear when chicken is pierced with a fork, about 7 minutes; turn chicken over after 4 minutes and rotate casserole ¼ turn. Let chicken cool until warm; cut into 2.5cm (1in) pieces.

Microwave walnuts in glass pie dish, uncovered, at High 2–3 minutes until toasted, stirring every minute. Slice (Slicing Disc) water chestnuts; remove. Process (Steel Knife) walnuts until finely chopped; process chicken until coarsely chopped. Combine water chestnuts, walnuts and chicken in medium bowl. Process (Steel Knife) parsley using on/off technique until minced; add vinegar, salt and peper to bowl. With machine running (Steel Knife), add oil through feed tube. Pour dressing over chicken mixture and toss. Refrigerate covered 1 hour for flavours to blend.

Make Cucumber mayonnaise; stir in sour cream, dillweed and mustard; spoon over chicken mixture and toss. Spoon into serving bowl; garnish with hard-boiled egg.

*Tips*
1 Because this is a fine-textured chicken salad, it makes an excellent appetiser or sandwich spread.
2 Chicken and mayonnaise mixtures can be prepared 1 day in advance; refrigerate separately, covered, and combine just before serving.
3 Serve Double-dressed chicken salad with Garlic-herb toast (see Index), if you wish. Alternatively, spread the salad in pita bread halves.

## Moulded vegetable salad

Total Preparation Time: 27–8 min
(plus chilling time)
Microwave Time: 5–6 min
Serves: 8

*A pretty vegetable mould can be made remarkably quickly with a microwave and food processor to produce a delicious summer dish.*

225ml (8fl oz) hot water
75g (3oz) gelatine
50ml (2fl oz) dry white wine
100ml (4fl oz) cold water
pinch of dried basil
pinch of dried tarragon
¼ medium head cauliflower, cut into florets
4 medium mushroom caps, fluted if desired
25g (1oz) fresh spinach, stems discarded
50g (2oz) mushrooms
¼ medium cucumber, cut to fit feed tube
¼ large red or green pepper, seeded, cut into 2.5cm (1in) pieces
½ small onion, peeled, cut into 2.5cm (1in) pieces
1 × 15ml tbsp (1tbsp) water
lettuce leaves

Microwave 225ml (8fl oz) hot water in glass measure at High until boiling; stir in gelatine until dissolved. Stir in wine, 100ml (4fl oz) cold water, basil and tarragon. Pour 100ml (4fl oz) of the gelatine mixture in bottom of lightly greased 1½ litre (2½pt) ring mould; refrigerate.

Reserve 5 florets and the mushroom caps; slice (Slicing Disc) remaining cauliflower, the spinach, mushrooms and cucumber separately. Process (Steel Knife) red pepper and onion using on/off technique until coarsely chopped. Microwave reserved florets, sliced cauliflower and 1 × 15ml tbsp (1tbsp) water in 1 litre (1¾pt) casserole, covered, at High for 3 minutes. Rinse with cold water and drain. Arrange florets and fluted mushroom caps on gelatine in mould; layer remaining vegetables in mould. Pour remaining gelatine mixture over vegetables; refrigerate until set, 6–8 hours.

Loosen edge of mould with tip of sharp knife; dip mould briefly in warm water. Unmould on lettuce leaves on serving plate.

*Tip*
To flute mushroom caps, hold each mushroom by the stem and use a sharp knife to peel away a thin strip of the cap. Hold the knife blade diagonally and cut from the crown of the cap to the edge. Rotate the mushroom and continue cutting away strips until you have a pinwheel pattern. Remove stem and reserve for other use.

# Fruit salad with pineapple-cream dressing

Total Preparation Time: 18–20 min
(plus chilling time)
Microwave Time: 3–5 min
Serves: 6–8

*An unusual summer starter. For a buffet party, arrange the fruit on a serving plate and allow guests to help themselves to the dressing separately. Substitute any fruit in season; melon, oranges, apples, pears, blackberries and grapes (unsliced) would all be delicious.*

Pineapple-cream dressing (recipe follows)
1 pineapple, peeled, cored, cut to fit feed tube
2 medium bananas, peeled, cut to fit feed tube
500ml (1pt) strawberries, hulled
lettuce leaves
mint sprigs (optional)

Make Pineapple-cream dressing. Slice (Slicing Disc) fruits; arrange fruits attractively on salad plates lined with lettuce leaves. Spoon dressing over; garnish with mint sprigs.

### Pineapple-cream dressing

Makes: 300ml (12fl oz)

25g (1oz) butter or margarine
2 × 15ml tbsp (2tbsp) cornflour
150ml (6fl oz) whipping cream
100ml (4fl oz) pineapple juice
2 × 15ml tbsp (2tbsp) lemon juice
50g (2oz) sugar
pinch of dry mustard
pinch of paprika
salt

Microwave butter in 1 litre (1¾pt) measure at High until melted. Stir in cornflour; stir in remaining ingredients. Microwave uncovered at High until thickened, 2–3 minutes, stirring with a whisk every minute. Cool to room temperature. Refrigerate until chilled.

*Tip*
Pineapple-cream dressing may be made 1 day in advance; refrigerate covered. Slice fruit as close to serving time as possible; if salad is to be served at a buffet, substitute a fruit that will not darken, such as oranges or honeydew melon, for the bananas.

# Courgette salad with pineapple dressing

Total Preparation Time: 18–19 min
Microwave Time: 3–4 min
Serves: 8

*Use whatever salad greens are available to make this an all-the-year-round salad. It goes well with meat loaf, lamb or chicken.*

100ml (4fl oz) pineapple conserve or jam
50ml (2fl oz) tarragon vinegar
50ml (2fl oz) vegetable oil
pinch of dried mint
100g (4oz) Gruyère cheese, chilled, cut to fit feed tube
2 medium courgettes, cut to fit feed tube
1 small onion, peeled, cut to fit feed tube
2 × 15ml tbsp (2tbsp) water
1kg (2lb) assorted salad greens, cut into bite-size pieces

Microwave jam, vinegar, oil and mint in ½ litre (1pt) measure uncovered at 50% (Medium) until jam has melted and mixture just comes to a boil, about 1 minute. Stir; let stand until room temperature.

Shred (Shredding Disc) cheese; reserve. Slice (Slicing Disc) courgettes and onion separately. Microwave courgettes and water in 1 litre (1¾pt) casserole, covered, at High 2 minutes. Drain; cool to room temperature.

Combine greens, reserved cheese, courgettes and onion in salad bowl; pour dressing over and toss.

*Tips*
1 Mature Cheddar can be substituted for the Gruyère.
2 Dressing may be prepared hours in advance and allowed to stand covered at room temperature. But do not toss with vegetables until ready to serve.

# Salade niçoise

Total Preparation Time: 40–5 min
Microwave Time: 18–21 min
Serves: 4

*Chicken replaces the more traditional anchovies or tuna in this salad. The microwaved dressing is absorbed quickly and thoroughly by the cooked, sliced vegetables, eliminating the need to marinate for fullest flavour.*

450g (1lb) boneless chicken breast halves, skinned
pinch of ground nutmeg
225g (8oz) fresh green beans, trimmed
50ml (2fl oz) water
2 medium potatoes, peeled, cut to fit feed tube
2 × 15ml tbsp (2tbsp) water
12 pitted olives, stoned
½ small head iceberg lettuce, cut into wedges to fit
    feed tube
1 small onion, peeled, cut to fit feed tube
2 tomatoes, seeded, cut into 2.5cm (1in) pieces
100ml (4fl oz) olive or vegetable oil
50ml (2fl oz) white wine vinegar
1 × 5ml level tsp (1 level tsp) dried tarragon
salt
pepper
2 hard-boiled eggs, shelled, cut into quarters

Arrange chicken in baking dish. Sprinkle chicken with nutmeg. Microwave covered with clingfilm at High until chicken is done and juices run clear when chicken is pierced with a fork, about 7 minutes; turn chicken over after 4 minutes and rotate dish ¼ turn. Drain and cool to room temperature. Cut into strips; refrigerate covered.

Slice (Slicing Disc) green beans, arranging beans horizontally in feed tube. Microwave beans and water, covered, at High until beans are crisp-tender, about 5 minutes, stirring after 3 minutes. Drain and cool to room temperature; refrigerate covered. Slice (Slicing Disc) potatoes. Microwave potatoes and 2 × 15ml tbsp (2tbsp) water in baking dish, covered, at High until tender, about 5 minutes, rotating dish ¼ turn after 3 minutes drain. Cool to room temperature; refrigerate.

Slice (Slicing Disc) olives, lettuce and onion separately. Process (Steel Knife) tomatoes using on/off technique until coarsely chopped.

Arrange lettuce on serving plate; arrange chicken and vegetables attractively on lettuce. Microwave oil, vinegar, tarragon, salt and pepper in a small bowl, uncovered, at High just until boiling; stir with whisk and sprinkle over salad. Garnish with egg.

*Tip*
Do not attempt to hard-boil eggs in the microwave oven; for conventional cooking instructions see Index.

*Hot Devilled Eggs (page 25); Food Processor Mayonnaise (page 100); Chocolate Mousse Pie (page 117)*

# When Calories Count

## Vegetable-stuffed aubergine Parmesan
### (about 275 calories per serving)

Total Preparation Time: 28–33 min
Microwave Time: 11–14 min
Serves: 4

*Because of its lightness, this is an unusually appealing way to serve aubergine. Those who aren't counting calories would enjoy smaller portions as a side dish with Mediterranean-flavoured entrées, such as Veal rolls with prosciutto or Lemon meat loaf (see Index).*

1 aubergine (about 450g [1lb])
50g (2oz) Parmesan cheese, cut into 2.5cm (1in) pieces
100g (4oz) Cheddar cheese, chilled, cut to fit feed tube
2 sprigs watercress or parsley
1 clove garlic, peeled
50g (2oz) walnuts
½ medium onion, peeled, cut into 2.5cm (1in) pieces
1 carrot, peeled, cut into 2.5cm (1 in) pieces
1 stick celery, cut into 2.5cm (1in) pieces
1 × 15ml tbsp (1tbsp) water
1 tomato, seeded, cut into 2.5cm (1in) pieces
½ × 5ml tsp (½tsp) dried basil
salt
pepper

Prick aubergine in several places with fork. Microwave on kitchen paper at High until tender, 5–6 minutes. Process (Steel Knife) Parmesan cheese until finely grated; remove. Shred (Shredding Disc) Cheddar cheese; remove. Process (Steel Knife) watercress using on/off technique until minced. With machine running (Steel Knife), add garlic through feed tube; process until minced. Add walnuts, onion, carrot and celery to bowl; process using on/off technique until finely chopped. Remove Steel Knife; microwave vegetable mixture and water in food processor bowl, covered with clingfilm at High until the vegetables are crisp-tender, about 3 minutes. Drain thoroughly.

Cut aubergine lengthwise into halves; scoop out interior and cut into 2.5cm (1in) pieces. Add aubergine pieces, tomato, Parmesan cheese, basil, salt and pepper to food processor bowl; process using

*Mustard Roast Beef (page 59); Pork Chops Gruyère (page 61); Fresh Tomato Sauce (page 96)*

87

on/off technique until aubergine is chopped. Stir aubergine mixture and half of the Cheddar cheese into vegetable mixture; spoon into aubergine shells. Place in glass baking dish. Microwave uncovered at High until hot through, 2–3 minutes. Sprinkle with remaining Cheddar cheese; microwave uncovered at High until cheese melts, about 1 minutes. Cut each shell into halves to serve.

*Tip*

If you are on a low-sodium diet, you may wish to omit the salt and reduce the amount of Parmesan cheese; the aubergine mixture will still taste good.

## Marinated shrimp and orange salad
### (about 265 calories per serving)

Total Preparation Time: 16–18 min
(plus chilling time)
Microwave Time: 9–10 min
Serves: 6

*Although low in calories, this light, refreshing salad will appeal to slimmers and non-slimmers alike.*

2 large sprigs parsley
1 clove garlic, peeled
1 medium onion, peeled, cut to fit feed tube
50ml (2fl oz) vegetable oil
100ml (4fl oz) cider vinegar

2 × 15ml tbsp (2tbsp) lemon juice
2 × 15 tbsp (2tbsp) ketchup
1½ × 15ml tbsp (1½tbsp) brown sugar
1 × 15ml tbsp (1tbsp) lime juice
1 × 5ml tsp (1tsp) soy sauce
½ × 5ml tsp (½tsp) dry mustard
pinch of paprika
pinch of cayenne pepper
550g (1¼lb) shelled, deveined, uncooked shrimps
2 medium oranges, peeled, cut vertically into halves
½ medium head lettuce, cut into wedges to fit feed tube

Process (Steel Knife) parsley using on/off technique until minced. With machine running, drop garlic through feed tube, processing until minced; remove. Slice (Slicing Disc) onion. Microwave garlic mixture, onion and oil in 1½ litre (2½pt) casserole, covered, at High until onion is tender, about 5 minutes, stirring after 2½ minutes. Stir in remaining ingredients except shrimps, oranges and lettuce. Microwave covered at High until boiling, about 3 minutes. Stir in shrimps; microwave covered at High until they turn pink, 1–2 minutes. Slice (Slicing Disc) oranges; stir into shrimp mixture. Refrigerate until chilled, about 2 hours.

Slice (Slicing Disc) lettuce; arrange on individual serving plates. Drain shrimp mixture and spoon over lettuce.

## Garden-baked fish fillets
### (about 130 calories per serving)
Total Preparation Time: 15–18 min
Microwave Time: 4–5 min
Serves: 4

*Chopped and shredded vegetables add bulk and flavour to this low-calorie dish.*

4 sprigs parsley
1 clove garlic, peeled
3 × 15ml tbsp (3tbsp) lemon juice
½ × 5ml tsp (½tsp) soy sauce
½ × 5ml tsp (½tsp) dried dillweed
½ × 5ml tsp (½tsp) dried basil
¼ × 5ml tsp (¼tsp) Dijon mustard
1 small cucumber, peeled, seeded, cut into 2.5cm
     pieces
450g (1lb) turbot or other white fish fillets
1 carrot, peeled, cut to fit feed tube
2 radishes, ends trimmed

Process (Steel Knife) parsley using on/off technique until minced. With machine running, drop garlic through feed tube, processing until minced. Add lemon juice, soy sauce, dillweed, basil and mustard to bowl; process until blended. Add cucumber to bowl; process using on/off technique until chopped.

Layer fish in 30 × 20cm (12 × 8in) baking dish, folding thin ends of fillets under. Spoon cucumber mixture evenly over fish.

Shred (Shredding Disc) carrot and radishes; sprinkle evenly over fish. Microwave covered with clingfilm at High until fish is tender and flakes with a fork, 4–5 minutes, rotating dish ¼ turn after 2 minutes. Arrange on serving plate.

## Oriental roast beef salad
### (about 175 calories per serving)
Total Preparation Time: 23–6 min
(plus chilling time)
Microwave Time: 6–8 min
Serves: 4

*An easy-to-prepare, tasty lunch dish for all the family using only a small quantity of beef. The potato and dressing are cooked in the food processor bowl to save washing-up time.*

225g (8oz) thinly sliced, cooked, lean roast beef
1 medium potato, peeled, cut to fit feed tube
2 × 15ml tbsp (2tbsp) water
1 medium green pepper, seeded, cut to fit feed tube
1 medium onion, peeled, cut to fit feed tube
100g (4oz) mushrooms
2 sprigs fresh coriander or ½ × 5ml tsp (½tsp) dried
     coriander

1 clove garlic, peeled
100ml (4fl oz) water
75ml (3fl oz) red wine vinegar
1 beef stock cube
2 × 5ml tsp (2tsp) soy sauce
pinch of dried marjoram
pinch of dried oregano
pinch of ground ginger
pepper

Arrange beef in 30 × 20cm (12 × 8in) baking dish. Slice (Slicing Disc) potato. Microwave potato and 2 × 15ml tbsp (2tbsp) water in a casserole, covered, at High until tender, about 4 minutes; add to beef. Slice (Slicing Disc) green pepper, onion and mushrooms; add to beef.

Process (Steel Knife) coriander using on/off technique until minced. With machine running, drop garlic through feed tube, processing until minced. Add remaining ingredients to bowl, processing until blended. Remove Steel Knife; microwave mixture in food processor bowl, uncovered, at High just to boiling, about 2 minutes. Pour over meat mixture and toss. Let stand until room temperature; refrigerate until chilled.

*Tip*
Oriental roast beef salad can be prepared 1 day in advance; refrigerate covered. It is an excellent choice for picnics, as all ingredients travel well. If you wish to double the recipe, microwave the potato slices about 6 minutes and proceed as above.

## Steak in onion gravy
### (about 315 calories per serving)
Total Preparation Time: 40–2 min
Microwave Time: 22–4 min
Serves: 6

*Everything you ever wanted on a diet but were afraid to touch—beef, beer and a thick onion gravy. You can fool everyone with this dish, including yourself!*

675g (1½lb) lean, boneless beef round or topside,
     cut into 1.25cm (½in) strips
225ml (8fl oz) beer
4 medium onions, peeled, cut to fit feed tube
40g (1½oz) butter or margarine
2 × 5ml tsp (2tsp) brown sugar
3 × 15ml tbsp (3tbsp) flour
½ × 5ml tsp (½tsp) dry mustard
100ml (4fl oz) beef stock
pinch of dried marjoram
pinch of dried oregano
pinch of dried thyme
pinch of dried savory
browning and seasoning sauce

Combine beef and beer in 2 litre (3½pt) casserole; let stand for 15 minutes. Drain, reserving 100ml (4fl oz) beer.

Slice (Slicing Disc) onions. Microwave onions, butter and sugar in 2 litre (3½pt) casserole, covered, at High until onions are golden, about 10 minutes, stirring every 3 minutes. Stir in flour and mustard; microwave uncovered at High 2 minutes. Stir in reserved beer, the stock, marjoram, oregano, thyme, savory and a few drops browning sauce; microwave uncovered at High 2 minutes. Stir in beef; microwave covered at High until meat loses pink colour and is tender, 8–10 minutes, stirring every 3 minutes. Let stand covered 10 minutes before serving.

*Tip*

Because round or topside beef is not a tender cut, it is important to cut it into very thin strips. If you wish to slice the meat in the food processor, cut it into pieces to fit the feed tube; be sure that the grain of the meat is lengthwise, so that you will slice across it. Place the pieces on a baking sheet lined with aluminium foil and freeze until semi-firm (you should still be able to pierce it with a knife). Insert pieces in the feed tube and slice (Slicing Disc) with firm pressure.

## Yogurt chicken
## (about 175 calories per serving)
Total Preparation Time: 28–30 min
(plus marinating time)
Microwave Time: 13–18 min
Serves 4

*This dish tastes much, much richer than it is, due to the variety of spices and the creaminess of the sauce. Marinate the chicken at least an hour, or overnight, for the seasonings to blend. The salt can easily be omitted for low-sodium diets.*

2 sprigs fresh coriander or ½ × 5ml (½tsp) dried coriander
1 small clove garlic, peeled
100ml (4fl oz) low-fat yogurt
1 × 5ml tsp (1tsp) paprika
½ × 5ml tsp (½tsp) ground cinnamon
pinch of ground nutmeg
pinch of ground cardamom
1 × 5ml tsp (1tsp) salt
pinch of cayenne pepper
4 small chicken breast halves, skinned (about 675g [1½lb])
50ml (2fl oz) chicken stock
1 × 15ml tbsp (1tbsp) flour
2 × 15ml tbsp (2tbsp) water
1 small lemon, cut to fit feed tube
coriander or parsley sprigs

Process (Steel Knife) 2 sprigs coriander using on/off technique until minced. With machine running, drop garlic through feed tube, processing until minced. Add yogurt, paprika, cinnamon, nutmeg, cardamom, salt and cayenne papper to bowl; process (Steel Knife) using on/off technique until mixed. Arrange chicken in glass baking dish, with meatiest portions towards edges of dish. Pour yogurt marinade over chicken. Refrigerate covered with greaseproof paper 1–2 hours. Microwave chicken in baking dish with yogurt marinade, covered with greaseproof paper until chicken is tender and juices run clear when chicken is pierced with a fork in thickest parts, 10–13 minutes; rearrange chicken pieces and coat with marinade after 6 minutes.

Arrange chicken on serving plate; cover loosely with aluminium foil. Pour juices and marinade into glass measure; add chicken stock to make 100ml (4fl oz). Stir in combined flour and water to make sauce. Microwave uncovered at 50% (Medium) just until boiling, 3–4 minutes, stirring every 2 minutes. Pour sauce over chicken. Slice (Slicing Disc) lemon. Garnish chicken with lemon and coriander or parsley sprigs.

# Sandwiches and Snacks

## Sloppy Joes
Total Preparation Time: 25–8 min
Microwave Time: 10–13 min
Serves: 6

*American Sloppy Joes offer a very good reason to buy extra beef when it is cheap and keep it ready in the freezer. The sliced pepper garnish may be omitted.*

450g (1lb) boneless sirloin of beef
1 medium onion, peeled, cut into 2.5cm (1in)
   pieces
1 stick celery, cut into 2.5cm (1in) pieces
1 large green pepper, seeded, cut into 2.5cm (1in)
   pieces
150ml (6fl oz) chilli sauce
2 × 15ml tbsp (2tbsp) light brown sugar
1 × 15ml tbsp (1tbsp) cider vinegar
1 × 5ml tsp (1tsp) Worcestershire sauce
½ × 5ml tsp (½tsp) Garlic salt (see Index)
pinch of dry mustard
pepper
1 large green pepper, seeded, cut to fit feed tube
6 hamburger buns or baps

Trim excess fat from meat; cut meat into 2.5cm (1in) pieces. Process (Steel Knife) meat using on/off technique until finely chopped. Process (Steel Knife) onion, celery and green pepper pieces using on/off technique until chopped. Microwave meat and vegetables in 1½ litre (2½pt) casserole, covered, at High until meat loses pink colour and vegetables are tender, about 5 minutes, stirring after 2½ minutes. Stir in remaining ingredients except large green pepper and rolls; microwave covered at High until hot, about 5 minutes, stirring after 2 minutes.

   Slice (Slicing Disc) large green pepper. Spoon meat mixture onto bottoms of rolls; top with green pepper slices and roll tops.

*Tips*
1 Unless you have a large-model food processor, do not chop more than 225g (8oz) beef at a time.
2 The cooked meat mixture can be frozen in a covered container up to 1 month.
3 To warm rolls, arrange them in a circle on kitchen paper; microwave at 70% (Medium High) until just warm to the touch, 30–40 seconds.

## Rye bread open sandwiches
Total Preparation Time: 18–20 min
Microwave Time: 8–10 min
Serves: 6

*Four delicious layers in one sandwich. This recipe makes most economical use of costly ingredients with food processor chopping, blending and shredding.*

100g (4oz) Gruyère or Cheddar cheese, chilled, cut
   to fit feed tube
225g (8oz) cooked corned beef, cut into 2.5cm (1in)
   pieces
4 slices pickled betroot, well drained
¼ medium onion, peeled, cut into 2.5cm (1in) pieces
2 medium pickled gherkins, cut into 2.5cm (1in)
   pieces
50ml (2fl oz) mayonnaise or salad dressing
2 × 15ml tbsp (2tbsp) ketchup
6 slices rye bread
1 × 397g (14oz) tin sauerkraut, well drained

Shred (Shredding Disc) cheese; remove. Process (Steel Knife) corned beef and beetroot using on/off technique until coarsely chopped; remove. Process (Steel Knife) onion, gherkins, mayonnaise and ketchup until onion is finely chopped.

   Spread bread slices with onion mixture; top with sauerkraut, corned beef mixture and shredded cheese. Place sandwiches on 2 plates lined with kitchen papper; microwave at 70% (Medium High) until hot through, 8–10 minutes, rotating plates ¼ turn after 5 minutes. Serve immediately.

## Beef and pepper rolls
Total Preparation Time: 25–30 min
Microwave Time: 18–21 min
Serves: 4

*A herb sauce makes the most of leftover roast beef. Prepare it without the tomato sauce for a beef-in-gravy-style sandwich.*

2 cloves garlic, peeled
2 small onions, peeled, cut into 2.5cm (1in) pieces
15g (½oz) butter or margarine
300ml (12fl oz) water

225ml (8fl oz) tomato sauce (optional)
50ml (2fl oz) red wine vinegar
1 beef stock cube
1 × 15ml tbsp (1 tbsp) brown sugar
1 × 15ml tbsp (1 tbsp) crushed dried red pepper
1 × 5ml tsp (1 tsp) dried basil
$\frac{1}{2}$ × 5ml tsp ($\frac{1}{2}$tsp) dried oregano
2 medium green peppers, seeded, cut to fit feed tube
225g (8oz) thinly sliced, cooked roast beef
4 large finger rolls, split

With machine running (Steel Knife), drop garlic through feed tube, processing until minced. Add onions to bowl; process using on/off technique until chopped. Microwave onion mixture and butter in 2 litre (3$\frac{1}{2}$pt) casserole, uncovered, at High until onions are tender, about 4 minutes. Stir in remaining ingredients except green peppers, beef and rolls; microwave covered at High until boiling, 4–5 minutes.

Slice (Slicing Disc) green peppers; stir into sauce. Microwave covered at High until peppers are tender, 5–7 minutes. Stir in beef; microwave covered at High until hot through, about 4 minutes.

Place rolls in oven on kitchen paper; microwave at 70% (Medium High) 30 seconds. Spoon meat mixture into rolls.

## Continuous cheese dip

Total Preparation Time: 9–12 min
Microwave Time: 1–3 min
Makes: 300ml (12fl oz)

*An extremely tasty way of using up pieces of leftover cheese. Use any combination of firm cheeses, nuts, herbs and spices, and renew the blend weekly or monthly, as bits of cheese accumulate.*

100g (4oz) cheese (Cheddar, Cheshire, Leicester, etc) cut into 2.5cm (1in) pieces
75g (3oz) cream cheese, cut into quarters, softened
50g (2oz) nuts (almonds, walnuts, hazelnuts, cashews, etc)
25g (1oz) butter or margarine
$\frac{1}{2}$ × 5ml tsp ($\frac{1}{2}$tsp) Basil salt (optional; see Index)
1–2 × 15ml tbsp (1–2tbsp) brandy, cognac or dry sherry
crackers, toast triangles, courgette and cucumber slices, medium mushroom caps

Process (Steel Knife) cheeses, nuts, butter, Basil salt and brandy until smooth, scraping side of bowl with rubber spatula if necessary. Spread cheese mixture generously on crackers or toast, spoon onto vegetable slices, or fill mushroom caps. Microwave on glass serving plate, uncovered, at High until cheese is hot and beginning to melt, 1 minute for 12 crackers or vegetable slices, about 3 minutes for 12 mushrooms caps. Serve hot.

*Tip*
Refrigerate cheese blend in a tightly covered container; add any cheeses, nuts or herbs, as desired. If the flavour of the mixture becomes too sharp, add cream cheese or butter. To add to the cheese mixture, microwave mixture in glass bowl at 50% (Medium) just until softened; transfer to food processor bowl. Add new ingredients and process as directed above. To keep the renewed cheese mixture longer than 2 months, add 1–2 × 15ml tbsp (1–2tbsp) brandy, cognac or sherry every 6–8 weeks.

## Twice-baked potato skins

Total Preparation Time: 33–5 min
Microwave Time: 22–5 min
Serves: 4

*An absolutely habit-forming treat—either a high-calorie treat or an economical source of nutrition, depending on your point of view!*

3 medium potatoes
3 slices bacon
50g (2oz) butter or margarine
$\frac{1}{2}$ × 5ml tsp ($\frac{1}{2}$tsp) Dill salt (see Index) or salt
1–2 dashes Tabasco
50g (2oz) Cheddar cheese, chilled, cut to fit feed tube
$\frac{1}{2}$ small onion, peeled, cut into 2.5cm (1in) pieces
$\frac{1}{4}$ green pepper, seeded, cut into 2.5cm (1in) pieces
$\frac{1}{4}$ red or green pepper, seeded, cut into 2.5cm (1in) pieces

Prick potatoes several times with fork. Microwave on kitchen paper at High until tender, 8–9 minutes. Let stand 5 minutes. Microwave bacon in glass baking dish, covered with kitchen paper, at High until crisp, about 3 minutes; drain and crumble.

Cut potatoes lengthwise into quarters to make wedges. Carefully cut out potato, leaving 0.5cm ($\frac{1}{4}$in) potato on skins (reserve cut-out potato for other use). Microwave butter in small glass bowl at High until melted; stir in salt and Tabasco. Brush butter mixture on both sides of potato skins. Place skin sides up on kitchen paper in glass baking dish; microwave uncovered at High 8 minutes, rotating dish $\frac{1}{2}$ turn after 4 minutes.

Shred (Shredding Disc) cheese; remove. Process (Steel Knife) onion and peppers using on/off technique until chopped. Turn potato skins over; sprinkle with cheese. Top with chopped vegetables and bacon. Microwave uncovered at High until cheese is melted, about 2 minutes. Serve hot.

*Tips*

1 Remove cut-out potato in large pieces for use in French-style vegetable purée (see Index). Two medium potatoes will give the amount of peeled, cooked potato required for the purée.

2 If you are preparing baked potatoes for another use that does not require the skins, you can freeze the skins for use in this recipe. Remove the potato as directed above. Freeze skins on a baking sheet until firm; then transfer to a plastic bag, seal and freeze up to 3 months.

## Mushroom squares

Total Preparation Time: 27–30 min
Microwave Time: 7–9 min
Serves: 8

*This cross between an omelette and a creamy custard makes an ideal snack or light lunch.*

100g (4oz) Cheddar cheese, chilled, cut to fit feed tube
225g (8oz) mushrooms
2 large sprigs watercress or parsley
1 small onion, peeled, cut into 2.5cm (1in) pieces
1 spring onion and top, cut into 2.5cm (1in) pieces
75g (3oz) cream cheese, cut into quarters, softened
3 eggs
2 × 15ml tbsp (2tbsp) flour
2 × 15ml tbsp (2tbsp) dry sherry
1 × 5ml tsp (1tsp) drained capers
2 dashes Worcestershire sauce
salt
pepper

Shred (Shredding Disc) Cheddar cheese; remove. Slice (Slicing Disc) mushrooms; remove. Process watercress using on/off technique until minced. Add onions, cream cheese, eggs, flour, sherry, capers, Worcestershire sauce, salt and pepper to bowl; process (Steel Knife) until mixture is smooth. Add shredded cheese; process using on/off technique until blended.

Arrange mushrooms in 30 × 20cm (12 × 8in) glass baking dish; pour egg mixture over. Microwave uncovered at High 4 minutes, rotating dish ¼ turn every 2 minutes. Protect corners of pan with aluminium foil; microwave uncovered at High until mixture is almost set, 3–5 minutes, rotating dish ¼ turn every 2 minutes. Let stand loosely covered 5 minutes. Cut into squares; serve hot.

## Ham salad rolls

Total Preparation Time: 15–19 min
Microwave Time: 4–6 min
Serves: 4

*A delicious, crunchy ham salad dressed up with lightly sweetened Dill sauce.*

50g (2oz) walnuts
225g (8oz) smoked ham, cut into 2.5cm (1in) pieces
½ medium onion, peeled, cut into 2.5cm (1in) pieces
2 small sweet pickled gherkins, cut into 2.5cm (1in) pieces
1 stick celery, cut into 2.5cm (1in) pieces
50–75ml (2–3fl oz) sour cream
½ × 5ml tsp (½tsp) Dijon mustard
2 French or hard long rolls
Dill sauce (optional; see Index)
2 × 5ml tsp (2tsp) honey (optional)

Process (Steel Knife) walnuts using on/off technique until chopped; reserve 1½ × 15ml tbsp (1½tbsp). Add ham, onion, gherkins, celery, sour cream and mustard to walnuts in bowl; process (Steel Knife) using on/off technique until finely chopped.

Cut rolls lengthwise into halves; scoop out centres (reserve cut-out parts for breadcrumbs or other use). Fill rolls with ham mixture.

Make Dill sauce, stirring in honey. Microwave rolls on kitchen paper at 70% (Medium High) until hot through, 4–6 minutes; spoon sauce over. Sprinkle with reserved walnuts.

*Tip*
For a cold sandwich or appetiser spread, follow the first paragraph of the recipe; do not reserve walnuts. Substitute mayonnaise for the sour cream, if you wish.

## Hot turkey surprise

Total Preparation Time: 16–21 min
Microwave Time: 4–6 min
Serves: 4

*A mouth-watering combination of turkey, chopped apple and chutney topped with a savory meringue. Process egg whites first to avoid washing the food processor bowl.*

2 egg whites
pinch of dry mustard
25g (1oz) blanched almonds
1 medium apple, cored, cut into 2.5cm (1in) pieces
3 × 15ml tbsp (3tbsp) chutney
225g (8oz) thinly sliced, cooked turkey
4 slices bread

Process (Steel Knife) egg whites and mustard until stiff peaks form; reserve. Process (Steel Knife) almonds using on/off technique until chopped; remove. Process (Steel Knife) apple using on/off technique until chopped; add chutney to bowl. Process until just blended.

Microwave almonds in glass pie dish, uncovered, at High until toasted, 2–3 minutes, stirring after 1 minute.

Arrange turkey on bread; spoon apple mixture over turkey. Spoon meringue over apple mixture; sprinkle with almonds. Microwave on kitchen paper, uncovered, at High until meringue is firm to touch, 2–3 minutes. Serve hot.

*Tip*
Microwave sandwich only until meringue is firm; the meringue will not brown.

## Pita pockets

Total Preparation Time: 22–4 min
Microwave Time: 16–17 min
Serves: 6

*Pita bread is ideal for holding a tasty Oriental stir-fry filling.*

225g (8oz) lean boneless pork, cut into 0.5cm (¼in) strips
1 × 15ml tbsp (1tbsp) vegetable oil
2 sticks celery, cut to fit feed tube
3 spring onions and tops, cut to fit feed tube
150g (6oz) water chestnuts, drained
225g (8oz) fresh or tinned bean sprouts, rinsed, well drained
2 × 15ml tbsp (2tbsp) soy sauce
1 × 15ml tbsp (1tbsp) cornflour
50ml (2fl oz) cold water
2 × 5ml tsp (2tsp) sesame seeds
3 pita breads, cut into halves

Microwave pork and oil in a suitable casserole, uncovered, at High until pork loses pink colour, about 6 minutes, stirring after 3 minutes. Slice (Slicing Disc) celery, onions and water chestnuts; stir into pork. Stir bean sprouts and soy sauce into pork mixture. Microwave uncovered at High 5 minutes, stirring after 3 minutes. Mix cornflour and cold water; stir into pork mixture. Microwave uncovered at High 5 minutes, until thickened, about 3 minutes, stirring after 1½ minutes.

Microwave sesame seeds in glass pie dish uncovered at High until toasted, about 2 minutes, stirring after 1 minute. Open pockets in breads; fill with pork mixture. Sprinkle with sesame seeds.

*Tip*
To crisp tinned bean sprouts, place them in iced water for 10 minutes, or as long as time allows.

## Honey fruit snack mix

Total Preparation Time: 20–2 min
Microwave Time: 16–18 min
Makes: 4 cups

*A nourishing snack, without the additives or cost of packet mixtures. Equally satisfying for late-night snacks, picnics and impromptu parties.*

100g (4oz) dry wholewheat breadcrumbs (see Index)
50g (2oz) walnuts
50g (2oz) dried apricots
50g (2oz) prunes, stoned
150g (6oz) rolled oats
40g (1½oz) shredded coconut
1 × 5ml tsp (1tsp) ground cinnamon
25g (1oz) butter or margarine
25g (1oz) honey
2 × 15ml tbsp (2tbsp) maple syrup or honey
40g (1½oz) sultanas

Make breadcrumbs. Process (Steel knife) walnuts until coarsely chopped; remove. Process (Steel Knife) apricots and prunes until coarsely chopped.

Microwave oats in 30 × 20cm (12 × 8in) baking dish, uncovered, at High 2 minutes, stirring after 1 minute. Stir in breadcrumbs, walnuts, coconut and cinnamon; mix well. Microwave butter in small glass dish at High until melted; stir butter, honey and maple syrup into oatmeal mixture. Microwave uncovered at 70% (Medium High) 7 minutes, stirring every 2 minutes. Stir in apricots, prunes and sultanas; microwave uncovered at 70% (Medium High) 2 minutes. Cool to room temperature. Store at room temperature in airtight container up to 2 weeks.

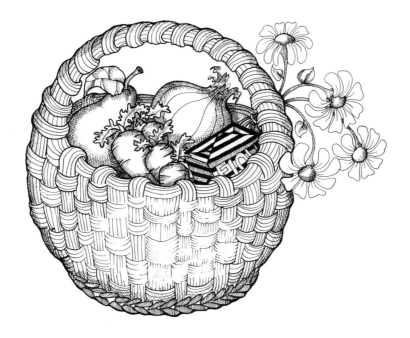

# Sauces and Ready Prepared Mixtures

## Fresh tomato sauce

Total Preparation Time: 30–3 min
Microwave Time: 20–3 min
Makes: 400ml (16fl oz)

*This sauce is so useful, both alone and as an ingredient in other recipes, that you might want to make an extra batch for the freezer when tomatoes are lush and ripe.*

4 sprigs parsley
1 clove garlic, peeled
2 spring onions and tops, cut into 2.5cm (1in)
　　pieces
1kg (2lb) tomatoes, seeded, cut into 2.5cm (1in)
　　pieces
2 × 15ml tbsp (2tbsp) tomato paste
2 × 5ml tsp (2tsp) light brown sugar
pinch of dried tarragon
pinch of dried thyme
salt
pepper

Process (Steel Knife) parsley until minced. With machine running, drop garlic through feed tube; process using on/off technique until minced. Add onions and tomatoes to bowl; process using on/off technique until chopped. Transfer mixture to 1 litre (1¾pt) casserole; stir in remaining ingredients. Microwave uncovered at High until sauce has thickened, about 20 minutes, stirring every 5 minutes.

*Tips*
1 To seed tomatoes, cut them into halves crosswise and squeeze halves gently. Ripen tomatoes at room temperature, stem ends up, away from direct sunlight.
2 To avoid spattering, lay a sheet of greaseproof paper over the casserole.

## Horseradish cocktail sauce

Total Preparation Time: 8–10 min
Microwave Time: 4–5 min
Makes: about 250ml (½pt)

*Serve hot or chilled with shrimps, other seafood and grilled meats.*

½ medium onion, peeled, cut into 2.5cm (1in) pieces
2 × 5ml tsp (2tsp) cider vinegar
1 medium dill pickle, cut into 2.5cm (1in) pieces
225ml (8fl oz) chilli sauce
1 × 15ml tbsp (1tbsp) horseradish
2 × 5ml tsp (2tsp) Worcestershire sauce
1 × 5ml tsp (1tsp) Dijon mustard
pepper
2–3 dashes Tabasco

Process (Steel Knife) onion and vinegar using on/off technique until chopped; remove Steel Knife. Microwave onion mixture in food processor bowl, covered with clingfilm, at High 2 minutes. Insert Steel Knife and add pickle to bowl; process using on/off technique until finely chopped. Add remaining ingredients to bowl; process (Steel Knife) until smooth. Microwave in glass serving bowl, covered, at High until hot, about 2 minutes.

## Chilli steak sauce

Total Preparation Time: 7–9 min
Microwave Time: 3–4 min
Makes: about 225ml (8fl oz)

*A sauce well worth the careful stirring required to heat it. It is superb with grilled beef or chicken.*

2 spring onions and tops, cut into 2.5cm (1in)
　　pieces
100ml (4fl oz) mayonnaise or salad dressing
100ml (4fl oz) chilli sauce
1 egg white
1 × 15ml tbsp (1tbsp) Worcestershire sauce
1–2 × 5ml tsp (1–2tsp) prepared horseradish
1 × 15ml tbsp (1tbsp) chilli powder
½ × 5ml tsp (½tsp) curry powder
½ × 5ml tsp (½tsp) salt

Process (Steel Knife) spring onions using on/off technique until finely chopped. Add remaining ingredients to bowl; process using on/off technique until blended. Microwave in a glass measure, uncovered, at 50% (Medium) just until hot, 3–4 minutes, stirring with whisk every 30 seconds (do not overcook or mixture will separate). Serve hot.

# Hollandaise sauce

Total Preparation Time: 4–5 min
Microwave Time: 2–3 min
Makes: about 225ml (8fl oz)

*Not only fast, but fail-safe. You can make this sauce up to 2 days in advance, refrigerate it, and reheat it. It is blended and cooked in the food processor bowl. Classic sauce to serve with poached fish, asparagus or eggs Benedict.*

100g (4oz) cold butter, cut into pieces
2 × 15ml tbsp (2tbsp) lemon juice
$\frac{1}{2}$ × 5ml tsp ($\frac{1}{2}$tsp) Dijon mustard (optional)
2 dashes Tabasco
2 egg yolks, room temperature

Arrange butter pieces around bottom of food processor bowl without Steel Knife; microwave uncovered at High until butter is soft, but not melted, about 1 minute. Insert Steel Knife; add lemon juice, mustard and Tabasco to bowl. Process until mixture is blended. With machine running, add yolks through feed tube 1 at a time, processing 30 seconds after each addition.

Remove Steel Knife; microwave uncovered at 50% (Medium) until thickened, about 1½ minutes, stirring after 1 minute. Stir and serve.

*Tips*

1 For Lime hollandaise, substitute lime juice for the lemon juice and omit the mustard.
2 Whole eggs or 1 egg and 1 egg yolk can be substituted for the yolks; sauce made with whole eggs will require about 15 seconds more cooking time. It is important that the eggs be at room temperature; to do this, place them in a bowl of warm water and let stand 5 minutes.
3 If a fluffier sauce is required, sauce can be processed with Steel Knife halfway through cooking time and again at the end.
4 If sauce should separate or curdle during cooking, process with Steel Knife until smooth.
5 Sauce can be made up to 30 minutes in advance and left in the food processor bowl, covered, at room temperature. To reheat, microwave as above about 1 minute, stirring after 30 seconds. If sauce thickens too much upon standing, process with Steel Knife until smooth; with machine running, add 1 × 15ml tbsp (1tbsp) warm water through feed tube before reheating.
6 Sauce can be refrigerated covered up to 2 days. Before reheating, process (Steel Knife) to blend; with machine running, add 1 × 15ml tbsp (1tbsp) warm water through feed tube. Remove Steel Knife; scrape down side of bowl. Microwave uncovered at 50% (Medium) 1½ minutes, stirring after 30 seconds.

# Béarnaise sauce

Total Preparation Time; 10–11 min
Microwave Time: 3–4 min
Makes: about 225ml (8fl oz)

*This tarragon-seasoned version of Hollandaise sauce is just as easy to make and tastes delicious with grilled steaks, poached salmon and roast beef.*

1 shallot or $\frac{1}{2}$ small white onion, peeled, cut into
    2.5cm (1in) pieces
1½ × 15ml tbsp (1½tbsp) white tarragon vinegar
1½ × 15ml tbsp (1½tbsp) dry white wine
1 × 15ml tbsp (1tbsp) dried tarragon
100g (4oz) cold butter, cut into pieces
2 egg yolks, room temperature

With machine running (Steel Knife), drop shallot through feed tube, processing until minced. Add vinegar, wine and tarragon to bowl; process until blended.

Remove Steel Knife; scrape sides of bowl. Microwave covered at High 1 minute. Arrange butter pieces evenly around bottom of bowl; microwave uncovered at 50% (Medium) until butter is soft but not melted, about 1 minute. Cool to room temperature.

Insert Steel Knife. With machine running, add yolks through feed tube one at a time, processing 30 seconds after each addition. Remove Steel Knife; microwave uncovered at 50% (Medium) until thickened, about 1½ minutes, stirring after 30 seconds. Stir and serve.

*Tip*
See cooking and storage tips for Hollandaise sauce.

# Twice-as-fast sauce mix

Total Preparation Time: 5–6 min
Microwave Time: $\frac{1}{2}$–1 min
Makes: about 375ml ($\frac{3}{4}$pt)

*This basic mixture provides quick thickening for microwave-smooth sauces, soups and gravies. Keep a supply in the refrigerator for use in the following sauces as well as other recipes in this book.*

225g (8oz) butter or margarine, cut into pieces
100g (4oz) plain flour
1½ × 5ml tsp (1½tsp) salt
1 chicken stock cube

Arrange butter in bottom of food processor bowl without Steel Knife; microwave at High until butter is soft, about 30 seconds. Insert Steel Knife; add flour, salt and crumbled stock cube. Process until thoroughly blended. Refrigerate in covered container.

## Garlic sauce

Total Preparation Time: 22–4 min
Microwave Time: 10–12 min
Makes: 150ml (6fl oz)

*An irresistible sauce for all garlic-lovers. Serve it with fish or chicken. When cooked, the whole cloves of garlic become mild and delicious.*

2 heads garlic
1 small onion, peeled, cut into 2.5cm (1in) pieces
125g (5oz) butter or margarine

Peel cloves of garlic. With machine running (Steel Knife), drop half the cloves through feed tube, processing until minced. Add onion to bowl; process using on/off technique until minced.

Microwave minced garlic mixture and butter in 1 litre (1¾pt) casserole, covered, at 50% (Medium), 5 minutes, stirring after 2½ minutes. Stir in whole garlic cloves; microwave covered at 50% (Medium) just until turning golden, 5–7 minutes, stirring every 2½ minutes (do not overcook as garlic can burn easily).

*Tips*
1 To make Garlic butter, increase butter to 450g (1lb) and proceed as above. Strain the butter and keep it refrigerated. It has hundreds of uses. It will gently season mushrooms, onions, green beans, spinach and other vegetables sautéed in it, and it is an excellent basting sauce for grilled or roast lamb and poultry.
2 If you wish, you can add the cooked whole cloves of garlic to the aubergine when you are processing Aubergine dip (see Index).

## Mushroom sauce

Total Preparation Time: 12–13 min
Microwave Time: 6–7 min
Makes: 250ml (½pt)

3 × 15ml tbsp (3tbsp) Twice-as-fast sauce mix (see Index)
50g (2oz) mushrooms
225ml (8fl oz) milk
1 × 5ml tsp (1tsp) Worcestershire sauce
pepper
50g (2oz) Gruyère cheese, cut to fit feed tube

Microwave sauce mix in a glass measure, uncovered, at High 2 minutes. Process (Steel Knife) mushrooms until chopped; stir into sauce mix. Microwave uncovered at High 1 minute. Stir in milk, Worcestershire sauce and pepper. Microwave uncovered at High until sauce boils and thickens, 3–3½ minutes, stirring with whisk every minute. Shred (Shredding Disc) cheese; stir into sauce until melted. Serve with cooked vegetables or meats.

## Brandy sauce

Total Preparation Time: 8 min
Microwave Time: 5 min
Makes: about 225ml (8fl oz)

65g (2½oz) butter or margarine
50g (2oz) granulated sugar
50g (2oz) light brown sugar
100ml (4fl oz) whipping cream
2 egg yolks, beaten
2 × 15ml tbsp (2tbsp) brandy

Microwave butter in glass measure at High until melted, about 2 minutes. Stir in sugars, cream and egg yolks. Microwave uncovered at High 3 minutes, or until thickened, stirring with whisk every 30 seconds. Stir in brandy.

## Dill sauce

Total Preparation Time: 7–8 min
Microwave Time: 5–6 min
Makes: about 300ml (12fl oz)

3 × 15ml tbsp (3tbsp) Twice-as-fast sauce mix (see Index)
250ml (½pt) milk
1 × 5ml tsp (1tsp) Dijon mustard
½ × 5ml tsp (½tsp) dried chives
½ × 5ml tsp (½tsp) dried dillweed
pepper

Microwave sauce mix in a glass measure, uncovered, at High 2 minutes. Stir in milk and remaining ingredients; microwave at High until mixture boils and thickens, 3–3½ minutes, stirring with whisk every minute.

## Sweet and sour sauce

Total Preparation Time: 10–11 min
Microwave Time: 6–7 min
Makes: about 250ml (½pt)

3 × 15ml tbsp (3tbsp) Twice-as-fast sauce mix (see Index)
¼ medium onion, peeled, cut into 2.5cm (1in) pieces
¼ green pepper, seeded, cut into 2.5cm (1in) pieces
225ml (8fl oz) orange juice
2 × 15ml tbsp (2tbsp) light brown sugar
2 × 15ml tbsp (2tbsp) cider vinegar

Microwave sauce mix in a glass measure, uncovered, at High 2 minutes. Process (Steel Knife) onion and pepper using on/off technique until finely chopped; stir into sauce mix. Microwave uncovered at High 1 minute. Stir in orange juice, sugar and vinegar; microwave uncovered until mixture boils and thickens, 3–3½ minutes, stirring with whisk every minute.

## Butter sauce

Total Preparation Time: 7–9 min
Microwave Time: 4–5 min
Makes: about 300ml (12fl oz)

*A suitably simple accompaniment for grilled fish, Three-vegetable terrine or Tomato timbales (see Index). The softened butter added at the end, through the food processor feed tube, produces a light, fluffy consistency.*

50g (2oz) butter or margarine
2 × 15ml tbsp (2tbsp) flour
225ml (8fl oz) chicken stock
1–3 × 5ml tsp (1–3tsp) lemon juice
salt
25–40g (1–1½oz) butter or margarine, softened

Microwave 50g (2oz) butter in a glass measure, uncovered, at High until melted; stir in flour. Microwave uncovered at High 30 seconds. Stir in chicken stock; microwave at High until mixture boils and thickens, 2–3 minutes, stirring after 1 minute. Stir in lemon juice and salt to taste.

Insert Steel Knife in food processor bowl. Transfer butter mixture to bowl. With machine running, add remaining butter, a little at a time, through feed tube, until blended.

## Fresh pineapple and cranberry sauce

Total Preparation Time: 28–30 min
Microwave Time: 18–20 min
Makes: 1 litre (1¾pt)

*A fruity relish for poultry and ham. Any surplus sauce will freeze well in covered container.*

75g (3oz) walnuts
1 large pineapple (approx 1kg [2–2½lb]), peeled, cored, cut into 2.5cm (1in) pieces
300g (12oz) fresh or frozen, thawed cranberries
150g (6oz) light brown sugar
1 × 5ml tsp (1tsp) mixed spice
1 stick cinnamon
2 × 15ml tbsp (2tbsp) cornflour
50ml (2fl oz) cold water

Process (Steel Knife) walnuts; reserve. Process (Steel Knife) pineapple until coarsely chopped. Process (Steel Knife) half the cranberries until chopped. Mix all ingredients except walnuts, cornflour, and water in glass measure; microwave uncovered at High 15 minutes, stirring every 5 minutes. Stir in combined cornflour and water; microwave uncovered at High until thickened, about 3 minutes, stirring after 1½ minutes. Stir in walnuts.

## Sherry beef sauce

Total Preparation Time: 9–10 min
Microwave Time: 7–8 min
Makes: about 250ml ($\frac{1}{2}$pt)

*This delicious sauce will lift your roast beef into the gourmet class!*

3 × 15ml tbsp (3tbsp) Twice-as-fast sauce mix (see Index)
$\frac{1}{2}$ clove garlic, peeled
$\frac{1}{4}$ medium onion, peeled, cut into 2.5cm (1in) pieces
225ml (8fl oz) beef stock
$\frac{1}{2}$ × 5ml tsp ($\frac{1}{2}$tsp) dried chervil
$\frac{1}{2}$ × 5ml tsp ($\frac{1}{2}$tsp) Worcestershire sauce
1 egg yolk
1 × 15ml tbsp (1tbsp) dry sherry or vermouth

Microwave sauce mix in a glass measure, un-covered, at High 2 minutes. Process (Steel Knife) garlic and onion using on/off technique until minced; stir into sauce mix. Microwave uncovered at High 1 minute. Stir in beef stock, chervil and Worcestershire sauce. Microwave uncovered at High until mixture thickens and boils, 3–3$\frac{1}{2}$ minutes, stirring with whisk every minute. Stir about 50ml (2fl oz) mixture into egg yolk; stir yolk mixture into sauce. Microwave uncovered at High 1 minute, stirring after 30 seconds; stir in sherry. Serve with beef and game.

## Sour-cream onion sauce

Total Preparation Time: 9–10 min
Microwave Time: 6-7 min
Makes: about 225ml (8fl oz)

3 × 15ml tbsp (3tbsp) Twice-as-fast sauce mix (see Index)
2 spring onions and tops, cut into 2.5cm (1in) pieces
150ml (6fl oz) milk
1 × 5ml tsp (1tsp) soy sauce
$\frac{1}{2}$ × 5ml tsp ($\frac{1}{2}$tsp) made mustard
$\frac{1}{2}$ × 5ml tsp ($\frac{1}{2}$tsp) dried mixed herbs
pepper
50–75ml (2–3fl oz) sour cream

Microwave sauce mix in a glass measure, un-covered, at High 2 minutes. Process (Steel Knife) onions using on/off technique until finely chopped; stir into sauce mix. Microwave uncovered at High 1 minute. Stir in milk, soy sauce, mustard, mixed herbs and pepper. Microwave uncovered at High until sauce boils and thickens, 3–3$\frac{1}{2}$ minutes, stirring with whisk every minute. Stir in sour cream until blended. Serve over cooked vegetables or poultry.

## Calvados sauce

Total Preparation Time: 9–11 min
Microwave Time: 6–8 min
Makes: about 300ml (12fl oz)

2 cloves garlic, peeled
2 large shallots, peeled, or $\frac{1}{4}$ small onion, peeled, cut into 2.5cm (1in) pieces
2 × 15ml tbsp (2tbsp) chicken or pork fat, or butter or margarine
3 × 15 tbsp (3tbsp) Twice-as-fast sauce mix (see Index)
225ml (8fl oz) whipping cream
3–4 × 15ml tbsp (3–4tbsp) Calvados or brandy

With machine running (Steel Knife), drop garlic and shallots through feed tube, processing until minced. Microwave garlic mixture and fat in a glass measure, uncovered, at high 2 minutes. Stir in sauce mix; microwave 1 minute. Stir in cream; microwave uncovered at 50% (Medium) until just boiling, 3–5 minutes, stirring with whisk every minute. Stir in Calvados; serve hot sauce with pork or chicken.

## Food processor mayonnaise and variations

Total Preparation Time: 3–4 min
Makes: about 300ml (12fl oz)

*Homemade mayonnaise is worlds apart in taste and texture from commercial blends. Not only does it lighten chicken, seafood, ham and egg salads but it also serves as a beautiful sauce for cold meats, poultry and fish. Choose among the variations for 'instant' dips and accompaniments. Try the Walnut mayonnaise with cold chicken, the Green mayonnaise with cold poached fish, the Sesame mayonnaise as a dip with crisp vegetables and the Horseradish mayonnaise on turkey sandwiches. Cream-enriched Chantilly mayonnaise is delicious with cold roast beef or lamb. Unless the recipe specifies otherwise, you can use either homemade or commercial mayonnaise in the recipes in this book but the food processor blend will always give finer results.*

2 egg yolks, room temperature
1 × 15ml tbsp (1tbsp) lemon juice
1 × 15ml tbsp (1tbsp) white wine vinegar
1 × 5ml tsp (1tsp) Dijon mustard
salt
pepper
250ml ($\frac{1}{2}$pt) vegetable oil

Process (Steel Knife) egg yolks, lemon juice, vinegar, mustard, salt and pepper until blended. With machine running, slowly pour oil through feed tube, pouring more quickly as mayonnaise in bowl thickens. Refrigerate in covered container up to 10 days.

## Variations

**Walnut:** Process (Steel Knife) 50g (2oz) toasted walnuts until chopped prior to making mayonnaise and reserve; stir into mayonnaise. Alternatively use flaked almonds.

**Sesame:** Microwave 1–2 × 15ml tbsp (1–2tbsp) sesame seeds in glass pie dish, uncovered, at High until toasted, 2–3 minutes, stirring after every minute; cool and stir into mayonnaise.

**Thousand Island:** Make mayonnaise as above. Add 65ml (2½fl oz) ketchup; pickled gherkins, cut into 2.5cm (1in) pieces; 1 hard-boiled egg, cut into quarters; and ½–1 × 5ml tsp (½–1tsp) prepared horseradish to bowl. Process (Steel Knife) using on/off technique until egg is coarsely chopped. Serve chilled or hot. To heat, microwave in a glass measure, uncovered, at 10% (Low) until hot through, 2½–3 minutes, stirring with whisk after 1½ minutes (do not overcook, or mayonnaise will separate).

**Shallot:** With machine running (Steel Knife), drop 2 shallots through feed tube, processing until minced. Proceed with recipe as above, substituting red wine for the white wine vinegar.

**Green:** Process (Steel Knife) 3 sprigs parsley, 2 sprigs coriander and 4–6 spinach leaves until minced; reserve. Make mayonnaise as above; stir in minced herbs and spinach.

**Cucumber:** Process (Steel Knife) ½ medium cucumber, peeled, seeded and cut into 2.5cm (1in) pieces, using on/off technique, until chopped; reserve. Make mayonnaise as above; stir in cucumber and ½ × 5ml tsp (½tsp) dried dillweed.

**Garlic:** With machine running (Steel Knife), drop garlic through feed tube, processing until minced. Proceed with mayonnaise recipe as above.

**Horseradish:** Make mayonnaise as above; add 50g (2oz) currant jelly and 1–2 × 15ml tbsp (1–2tbsp) prepared horseradish to bowl; process (Steel Knife) using on/off technique until blended.

**Chantilly:** Process (Steel Knife) 225ml (8fl oz) whipping cream until thick; reserve. Make mayonnaise as above; fold in cream.

*Tips*

1 To ensure good results, start with all ingredients at room temperature.
2 When adding oil through feed tube, pour very slowly at first—only a few drops at a time— until mixture begins to thicken. If mayonnaise fails to thicken, pour it into a 500ml (1pt) measure and use this quick 'rescue' technique: process (Steel Knife) an additional egg yolk until beaten. With the machine running, slowly pour the mayonnaise mixture through the feed tube and process until thickened.

## Food processor butter and variations

Total Preparation Time: 5–8 min
Makes: about 150ml (6fl oz)

*The most delicious butter is easily 'churned' in the food processor. Mimic the fresh taste, if you wish, by blending purchased butter with sour cream. Either way, you can add sweet or savoury seasonings to make superb toppings for vegetables, meats, pancakes, toast and dinner rolls.*

400ml (16fl oz) whipping cream

Process (Steel Knife) cream until mixture becomes grainy in appearance and water begins to separate; continue processing until mixture returns to a smooth consistency and becomes pale yellow in colour, 8–10 minutes. Rinse in cold water; drain in strainer. Pack butter into covered container and refrigerate.

### Variations

**Mock food processor butter:** Process (Steel Knife) 150g (6oz) unsalted butter, slightly softened, and 1 × 15ml tbsp (1tbsp) sour cream until fluffy; pack into covered container and refrigerate.

**Strawberry butter:** Process (Steel Knife) 150g (6oz) butter, 75g (3oz) cream cheese, 100–125g (4–5oz) hulled fresh strawberries, 3 × 15ml tbsp (3tbsp) honey, and 2 × 5ml tsp (2tsp) grated lemon rind until fluffy. Serve with baked potatoes, waffles or pancakes.

**Chutney butter:** Process (Steel Knife) 150g (6oz) butter, 2 × 15ml tbsp (2tbsp) chutney, 1 × 5ml tsp (1tsp) plain yogurt, and a pinch of curry powder until fluffy; add 40g (1½oz) peanuts and process (Steel Knife) using on/off technique until peanuts are chopped. Serve with baked potatoes; roast lamb, pork or chicken; steamed asparagus, courgettes or carrots.

**Parmesan-garlic butter:** Process (Steel Knife) 2 large sprigs parsley using on/off technique until minced. With machine running, drop 15g (½oz) cubed Parmesan cheese and 1 clove garlic through feed tube, processing until finely grated. Add 150g (6oz) butter, 1 × 15ml tbsp (1tbsp) sour cream, pinch of dried marjoram, dried oregano and dried thyme to bowl; process (Steel Knife) until smooth. Serve with baked potatoes, cooked green vegetables or grilled meats.

101

## Clarified butter and variation

Total Preparation Time: 3–4 min
Microwave Time: 2–3 min
Makes: about 150ml (6fl oz)

*It's much easier to clarify or brown butter without burning it in the microwave oven. Some cooks prefer Clarified butter for sauces, and most agree that it produces the best fillo pastries. The toasted taste of Brown butter will highlight any plain, cooked vegetable.*

Microwave 225g (8oz) butter in glass measure at High until melted and bubbly. Let stand several minutes for milk solids to collect at bottom. Skim foam from top and pour clear butter into container; discard milk solids.

### Variation

**Brown butter:** Microwave Clarified butter in glass measure at High until butter turns brown in colour, 2–3 minutes. Serve over cooked vegetables.

## Garlic salt and variations

Total Prepararation Time: 12–14 min
(plus refrigeration time)
Microwave Time: 3 min
Makes: 225ml (8fl oz)

*Sprinkle these seasoning salts on meats and vegetables—wrap up extra jars as gifts for friends who cook.*

2 cloves garlic, peeled
225g (8oz) coarse salt

With machine running (Steel Knife), drop garlic through feed tube, processing until minced. Add salt to bowl; process using on/off technique until mixture is very finely ground. Refrigerate covered overnight.

Pour salt mixture into glass pie dish; microwave uncovered at High 3 minutes, stirring every minute. Cool to room temperature; process (Steel Knife) until smooth. Store in airtight container at room temperature.

### Variations

**Dill:** Follow above recipe, substituting 1 × 5ml tsp (1tsp) dried dillweed for the garlic; add dillweed to food processor bowl with salt.

**Basil:** Follow above recipe, substituting 1 × 5ml tsp (1tsp) dried basil leaves, $\frac{1}{2}$ × 5ml tsp ($\frac{1}{2}$tsp) paprika and a pinch of turmeric for the garlic; add basil, paprika and turmeric to bowl with salt.

**Mustard:** Follow above recipe, substituting $\frac{1}{2}$ × 5ml tsp ($\frac{1}{2}$tsp) dry mustard for the garlic; add mustard to food processor bowl with salt.

*Ratatouille (page 73); Shredded Carrot Casserole (page 78); Green Beans and Tomatoes (page 77)*

## Breadcrumbs and variations

Total Preparation Time: 8–11 min
Microwave Time: 3–4 min
Makes: about 100g (4oz) fresh crumbs,
50–75g (2–3oz) dry crumbs

*Fresh and dried breadcrumbs are extremely useful in all kinds of dishes and no kitchen should be without a supply. Make these with any kind of leftover bread. The amount will vary, depending on the type of bread.*

100g (4oz) French bread, torn into pieces

Process (Steel Knife) bread using on/off technique until fine crumbs are formed. Refrigerate fresh crumbs in airtight container up to 1 month.

To make dry crumbs, spread fresh crumbs in thin layer in 30 × 20cm (12 × 8in) baking dish. Microwave uncovered at High until dry, 3–4 minutes, stirring after 2 minutes; cool. If desired, process (Steel Knife) to finer texture. Store dry crumbs in airtight container at room temperature up to 2 months.

### Variations

**Wheat and walnut:** Process (Steel Knife) 4 large sprigs parsley until minced; add 100g (4oz) wholewheat bread, torn into pieces, to bowl. Process as above. Add 100g (4oz) uncooked oats, 25g (1oz) walnuts, pinch of ground cinnamon, pinch of ground mace and pinch of ground nutmeg to bowl. Process 2 seconds. Store fresh crumbs or make dry crumbs as above.

**Currant:** Process (Steel Knife) 100g (4oz) currant bread, torn into pieces, 25g (1oz) walnuts, pinch of mixed spice and pinch of cloves using on/off technique as above. Store fresh crumbs or make dry crumbs as above.

**Garlic-herb:** With machine running (Steel Knife), drop 1 clove peeled garlic through feed tube, processing until minced. Add 100g (4oz) French or Italian bread, torn into pieces, to bowl; add 1 × 5ml tsp (1tsp) dried chives, ½ × 5ml tsp (½tsp) dried basil, pinch of dried oregano and pinch of dried marjoram to bowl. Process as above; store fresh crumbs or make dry crumbs as above.

**Spicy wholewheat:** Process (Steel Knife) 1 small spring onion, cut into 2.5cm (1in) pieces, using on/off technique until chopped. Add 100g (4oz) wholewheat bread, torn into pieces, pinch of cayenne pepper, pinch of ground cumin and pinch of paprika to bowl. Process as above; store fresh crumbs or make dry crumbs as above.

**Parmesan:** With machine running (Steel Knife), drop 25g (1oz) Parmesan cheese, cut into 2.5cm (1in) pieces, through feed tube, processing until finely grated. Add 100g (4oz) wholewheat bread,

*Spaghetti Carbonara with large tossed salad (page 70); Coconut-banana Cream Pie (page 118); Chocolate Rum Truffles (page 123)*

torn into pieces, and $\frac{1}{2} \times 5$ ml tsp ($\frac{1}{2}$tsp) dried tarragon to bowl; process as above. Store fresh crumbs or make dry crumbs as above.

**Sesame:** Process (Steel Knife) 3 large sprigs parsley using on/off technique until minced. Add 100g (4oz) French bread, torn into pieces, to bowl; process as above. Add $2 \times 15$ ml tbsp (2tbsp) sesame seeds and $\frac{1}{2} \times 5$ ml tsp ($\frac{1}{2}$tsp) chervil to bowl; process 2 seconds. Store fresh crumbs or make dry crumbs as above.

**Bread variations:** The above recipes can be made with French, wholewheat, rye or pumpernickel bread. Raisin bread can be used to make the plain or Wheat and walnut variation.

## Croûtons and variations

Total Preparation Time: 12–15 min
Microwave Time: 5–7 min
Makes: 150g (6oz)

*Both tasty and economical, homemade croûtons make ideal additions to casseroles, soups, salads and stuffings.*

50g (2oz) butter or margarine
6 sprigs parsley
100g (4oz) day-old or French bread, cut into scant
   1.25cm ($\frac{1}{2}$in) cubes

Microwave butter in $30 \times 20$cm ($12 \times 8$in) baking dish at High until melted. Process (Steel Knife) parsley using on/off technique until minced; stir into butter. Add bread cubes to baking dish, tossing to coat with butter mixture. Microwave uncovered at High until lightly browned and dry, 3–4 minutes, stirring every 2 minutes. Cool to room temperature (croûtons become more crisp as they cool); store in airtight container at room temperature up to 1 week or freeze up to 2 months.

### Variations

**Garlic:** With machine running (Steel Knife) drop 1 large clove peeled garlic through feed tube, processing until minced. Mix with melted butter and bread cubes and microwave as above.

**Herb:** Mix $1 \times 5$ ml tsp (1tsp) minced fresh or $\frac{1}{2} \times 5$ ml tsp ($\frac{1}{2}$tsp) dried herbs with melted butter and bread cubes and microwave as above. Use any favourite herb or combinations including tarragon, basil, dillweed, oregano, chervil, marjoram, rosemary or coriander.

**Sweet or savoury:** Mix a good pinch of ground spices with melted butter and bread cubes and microwave as above. Use cinnamon, mixed spice, nutmeg, mace or chilli powder.

**Parmesan:** With machine running (Steel Knife), drop 15g ($\frac{1}{2}$oz) Parmesan cheese through feed tube,

processing until grated. Toss warm croûtons with cheese; cool as above.

**Bread variations:** Croûtons can be made with any kind of bread. Rye, wholewheat and pumpernickel are excellent for garlic, herb or savoury croûtons; currant bread can be used for sweet croûtons.

## Baking mix

Total Preparation Time: 3–4 min
Makes: 450g (1lb)

*It makes no sense to buy baking mix when you can blend your own in seconds and store it without chemical preservatives. Use it to make Poppy seed scones, Cheese twists and Fresh fruit cobbler (see Index). Substitute half whole wheatflour for a change.*

450g (1lb) plain flour
$1\frac{1}{2} \times 15$ ml tbsp ($1\frac{1}{2}$tbsp) baking powder
$2 \times 5$ ml tsp (2tsp) sugar
$\frac{1}{2} \times 5$ ml tsp ($\frac{1}{2}$tsp) bicarbonate of soda
$\frac{1}{2} \times 5$ ml tsp ($\frac{1}{2}$tsp) salt
a small knob of vegetable fat

Process (Steel Knife) all ingredients using on/off technique until mixture is blended. Refrigerate in airtight container.

## Chicken stock

Total Preparation Time: 40–70 min
Microwave Time: 30–60 min
Makes: about 1 litre ($1\frac{3}{4}$pt)

*There is no comparison between the flavour of homemade stocks and commercial mixtures. Quantities should be cooked conventionally, but you may want to microwave this relatively fast chicken stock. Chop and add whatever fresh greens you have available, whether parsley, dill, celery leaves or carrot tops; these will enchance the flavour considerably.*

1 medium carrot, peeled, cut to fit feed tube
1 stick celery, cut to fit feed tube
1 medium onion, peeled, cut to fit feed tube
450g (1lb) chicken portions (wings, backs, necks)
$1\frac{1}{2}$ litres ($2\frac{1}{2}$pt) water
2 bay leaves
pinch of dried thyme

Slice (Slicing Disc) carrot, celery and onion. Microwave vegetables and remaining ingredients in 3 litre (5pt) casserole, uncovered, at High 30–60 minutes, depending upon desired strength of flavour.

   Strain; discard chicken pieces and vegetables. Cool to room temperature; refrigerate stock up to 4 days or freeze up to 2 months.

# Breads

## Date and walnut loaf

Total Preparation Time: 43–5 min
Microwave Time: 13–15 min
Makes: 1 loaf

*Spread slices of this with cream cheese or butter and serve with morning coffee or afternoon tea.*

150g (6oz) dates, stoned
150g (6oz) dark soft brown sugar
50g (2oz) walnuts
150ml (6fl oz) boiling water
1 × 5ml tsp (1tsp) bicarbonate of soda
50g (2oz) butter or margarine
1 egg
225g (8oz) plain flour
pinch of salt

Process (Steel Knife) dates and sugar using on/off technique until coarsely chopped. Add walnuts and process using on/off technique until coarsely chopped. Add water and soda to bowl; process (Steel Knife) 2 seconds using on/off technique. Let stand 10 minutes. Microwave butter or margarine in a small bowl until melted; add to bowl with egg. Process (Steel Knife) using on/off technique 3 seconds. Sprinkle flour and salt over ingredients in bowl. Process (Steel Knife) using on/off technique just until flour is blended into mixture.

Spread mixture into a 22.5 × 12.5cm (9 × 5in) greased loaf dish, base lined with greaseproof paper. Shield end of loaf with 5cm (2in) wide strips of foil, covering about 2.5cm (1in) of mixture and moulding rest of foil around dish handles. DO NOT ALLOW FOIL TO TOUCH ANY PART OF OVEN INTERIOR.

Place loaf dish on an inverted plate in the oven. Microwave uncovered at 50% (Medium) 8 minutes rotating dish every 2 minutes if the oven does not have a turntable. Remove foil and microwave at High for about 2–6 minutes until moistness has almost gone from centre of loaf. Leave to stand for 10 minutes before removing from dish to cool on a wire rack.

*Tip*
150g (6oz) raisins or mixed fruit can be substituted for the dates.

## Walnut streusel cake

Total Preparation Time: 27–9 min
Microwave Time: 7–9 min
Serves: 6–8

*This walnut cake is so tempting, it will disappear as quickly as it's baked!*

100g (4oz) walnuts
2 × 15ml tbsp (2tbsp) light brown sugar
1 × 15ml tbsp (1tbsp) flour
½ × 5ml tsp (½tsp) ground cinnamon
pinch of ground mace
100g (4oz) cold butter or margarine, cut into pieces
150g (6oz) granulated sugar
150ml (6fl oz) sour cream or buttermilk
1 egg
1 × 5ml tsp (1tsp) vanilla
150g (6oz) plain flour
1 × 5ml tsp (1tsp) baking powder
1 × 5ml tsp (1tsp) bicarbonate of soda

Process (Steel Knife) walnuts, brown sugar, 1 × 15ml tbsp (1tbsp) flour, the cinnamon and mace using on/off technique until nuts are finely chopped; remove.

Process (Steel Knife) butter and granulated sugar until smooth and fluffy. Add sour cream, egg and vanilla to bowl; process until smooth. Sprinkle 150g (6oz) flour, the baking powder and soda over ingredients in bowl; process using on/off technique just until blended.

Spoon half the batter into ungreased 1½ litre (2½pt) glass or plastic ring mould. Sprinkle with half the nut mixture. Repeat with remaining batter and nuts. Microwave on inverted saucer, uncovered, at 50% (Medium) 5 minutes, rotating mould ¼ turn every minute. Microwave uncovered at High until cake springs back when touched, 2–4 minutes, rotating mould ¼ turn every minute (cake may have moist spots on the top). Let stand on worktop 10 minutes. Serve warm.

*Tips*
1 Cake can be baked 1 day in advance; store covered at room temperature. The texture will become denser as the cake stands, and you may prefer it this way. If you bake the cake in a 2 litre

($3\frac{1}{2}$pt) casserole, with a glass placed open end up in the centre, you can remove it more easily for freezing. Let it stand at least 4 hours after baking; then remove, wrap in aluminium foil and freeze. To reheat, microwave slices on kitchen paper at High 30 seconds.

2 For most efficient processing, scrape down the side of the workbowl once or twice when combining butter and sugar. It is not necessary to combine dry ingredients before adding them to the food processor bowl; just sprinkle them over the ingredients in the bowl.

3 To make a delicious filling for baked apples, follow the first step of the above recipe. Prepare apples by coring and peeling a strip of skin from the top of each apple. Place apples in glass baking dish. Spoon walnut mixture into centres and top each with a thin pat of butter. Microwave covered with greaseproof paper at High 2–3 minutes per apple; let stand 3 minutes. Extra walnut mixture can be refrigerated covered up to 1 month.

## Poppy seed scones

Total Preparation Time: 16–18 min
Microwave Time: 4–6 min
Makes: about 10

*Easy to make and quick to bake, these scones should be eaten freshly cooked and warm.*

225g (8oz) Baking mix (see Index)
100–150ml (4–6fl oz) milk
15g ($\frac{1}{2}$oz) butter or margarine
2 × 15ml tbsp (2tbsp) dry breadcrumbs (see Index)
$\frac{1}{2}$ × 5ml tsp ($\frac{1}{2}$tsp) poppy seeds

Place Baking mix in food processor bowl with Steel Knife; with machine running, pour milk through feed tube until ingredients form ball of dough. Let dough spin around bowl 5 times.

Pat dough on lightly floured surface to 1.25cm ($\frac{1}{2}$in) thickness; cut scones with 5cm (2in) round cutter. Microwave butter in small cup at High until melted. Brush tops of scones with butter; sprinkle with combined breadcrumbs and poppy seeds.

Place scones on 2 plates lined with kitchen paper. Microwave 1 plate at a time uncovered at High until scones have risen and are slightly dry on top, 2–3 minutes, rotating plate $\frac{1}{4}$ turn every minute. Serve freshly cooked, warm with butter and jam.

*Tips*

1 If you have a browning dish, check the manufacturer's instructions for cooking scones; if scones are browned on the dish, breadcrumbs and poppy seeds may be omitted.

2 You may wish to keep honey-butter on hand for breakfast. Process (Steel Knife) honey and butter until fluffy; refrigerate tightly covered up to 1 month. Use 1 part honey to 3 parts butter or equal parts of honey and butter, depending on desired sweetness.

3 Strawberry butter (see Index) is another ideal spread for hot biscuits.

## Herbed-wheat crackers

Total Preparation Time: 26–8 min
Microwave Time: 6–8 min
Makes: about 3 dozen

*Not as dry as bought crackers, these fragile squares make good light nibbling on their own or with a soft cheese, such as ripe Camembert or Boursin.*

4 sprigs parsley
1 clove garlic, peeled
50g (2oz) plain flour
50g (2oz) wholewheat flour
$\frac{1}{2}$ × 5ml tsp ($\frac{1}{2}$tsp) dried savory
a pinch of dried thyme
salt
75g (3oz) cold butter or margarine, cut into pieces
3–4 × 15ml tbsp (3–4tbsp) iced water

Process (Steel Knife) parsley using on/off technique until minced. With machine running (Steel Knife), drop garlic through feed tube, processing until minced. Add flours, savory, thyme and salt to food processor bowl; process (Steel Knife) until mixed. Add butter to bowl; process using on/off technique until mixture is crumbly. With machine running, add water through feed tube until mixture holds together but is not sticky (dough will not form a ball).

Roll dough on floured surface into rectangle 40 × 25cm (16 × 10in): cut into 5cm (2in) squares. Place 10 crackers in greased baking dish; microwave uncovered at High until crisp, about 2 minutes. Cool on wire rack; crackers will become crisper as they cool. Repeat with remaining crackers. Store at room temperature in airtight container.

## Garlic-herb toast

Total Preparation Time: 24–33 min
Microwave Time: 15–18 min
Makes: 18 pieces

*This very easy Melba-type toast makes good use of leftover bread. It goes well with spreads, cheeses, salads and soups. Try it with Double-dressed chicken salad or Continuous cheese dip (see Index).*

2 large sprigs parsley
1 clove garlic, peeled
100g (4oz) cold butter or margarine, cut into pieces
$\frac{1}{2}$ × 5ml tsp ($\frac{1}{2}$tsp) dried basil leaves
pinch of dried oregano leaves
pinch of dried marjoram leaves
thin slices white bread (0.5cm [$\frac{1}{4}$in] thick)

Process (Steel Knife) parsley using on/off technique until minced. With machine running, drop garlic through feed tube; process until minced. Add butter, basil, oregano and marjoram to bowl; process until smooth. Microwave butter mixture in a glass bowl at High until melted. Lightly brush butter mixture on one side of bread slices. Microwave 6 bread slices on microwave roasting rack, uncovered, at High until bread is completely dry and beginning to brown, 4–7 minutes, turning bread slices over and rotating rack $\frac{1}{4}$ turn every 2 minutes. Cool on wire rack (bread will become crisper as it cools). Store at room temperature in airtight container up to 1 week.

*Tip*
To make plain Melba toast, omit herbs and proceed as above.

## Cheese twists
Total Preparation Time: 26–8 min
Microwave Time: 6–8 min
Makes: 1$\frac{1}{2}$ dozen

*Offer these to guests to nibble before dinner—they are just rich enough to soothe appetites without spoiling them. Also superb with soups and entrée salads.*

50g (2oz) Cheddar cheese, chilled, cut to fit feed
 tube
1 sprig parsley
1 × 5ml tsp (1tsp) Parmesan cheese
125g (5oz) Baking mix (see Index)
25g (1oz) butter or margarine
pinch of cayenne pepper
4–5 × 15ml tbsp (4–5tbsp) iced water
paprika

Shred (Shredding Disc) Cheddar cheese; remove. Process (Steel Knife) parsley using on/off technique until minced. With machine running, drop Parmesan cheese through feed tube; process until minced. Add Cheddar cheese, Baking mix, butter and cayenne pepper to bowl; process (Steel Knife) until mixture resembles coarse crumbs. With machine running, add water through feed tube until ingredients form ball of dough.

Roll dough on lightly floured surface into rectangle 0.5cm ($\frac{1}{4}$in) thick. Cut into strips 12.5 × 1.25cm (5 × $\frac{1}{4}$in). Twist strips. Microwave 6 strips at a time in baking dish, uncovered, at High until crisp, 2–2$\frac{1}{2}$ minutes, rotating dish $\frac{1}{4}$ turn after 1 minute. Sprinkle with paprika; let cool on wire rack (twists become crisper as they cool).

*Tip*
Cheese twists can be made 2 days in advance; store in a tightly covered container at room temperature. To crisp them up, microwave on kitchen paper, uncovered, at High until warm, about $\frac{1}{2}$–1 minute, and cool on wire rack. For most effective heating, arrange twists in a spoke pattern.

## Sour-cream scones
Total Preparation Time: 20–1 min
Microwave Time: 5–6 min
Makes: 1 dozen

*A British favourite, baked extra light with sour cream, invites a cup of tea any time.*

225g (8oz) plain flour
2 × 15ml tbsp (2tbsp) sugar
1 × 15ml tbsp (1tbsp) baking powder
$\frac{1}{4}$ × 5ml tsp ($\frac{1}{4}$tsp) bicarbonate of soda
1 × 5ml tsp (1tsp) salt
50g (2oz) cold butter or margarine, cut into pieces
50ml (2floz) whipping or single cream
100ml (4floz) sour cream
1 egg
1 × 15ml tbsp (1tbsp) sugar
pinch of ground cinnamon
pinch of ground mace
pinch of ground nutmeg
butter or margarine
orange marmalade

Process (Steel Knife) flour, 2 × 15ml tbsp (2tbsp) sugar, the baking powder, soda, salt and 50g (2oz) butter using on/off technique until mixture resembles coarse crumbs. Add cream, sour cream and egg to bowl; process using on/off technique just until mixed (dough will be soft).

Divide dough in half. Pat each half on lightly floured surface into 15cm (6in) circle; cut each circle into 6 wedges. Mix 1 × 15ml tbsp (1tbsp) sugar, the cinnamon, mace and nutmeg; sprinkle over scones.

Place 6 scones in circle with pointed ends towards centre on plate lined with kitchen paper. Microwave uncovered at High 2$\frac{1}{2}$–3 minutes, or until no longer doughy; let stand 2 minutes. Repeat with remaining scones.

Serve warm with butter and marmalade.

*Tip*
Sour-cream scones can be frozen for up to 3 months. To reheat, microwave on kitchen paper at High, 30 seconds per scone.

## Oatmeal bread

Total Preparation Time: 68–72 min
(plus 20 more, if needed)
Microwave Time: 28–30 min
(plus 10 more, if needed)
Makes: 1 loaf

*One loaf of this oat-enriched bread, with butter and jam, will not go very far! But if you don't consume it all straight from the oven, you'll have the perfect bread for all kinds of cheese sandwiches.*

7g ($\frac{1}{4}$oz) active dry yeast
2 × 15ml tbsp (2tbsp) sugar
50ml (2fl oz) warm water (43°C [110°F])
150ml (6fl oz) milk
25g (1oz) uncooked quick oats
225g (8oz) plain flour
25g (1oz) wholewheat flour
$\frac{1}{2}$ × 5ml tsp ($\frac{1}{2}$tsp) bicarbonate of soda
1 × 5ml tsp (1tsp) salt
25g (1oz) cold butter or margarine
2–3 × 15ml tbsp (2–3tbsp) cold water
milk
uncooked quick oats

Stir yeast and sugar into the warm water in small bowl; let stand 5 minutes. Microwave the milk in a measure at high just until boiling; stir in the oats and cool to room temperature.

Measure flours, soda, salt and butter into food processor bowl; process (Steel Knife) until mixture resembles coarse crumbs. Add yeast mixture and oat mixture to bowl; process (Steel Knife) using on/off technique until mixed. With machine running, add 2–3 × 15ml tbsp (2–3tbsp) cold water through feed tube for dough to form ball; let ball of dough spin around bowl 12–15 times. Remove Steel Knife; cover food processor bowl with clingfilm.

Place food processor bowl in glass baking dish; fill baking dish halfway with warm water. Microwave at 10% (Low) 10 minutes; let stand covered 10 minutes. Repeat procedure, if necessary, until dough has doubled in bulk. Knead dough

Grease 21.25 × 11.25cm ($8\frac{1}{2}$ × $4\frac{1}{2}$in) loaf dish; coat with oats. Shape dough into loaf; place in dish. Place loaf dish in glass baking dish with warm water. Microwave uncovered at 10% (Low) 10 minutes; let stand 10 minutes. Repeat procedure, if necessary, until bread has doubled in bulk. Remove loaf dish from baking dish.

Brush top of loaf lightly with milk; sprinkle with oats. Microwave uncovered at 70% (Medium High) until bread springs back when touched lightly, about 7 minutes, rotating dish $\frac{1}{4}$ turn after 4

minutes. Remove bread from dish immediately; cool upside down on wire rack (bottom and sides of the loaf may be a little sticky, but will dry upon standing).

*Tips*
1 For deeper colour, toast the oats in 22.5cm (9in) glass dish or pie plate. Microwave uncovered at High 3 minutes, rotating the dish $\frac{1}{4}$ turn halfway through.
2 Add water to dough cautiously; you need only enough water for dough to form a ball. If dough is too sticky to form a ball, add flour, 1 × 15ml tbsp (1tbsp) at a time; sprinkle flour over dough and process until mixed. If your food processor slows down, indicating that it cannot handle the full quantity, divide dough in half; process each half until it forms a ball and recombine dough by hand.
3 Oatmeal bread will not form a crust in the microwave oven. You can let the dough rise in the oven, as above, and bake it conventionally. Bake in preheated oven (400°F, 200°C, Gas 6) until top starts to brown and bread sounds hollow when tapped, about 25 minutes.

## Wholewheat cupcakes

Total Preparation Time: 15–20 min
Microwave Time: 6 min
Makes: 20–4 cupcakes

*These featherlight small cakes, so quickly and easily made, offer the goodness of wholewheat flour and black treacle.*

125g (5oz) plain wholewheat flour
50ml (2fl oz) black treacle
2 × 15ml tbsp (2tbsp) soft brown sugar
$1\frac{1}{2}$ × 5ml tsp ($1\frac{1}{2}$tsp) baking powder
pinch of salt
50ml (2fl oz) vegetable oil or melted margarine
50g (2fl oz) raisins (optional)

Process (Steel Knife) all ingredients together in bowl using on/off technique until just blended together.

Place 2 paper cake cases in each of six cups, or in a microwave muffin pan, and fill only half full with cake mixture. If using individual cups, arrange them, 6 at a time, in a circle in the oven. Microwave at High for about $1\frac{1}{2}$ minutes rotating cups during cooking if the oven does not have a turntable. Repeat with remaining mixture, cooking 6 cakes at a time. Remove cakes from cups immediately.

# Desserts

## Apple praline bundt cake
Total Preparation Time: 51–3 min
Microwave Time: 18–20 min
Serves: 12

*A moist, old-fashioned cake with a touch of glamour. The mock praline topping takes only a few minutes to make but adds tempting crunchiness.*

3–4 digestive biscuits, crumbled
75g (3oz) walnuts
450g (1lb) apples (about 3 medium), peeled, cored,
  cut to fit feed tube
150g (6oz) granulated sugar
125g (5oz) light brown sugar
225ml (8fl oz) vegetable oil
4 eggs
150g (6oz) plain flour
1½ × 5ml tsp (1½tsp) baking powder
1½ × 5ml tsp (1½tsp) bicarbonate of soda
2 × 5ml tsp (2tsp) ground cinnamon
pinch of ground nutmeg
pinch of ground allspice
Praline glaze (recipe follows)

Grease 2¾ litre (4¾pt) plastic fluted ring mould; coat with biscuit crumbs. Process (Steel Knife) walnuts using on/off technique until coarsely chopped; remove. Shred (Shredding Disc) apples; remove. Process (Steel Knife) sugars and oil until smooth; add eggs and process until smooth. Sprinkle flour, baking powder, soda, cinnamon, nutmeg and allspice evenly over sugar mixture. Process (Steel Knife) using on/off technique just until blended. Add 50g (2oz) of the walnuts and the apples to bowl; process using on/off technique just until blended into mixture. Pour mixture into prepared mould. Microwave raised on microwave roasting rack, uncovered, at 50% (Medium) 12 minutes, rotating pan ¼ turn every 5 minutes. Microwave uncovered at High until cake springs back when touched lightly (cake may have moist spots on surface), 4–6 minutes, rotating ¼ turn after 2 minutes. Let stand on worktop 15 minutes; turn out onto serving plate.
   Make Praline glaze. Pierce cake with skewer; spoon glaze over warm cake. Sprinkle with remaining walnuts and serve with fresh cream.

## Praline glaze
Makes: 150ml (6fl oz)

40g (1½oz) butter or margarine
65g (2½oz) light brown sugar
2 × 15ml tbsp (2tbsp) brandy
2 × 15ml tbsp (2tbsp) water

Microwave butter in small bowl at High until melted; stir in sugar, brandy and water. Microwave uncovered at High until boiling; boil 30 seconds. Stir until sugar is dissolved.

*Tip*
Apple praline bundt cake improves if you let it stand overnight, because the syrup will continue to soak into the cake.

## Cinnamon apple sauce
Total Preparation Time: 17–19 min
Microwave Time: 8–10 min

*You may never purchase apple sauce again! Homemade is incomparably better, and this recipe is much, much faster than most. Serve it for dessert, with plain biscuits, or to accompany roast lamb, poultry or pork.*

2¼kg (2½lb) tart cooking apples, peeled, cored, cut to
  fit feed tube
50ml (2fl oz) water
50g (2oz) sugar
1 × 15ml tbsp (1tbsp) brandy (optional)
½ × 5ml tsp (½tsp) ground cinnamon
pinch of ground mace
pinch of ground nutmeg

Slice (Slicing Disc) apples. Microwave apples and water in glass casserole, covered, at High until apples are tender, about 8 minutes, stirring after 4 minutes. Process (Steel Knife) apple mixture, sugar, brandy, cinnamon, mace and nutmeg until smooth. Cool to room temperature; refrigerate.

*Tips*
1 When apples are cheap, you may wish to make several batches of Cinnamon apple sauce and freeze the surplus. It can be frozen in covered containers up to 6 months.

2 Cinnamon apple sauce is delicious served in individual-portion Ginger crumb crusts. Make crumb mixture according to recipe (see Index) and press into bottoms of six 10cm (4in) shallow dishes; microwave according to recipe, rearranging dishes after 1 minute. Cool and spoon sauce into crusts. Make extra crumb mixture to sprinkle over sauce or garnish with thin slices of lemon.

## Whipped cream rice pudding

Total Preparation Time: 45–8 min
(plus chilling time)
Microwave Time: 28–31 min
Serves: 10–12

*Not only the creamiest, but also an extremely attractive rice pudding. Unmould it and garnish with fresh berries or peeled, sliced orange. Spoon some raspberry sauce (see Tip below) over the top, if you wish, and serve the rest separately.*

150g (6oz) uncooked long-grain rice
500ml (1pt) milk
6 egg yolks
150g (6oz) granulated sugar
300ml (12fl oz) single cream
1 × 15ml tbsp (1tbsp) orange-flavoured liqueur
   (optional)
few drops vanilla essence
15g ($\frac{1}{2}$oz) gelatine
100ml (4fl oz) water
50g (2oz) blanched hazelnuts or almonds
400ml (16fl oz) whipping cream
65g ($2\frac{1}{2}$oz) caster sugar

Microwave rice and milk in a casserole, covered, at High until rice is tender and milk is absorbed, about 15 minutes.

Process (Steel Knife) egg yolks and granulated sugar until thick and lemon coloured, 1$\frac{1}{2}$–2 minutes. Microwave single cream in glass measure uncovered at High until just boiling. With machine running, pour about 100ml (4fl oz) single cream through feed tube; stir egg mixture into remaining cream. Microwave uncovered at 50% (Medium) until thickened, 8–10 minutes, stirring every 2 minutes. Stir in liqueur and vanilla.

Stir gelatine into water in glass measure; microwave uncovered at High until gelatine is dissolved, 30–45 seconds. Stir gelatine mixture into custard; stir custard mixture into rice. Refrigerate until chilled but not set, 45–60 minutes.

Process (Steel Knife) hazelnuts using on/off technique until chopped. Microwave nuts in glass pie dish, uncovered, at High until toasted, 2–3 minutes, stirring every minute.

Process (Steel Knife) whipping cream and caster sugar until thick. Fold cream mixture and nuts into rice mixture; spoon into lightly greased 2 litre (3$\frac{1}{2}$pt) mould. Refrigerate until set, about 4 hours. Loosen edge of mould with tip of knife; dip mould briefly in warm water. Turn out onto serving plate.

*Tip*
Make raspberry sauce, by processing (Steel Knife) 250g (10oz) partially thawed raspberries with 1 × 15ml tbsp (1tbsp) sugar (optional) until smooth.

## Pineapple-cashew squares

Total Preparation Time: 28–31 min
Microwave Time: 9–10 min
Makes: 2 dozen

*A rich, crumbly mixture, glazed with conserve or jam.*

50g (2oz) cashew nuts
100g (4oz) cold butter or margarine, cut into pieces
75g (3oz) granulated sugar
65g (2$\frac{1}{2}$oz) light brown sugar
$\frac{1}{2}$ × 5ml tsp ($\frac{1}{2}$tsp) vanilla essence
100g (4oz) plain flour
75g (3oz) uncooked quick oats
1 × 5ml tsp (1tsp) baking powder
pinch of ground allspice
pinch of ground mace
pinch of ground ginger
100ml (4fl oz) pineapple conserve or jam
1 × 5ml tsp (1tsp) lemon juice

Process (Steel Knife) cashew nuts using on/off technique until finely chopped; reserve. Process (Steel Knife) butter, sugars and vanilla until mixture is fluffy. Sprinkle cashew nuts, flour, oats, baking powder, allspice, mace and ginger over ingredients in bowl; process using on/off technique until blended (mixture will be crumbly). Pat mixture evenly on bottom of greased 22.5cm (9in) square baking dish. Microwave uncovered at 50% (Medium) until crust is set and springs back when touched lightly, 6–7 minutes, protecting corners with aluminium foil and rotating dish $\frac{1}{4}$ turn after 3 minutes. Let stand on worktop 10 minutes.

Mix conserve or jam and lemon juice; spread over crust. Microwave uncovered at 50% (Medium) 3 minutes. Cool on wire rack; cut into squares.

*Tips*
1 Scrape down bowl at least once when processing butter and sugars to ensure smooth consistency.
2 It is not necessary to combine dry ingredients before adding them to the food processor bowl; just sprinkle them over the ingredients in the bowl.

# Citrus freeze

Total Preparation Time: 37–41 min
(plus freezing time)
Microwave Time: 6–7 min
Serves: 8

*A most refreshing sorbet, and a delightful source of vitamin C.*

250g (10oz) sugar
225ml (8fl oz) water
4–6 oranges
4–5 large lemons, peeled, cut into quarters
50ml (2fl oz) orange-flavoured liqueur
fresh mint sprigs (optional)

Mix sugar and water in a bowl. Microwave uncovered at High until mixture boils, about 5 minutes; continue microwaving 1 minute, or until sugar is dissolved. Cool to room temperature. Grate rind from 1 orange; stir into sugar syrup.

Peel oranges and cut into quarters. Process (Steel Knife) oranges until all juice is extracted; strain and discard pith and seeds. Measure 400ml (16fl oz) orange juice. Process (Steel Knife) lemons until all juice is extracted; strain and discard pith and seeds. Measure 225ml (8fl oz) lemon juice.

Stir orange and lemon juice into sugar syrup; stir in liqueur. Pour mixture into 2 ice-cube trays; freeze. Remove cubes from ice-cube trays; store in plastic bag in freezer.

To serve, process (Steel Knife) 6–8 cubes at a time until smooth. Serve immediately in small bowls.

*Tips*
1 You can crush the citrus cubes effectively in the food processor because they do not freeze hard.
2 Citrus freeze is tangy enough to serve as a palate-refresher between rich dinner courses.
3 One large pineapple, peeled, cored and cut into 2.5cm (1in) pieces can be substituted for the lemons; adjust sugar according to the sweetness of the pineapple.

## Lemon cream layer

Total Preparation Time: 45–50 min
(plus chilling time)
Microwave Time: 19–22 min
Serves: 12

*Well worth the time for a special celebration. The top glistens with chocolate glaze and the custard filling is smooth and lemony.*

Lemon filling (recipe follows)
100g (4oz) cold butter or margarine, cut into pieces
300g (12oz) sugar
2 eggs
225ml (8fl oz) milk
few drops vanilla essence
250g (10oz) plain flour
2 × 15ml tbsp (2tbsp) cornflour
1 × 15ml level tbsp (1 level tbsp) baking powder
$\frac{1}{2}$ × 5ml tsp ($\frac{1}{2}$tsp) salt
Chocolate cream glaze (recipe follows)

Make Lemon filling.

Process (Steel Knife) butter and sugar until very fluffy, about 1 minute, scraping side of bowl with rubber spatula after 30 seconds. Add eggs to bowl; process 1 minute. Add milk and vanilla to bowl; process just until blended. Sprinkle flour, cornflour, baking powder and salt evenly over ingredients in bowl; process using on/off technique just until flour disappears (do not overprocess).

Line bottom of 22.5cm (9in) deep round glass or plastic cake dish with greaseproof paper; spoon in half the mixture. Microwave uncovered at 50% (Medium) 6 minutes; rotating pan $\frac{1}{4}$ turn every 2 minutes. Microwave at High until cake springs back when touched lightly, 2–3 minutes (centre of cake will still look moist and unbaked). Let cake stand on worktop 5 minutes; remove from dish and cool on wire rack. Repeat with remaining mixture.

Make Chocolate cream glaze. Place 1 cake layer on serving plate; spread with Lemon filling. Place second cake layer on filling; spread top of cake with Chocolate cream glaze. Refrigerate until serving time. Serve with pouring or whipped cream.

### Lemon filling

75g (3oz) sugar
2 × 15ml tbsp (2tbsp) cornflour
salt
150ml (6fl oz) water
1 egg yolk, beaten
3 × 15ml tbsp (3tbsp) fresh lemon juice
2 × 5ml tsp (2tsp) grated lemon rind
15g ($\frac{1}{2}$oz) butter or margarine

Mix sugar, cornflour and salt in a glass measure; stir in water. Microwave uncovered at High until very thick, 2–3 minutes, stirring every minute. Stir about

3 × 15ml tbsp (3tbsp) cornflour mixture into egg yolk; stir yolk mixture into cornflour mixture. Microwave uncovered at 50% (Medium) 1 minute. Stir in lemon juice, lemon rind and butter until butter is melted. Cover mixture with clingfilm; refrigerate until chilled, about 2 hours.

### Chocolate cream glaze

25g (1oz) plain chocolate
15g ($\frac{1}{2}$oz) butter or margarine
75g (3oz) cream cheese
$\frac{1}{2}$ × 5ml tsp ($\frac{1}{2}$tsp) vanilla essence
75–100g (3–4oz) caster sugar

Microwave chocolate, butter and cream cheese in food processor bowl (without Steel Knife) uncovered at High until chocolate is softened, 1–2 minutes. Insert Steel Knife; process chocolate mixture and vanilla until smooth and fluffy, scraping side of bowl with spatula if necessary. Add half the sugar to bowl; process (Steel Knife) until sugar is blended into mixture. Add remaining sugar a few tablespoons at a time, processing until sugar is blended into mixture and mixture is of spreading consistency.

*Tips*

1 Lemon filling can be made 1 day in advance; refrigerate covered. Cake layers can be baked 1 day in advance; store at room temperature covered with clingfilm.
2 Cake layers can also be baked conventionally, in 2 greased, floured 22.5cm (9in) tins. Bake in preheated oven (375°F, 190°C, Gas 5) until skewer inserted in centre comes out clean, about 25 minutes.

## Chocolate shortbread cookies

Total Preparation Time: 30–2 min
Microwave Time: 8–10 min
Makes: 40

*Flecks of chocolate and chopped walnuts in a traditional, buttery shortbread. Serve with ice cream, or light whipped desserts.*

50g (2oz) chocolate, broken into pieces
75g (3oz) walnuts
300g (12oz) plain flour
75g (3oz) caster sugar
225g (8oz) cold butter or margarine, cut into pieces
vanilla essence (optional)
cocoa or caster sugar

Process (Steel Knife) chocolate using on/off technique until finely chopped. Add walnuts to bowl; process using on/off technique until finely chopped. Add flour, caster sugar, butter and a few drops of vanilla essence to bowl; process using on/off technique just until mixed and smooth (chocolate pieces will be visible in dough).

Divide dough into quarters; divide each quarter into 10 equal pieces. Roll 10 pieces into balls; place around edge of greaseproof-paper-lined 22.5cm (9in) quiche dish or baking dish. Flatten cookies with bottom of glass. Microwave uncovered at High until crisp, 2–2½ minutes, rotating dish ¼ turn after 1 minute. Let stand 5 minutes; remove and cool on wire rack (cookies will become crisper as they cool). Repeat with remaining dough. Sprinkle cookies with cocoa or caster sugar. Store at room temperature in airtight container.

*Tips*

1 Don't overprocess the dough; bits of chocolate should remain visible.
2 Chocolate shortbread dough, divided into quarters and wrapped in aluminium foil, can be frozen up to 2 months. For maximum convenience, freeze cookie-size balls of dough in a single layer on a baking sheet until firm; then transfer to a plastic bag and seal. Thaw dough balls on greaseproof paper in quiche dish and proceed as above.

## Fresh fruit cobbler

Total Preparation Time: 23–8 min
Microwave Time: 10–14 min
Serves: 6–8

*Keep Baking mix on hand to prepare this fresh fruit dessert in a matter of minutes. Use other fruit in season instead of apples or peaches, for a change.*

1kg (2lb) tart cooking apples or fresh peaches, peeled or skinned, cored or stoned, cut to fit feed tube
2 × 15ml tbsp (2tbsp) lemon juice
50g (2oz) raisins
1 × 5ml tsp (1tsp) grated orange or lemon rind
50g (2oz) granulated sugar
50g (2oz) light brown sugar
pinch of ground allspice
pinch of ground nutmeg
150g (6oz) Baking mix (see Index)
25g (1oz) butter or margarine
50g (2oz) light brown sugar
50ml (2fl oz) milk
1 × 15ml tbsp (1tbsp) granulated sugar
pinch of ground cinnamon

Slice (Slicing Disc) apples; place in 22.5cm (9in) square glass baking dish. Toss apples with lemon juice, raisins, orange rind, 50g (2oz) granulated and 50g (2oz) brown sugar, the allspice, nutmeg and 25g (1oz) of the Baking mix.

Microwave apple mixture uncovered at High until apples are crisp-tender, 6–8 minutes, rotating dish ¼ turn after 3 minutes.

Process (Steel Knife) remaining Baking mix, the butter and 50g (2oz) brown sugar until mixture is crumbly. Add milk to bowl; process using on/off technique just until blended. Spoon mixture around edges of glass baking dish; microwave uncovered at High until topping has baked, 4–6 minutes, rotating dish ¼ turn after 3 minutes. Sprinkle with combined 1 × 15ml tbsp (1tbsp) granulated sugar and the cinnamon. Serve warm with fresh cream, ice cream or custard.

## Orange 'n' spice steamed pudding

Total Preparation Time: 35–40 min
Microwave Time: 18–22 min
Serves: 8–10

*If you look forward to steamed pudding at holiday time but dread the chopping and long steaming ritual, you'll appreciate this 'unsteamed' pudding both for its speed and its fruity taste. Serve with brandy sauce (see Tips), if you wish.*

150g (6oz) mixed dried fruit
75g (3oz) currants or raisins
125g (5oz) sugar
225ml (8fl oz) orange juice
100ml (4fl oz) syrup
25g (1oz) butter or margarine
1 egg
1 × 15ml tbsp (1tbsp) grated orange rind
1 × 15ml tbsp (1tbsp) orange-flavoured liqueur or orange juice
few drops vanilla essence
50g (2oz) dry breadcrumbs
½ × 5ml tsp (½tsp) ground cinnamon
pinch of ground mace
pinch of ground nutmeg
100g (4oz) plain flour
1 × 5ml tsp (1tsp) bicarbonate of soda
salt
whipped cream

Process (Steel Knife) fruits, currants and 2 × 15ml tbsp (2tbsp) of the sugar using on/off technique until fruit is finely chopped. Microwave fruit mixture and orange juice in a casserole, covered, at High until fruit is softened, 6–8 minutes, stirring after 3 minutes.

Process (Steel Knife) remaining sugar, the syrup, butter, egg and orange rind until blended. Sprinkle remaining ingredients except whipped cream over mixture in bowl; process using on/off technique until blended. Add fruit mixture to bowl; process using on/off technique until blended. Spoon mixture into greased ring mould or 1½ litre (2½pt) casserole with glass placed open end up in centre. Microwave covered with clingfilm at 50% (Medium) until set and skewer inserted in centre comes out clean, 12–14 minutes, rotating mould $\frac{1}{4}$ turn every 5 minutes. Let stand covered on worktop 10 minutes. Turn out onto serving plate. Serve warm with whipped cream.

*Tips*

1 To make traditional hard sauce, process (Steel Knife) 100g (4oz) softened butter with 250g (10oz) sugar and 50ml (2fl oz) brandy until smooth, scraping down side of bowl once or twice.

2 Orange 'n' spice steamed pudding can be made 2 weeks in advance; refrigerate wrapped in aluminium foil. To reheat, microwave covered with clingfilm at 50% (Medium) until warm, about 5 minutes.

## Buttered crumb crust and variations

Total Preparation Time: 9–11 min
Microwave Time: 3–5 min
Makes: 1 pie crust

*This extremely quick pie crust provides the base for Chocolate mousse pie, Lemon cheesecake with raspberry sauce, and Apricot-glazed fruit tart. Vary the type of crumb to match the filling and use with your favourite pudding or custard fillings, too.*

150g (6oz) digestive biscuits, broken into pieces
75g (3oz) butter or margarine

Process (Steel Knife) biscuits using on/off technique until finely ground. Microwave butter in 22.5cm (9in) deep pie dish, uncovered, at High until melted; stir in crumb mixture and blend well. Press mixture on bottom and side of pie dish. Microwave uncovered at High 1$\frac{1}{2}$ minutes, rotating pie dish $\frac{1}{4}$ turn after 1 minute. Cool on wire rack.

*Tips*

1 Melt butter in the baking dish that the crumb crust will bake in, whether it is a glass pie dish, glass quiche dish, or glass or plastic cake dish.

2 For an almost instant dessert, fill the crumb crust with your favourite ice cream, softened, and freeze until firm. Spoon puréed raspberries or melted chocolate over each portion at serving time. To soften ice cream, microwave it in a glass bowl, uncovered, at 10% (Low).

### Variations

**Ginger:** Substitute 75g (3oz) gingersnaps, broken into halves, for half the digestive biscuits; if desired, 150g (6oz) gingersnaps can be substituted for all the digestive biscuits.

**Vanilla:** Substitute 150g (6oz) shortcake biscuits, broken into halves, for the digestive biscuits.

**Chocolate:** Substitute 150g (6oz) chocolate, broken into halves, for the digestive biscuits.

**Mixed:** Use 150g (6oz) of any combination of above crumbs in place of the digestive biscuits.

**Toasted nut:** Microwave 50g (2oz) desired nuts in glass pie dish, uncovered, at High until toasted, about 3 minutes, stirring after 1$\frac{1}{2}$ minutes. Substitute nuts for 50g (2oz) digestive biscuits in main recipe.

## Lemon cheesecake with raspberry sauce

Total Preparation Time: 24–5 min
(plus chilling time)
Microwave Time: 12–13 min
Serves: 12

*Processor blending and microwaves produce a fluffy cheesecake that goes perfectly with puréed raspberries.*

Ginger crumb crust (see previous recipe)
450g (1lb) cream cheese, cut into pieces, softened
225g (8oz) sugar
2 eggs
2 × 15ml tbsp (2tbsp) lemon juice
1 × 5ml tsp (1tsp) finely grated lemon rind
225ml (8fl oz) sour cream
2 × 15ml tbsp (2tbsp) sugar
1 lemon, ends trimmed, cut to fit feed tube
250g (10oz) frozen raspberries, slightly thawed
1 × 15ml tbsp (1tbsp) sugar (optional)

Make Ginger crumb crust, pressing crumb mixture onto bottom and 2.5cm (1in) up side of 22.5cm (9in) round cake dish. Microwave at High 1$\frac{1}{2}$ minutes, rotating dish $\frac{1}{4}$ turn after 1 minute. Cool on wire rack.

Process (Steel Knife) cream cheese, 225g (8oz) sugar, the eggs, lemon juice and rind until smooth and fluffy, scraping bowl with rubber spatula if necessary. Spread mixture in crumb crust. Microwave uncovered at High until set, 7–8 minutes, rotating dish $\frac{1}{4}$ turn every 2 minutes. Combine sour cream and 2 × 15ml tbsp (2tbsp) sugar; spread over cheesecake. Place cake dish on an inverted saucer. Microwave uncovered at 70% (Medium High) 3 minutes, rotating dish $\frac{1}{4}$ turn after 1$\frac{1}{2}$ minutes. Cool to room temperature; refrigerate until chilled, about 2 hours.

Slice (Slicing Disc) lemon; remove. Process (Steel Knife) raspberries and 1 × 15ml tbsp (1tbsp) sugar until smooth. Cut cheesecake into wedges; garnish with lemon slices. Serve with raspberry sauce.

## Tips

Raising the cake dish on an inverted saucer or microwave roasting rack for the last 3 minutes of baking ensures that the centre will cook evenly.

To get the most juice from a lemon or other citrus fruit, microwave at High 15 seconds. To soften cream cheese, remove from wrapping, place on glass plate, and cut blocks of cheese into pieces; microwave uncovered at High just until softened.

To make Chocolate cheesecake, process 50g (2oz) cocoa with cream cheese mixture. Substitute 2 × 15ml tbsp (2tbsp) orange juice for the lemon juice; substitute orange for the lemon rind and slices. Stir 2 × 15ml tbsp (2tbsp) cocoa into sour cream mixture. Follow above recipe to make cheesecake, substituting Chocolate crumb crust (recipe opposite), if desired.

## Chocolate mousse pie

Total Preparation Time: 22–4 min
(plus chilling time)
Microwave Time: 4–6 min
Serves: 8

*This pie has a delicious, silky-smooth filling. The sugar dissolves as the pie stands; so refrigerate overnight for smoothest texture.*

Buttered crumb crust or Chocolate crumb crust (see previous page)
75g (3oz) unsweetened chocolate, broken into pieces
100g (4oz) cold butter or margarine, cut into pieces
50g (2oz) light brown sugar
few drops vanilla essence
3 eggs
225ml (8fl oz) whipping cream

Make Buttered crumb crust using 22.5cm (9in) pie dish or flan dish.

Arrange chocolate pieces evenly in food processor bowl without Steel Knife. Microwave uncovered at High until chocolate is very soft, 2–3 minutes. Insert Steel Knife. Add butter and sugar to bowl; process until mixture is light and fluffy, about 15 seconds, scraping side of bowl with rubber spatula if necessary. Add vanilla to bowl. With machine running, add eggs one at a time through feed tube, blending well after each addition (sugar will not be dissolved). Spoon mixture into crust. Refrigerate until filling is set, 4–6 hours, or overnight. (Sugar will dissolve and filling will become smooth.)
Process (Steel Knife) cream until stiff. Garnish pie with whipped cream.

*Tip*
If desired, shred (Shredding Disc) 25g (1oz) chocolate and sprinkle over pie as garnish.

## Pie pastry and variations

Total Preparation Time: 13–17 min
(plus chilling time)
Microwave Time: 5–7 min
Makes: 1 pastry shell

*Microwave pastry is reliably tender and there is no need to fear overmixing or toughening the dough in the food processor. However, the pastry remains pale; so add food colouring, if you wish. Use the Sesame, Cheese and Herb variations with quiches. The Citrus variation is excellent for Coconut-banana cream pie or Individual fruit tarts (see Index).*

150g (6oz) plain flour
75g (3oz) frozen butter or margarine, cut into pieces
40g (1½oz) chilled vegetable fat
2 × 15ml tbsp (2tbsp) sugar
few drops yellow food colouring (optional)
3–4 × 15ml tbsp (3–4tbsp) iced water

Process (Steel Knife) flour, butter, fat and sugar using on/off technique until mixture resembles coarse meal. With machine running, add food colouring and water through feed tube until ingredients form ball of dough. Refrigerate dough covered 30 minutes.
Roll dough on lightly floured surface into round 2.5cm (1in) larger than inverted glass pie dish; ease pastry into pie dish. Flute and trim pastry; pierce bottom with tines of fork. Microwave uncovered at High until pastry is beginning to brown, 5–7 minutes, rotating dish ¼ turn every 3 minutes. Cool on wire rack.

**Tart shells:** Make pastry as above. Roll pastry on lightly floured surface into round 3mm (⅛in) thick. Invert 6 cups on dough; cut around cups to make rounds of dough. Shape pastry rounds on bottoms of cups; microwave as above. Remove shells from cups and cool on wire rack.

*Tip*
Refrigerating the dough makes it easier to roll; so does flouring the rolling pin.

### Variations

**Sesame:** Add 1 × 15ml tbsp (1tbsp) toasted sesame seeds to flour; make pastry as above.

**Nut:** Process (Steel Knife) the flour with 25g (1oz) nuts using on/off technique until nuts are finely chopped before adding other ingredients to the bowl. Make pastry as above.

**Cheese:** Add 25g (1oz) shredded Cheddar cheese to flour; omit sugar. Make pastry as above.

**Citrus:** Add 1 × 15 ml tbsp (1 tbsp) finely grated lemon, orange or lime rind to flour; make pastry as above.

**Herb:** Add $\frac{1}{2}$ × 5 ml tsp ($\frac{1}{2}$tsp) desired dried herbs to flour; omit sugar. Make pastry as above.

## Toffee pie

Total Preparation Time: 35–7 min
(plus chilling time)
Microwave Time: 9–13 min
Serves: 10–12

*A sinfully good party pie, easily flavoured with processor-chopped toffee bars. As long as you're indulging, you might want to make it with Nut pastry.*

1 Pie pastry (previous recipe)
7g ($\frac{1}{4}$oz) gelatine
50ml (2fl oz) cold milk
2 egg yolks
225ml (8fl oz) single cream
2 × 15ml tbsp (2tbsp) sugar
1 × 5ml tsp (1tsp) vanilla essence
salt
2 Crunchie bars, broken into 2.5cm (1in) pieces
225ml (8fl oz) whipping cream
2 × 15ml tbsp (2tbsp) sugar

Make Pie pastry using 22.5cm (9in) glass pie dish.

Stir gelatine into milk in glass measure. Microwave uncovered at High until gelatine is dissolved, 30–45 seconds.

Process (Steel Knife) egg yolks until thick and lemon coloured, about 2 minutes. Combine beaten yolks, single cream and 2 × 15ml tbsp (2tbsp) sugar in glass measure. Microwave uncovered at High until thickened, 4–6 minutes, stirring with whisk every 2 minutes. Stir in vanilla, salt and gelatine mixture. Refrigerate until chilled, but not set, 1$\frac{1}{2}$–2 hours.

Process (Steel Knife) Crunchie bars using on/off technique until finely chopped; remove. Process (Steel Knife) cream and 2 × 15ml tbsp (2tbsp) sugar until thick; fold into gelatine mixture. Fold chopped Crunchie bars into gelatine mixture; spoon into pastry shell. Refrigerate until set, about 4 hours.

## Individual fruit tarts

Total Preparation Time: 25–55 min
(plus chilling time)
Microwave Time: depends on pastry used
Serves: 6

*A very pretty alternative to a large fruit tart. The individual tarts are easier to serve than slices when the filling is whole blackberries or raspberries.*

$\frac{1}{2}$ recipe Pastry cream (recipe opposite)
Toasted nut crumb crust or Tart shells (see Index)
assorted fresh fruit (melon, peaches, pineapple, kiwi strawberries, bananas, etc)
150ml (6fl oz) peach or apricot conserve or jam

Make Pastry cream.

Make desired crust for tarts. If making crumb crust, press crumb mixture in bottoms of six 10cm (4in) tartlet dishes. Do not bake; refrigerate until ready to assemble tarts. Follow recipe directions for other crusts.

Select desired fruit. Peel, seed, core or hull fruit as necessary; cut fruit to fit feed tube. Slice (Slicing Disc) fruit. Spoon Pastry cream into tart crusts; arrange fruit decoratively over tops of tarts. Microwave conserve or jam in glass measure, uncovered, at High until melted, about 1 minute; brush over fruit. Refrigerate tarts until serving time.

*Tip*
Flavour will be best if tarts are assembled as close to serving time as possible.

## Coconut-banana cream pie

Total Preparation Time: 47–52 min
(plus chilling time)
Microwave Time: 19–22 min
Serves: 8

*The best of two flavours for those who love delicate cream pies. If you wish to use freshly grated coconut, see Index for preparation tip.*

Pastry cream (recipe opposite)
3 × 15ml tbsp (3tbsp) coconut- or banana-flavoured liqueur or 1 × 5ml tsp (1tsp) vanilla essence
Pie pastry (see Index)
50g (2oz) flaked coconut
2 medium bananas, peeled

Make Pastry cream, substituting coconut-flavoured liqueur for the almond-flavoured liqueur. Refrigerate until chilled.

Make Pie pastry, using 22.5cm (9in) glass pie dish. Microwave coconut in glass pie dish, uncovered, at High until toasted, 3–4 minutes, stirring every minute.

Slice (Slicing Disc) 1 banana; arrange in bottom of pastry. Spoon Pastry cream over banana; garnish edge of Pastry cream with coconut. Refrigerate until serving time.

At serving time, slice (Slicing Disc) remaining banana; garnish top of pie.

# Apricot-glazed fruit tart

Total Preparation time: 35–42 min
(plus chilling time)
Microwave Time: 9–12 min
Serves: 12

*A beautifully smooth Pastry cream is the key to this elegant tart. Make the crust and the cream days in advance, if you wish. But slice the fruit and assemble the tart just before you sit down to dinner.*

Pastry cream (recipe follows)
Toasted nut crumb crust (see Index)
¼ medium pineapple, peeled, cored, cut to fit feed tube
¼ medium cantaloupe or honeydew melon, peeled, seeded, cut to fit feed tube
225ml (½pt) strawberries, hulled
1 banana, peeled, cut to fit feed tube
50ml (2fl oz) apricot conserve or jam

Make Pastry cream.

Make Toasted nut crumb crust; pat onto 25cm (10in) serving plate or in bottom of 25cm (10in) quiche dish. Do not bake; refrigerate until ready to assemble tart.

Spread Pastry cream in crust. Slice (Slicing Disc) fruits separately; arrange decoratively over custard. Microwave conserve or jam in glass measure,

uncovered, at High until melted, about 1 minute; brush over fruit. Refrigerate tart until serving time.

**Pastry cream**
Makes: about ¾ litre (1¼pt)

225g (8oz) sugar
125g (5oz) plain flour
6 egg yolks
225ml (8fl oz) single cream
225ml (8fl oz) whipping cream
3 × 15ml tbsp (3tbsp) almond or orange-flavoured liqueur
1 × 5 ml tsp (1tsp) vanilla essence

Process (Steel Knife) sugar and flour using on/off technique until almost powdered. Add egg yolks to bowl; process until mixture is thick and lemon coloured, scraping side of bowl with spatula if necessary. Microwave single cream and whipping cream in glass measure, uncovered, at High just until boiling, 2–4 minutes. With machine running, slowly pour half the cream mixture through feed tube into egg mixture, processing until blended. Stir egg mixture into remaining cream mixture. Microwave uncovered at 70% (Medium High) until thickened, 6–8 minutes, stirring with whisk every 2 minutes. Stir in liqueur and vanilla. Cool to room temperature. Refrigerate until ready to use.

*Tips*

1 Flavour will be best if tart is assembled as close to serving time as possible.

2 Other soft fruits, such as sliced peaches, sliced kiwi, raspberries or blackberries can be substituted. Arrange fruit for maximum colour contrast; concentric circles will result in a portion of all fruits in each slice, but a pinwheel of 8 sections is very attractive also.

3 When slicing strawberries, arrange them sideways in the feed tube for long, attractive slices.

## Baklava

Total Preparation Time: 31–2 min
Microwave Time: 8–10 min
Serves: 8

*Bake this famous Greek pastry in small triangles for maximum crispness. Then pour hot honey syrup over the dessert at serving time to meld the wonderful flavours of spiced walnut filling and flaky pastry.*

75g (3oz) walnuts
25g (1oz) dry breadcrumbs (see Index)
3 × 15ml tbsp (3tbsp) sugar
$\frac{1}{2}$ × 5ml tsp ($\frac{1}{2}$tsp) ground cinnamon
pinch of ground cloves
65g (2$\frac{1}{2}$oz) butter or margarine
8 sheets fillo pastry
65ml (2$\frac{1}{2}$fl oz) honey
65g (2$\frac{1}{2}$oz) sugar
65ml (2$\frac{1}{2}$fl oz) water
1 × 5ml tsp (1tsp) grated orange rind

Process (Steel Knife) walnuts using on/off technique until finely chopped; add the breadcrumbs, 3 × 15ml tbsp (3tbsp) sugar, the cinnamon and cloves to bowl. Process (Steel Knife) until very finely chopped.

Microwave butter in small glass bowl, uncovered, at High until melted. Cut sheets of fillo lengthwise into 4 equal strips. Brush 1 strip with butter; top with second strip and brush with butter. Sprinkle 1 × 15ml tbsp (1tbsp) nut mixture over pastry; fold short end of pastry strip to side, forming triangle. Continue folding, flag-style. Repeat with remaining fillo, butter and nut mixture.

Place 8 pastries seam sides down in circle in glass dish or quiche dish; microwave uncovered at High 2 minutes, turning pastries over after 1 minute. Repeat with remaining 8 pastries. Cool on wire rack (pastries will become crisper as they cool). Store in airtight container at room temperature.

At serving time, microwave honey, 65g (2$\frac{1}{2}$oz) sugar, the water and orange rind in a glass measure, uncovered, at High until boiling. Place pastries in shallow glass baking dish; pour syrup over and let stand 5 minutes. (Do not let stand longer or pastries will become soggy.) Serve immediately.

*Tips*

1 Fillo pastry, very similar to strudel dough, can be found in the frozen food section of large supermarkets and delicatessens. Thaw fillo completely, according to packet directions, before using; unused portions can be tightly wrapped and refrozen. When working with strips of fillo, keep remaining pieces covered with a damp tea-towel to prevent them from drying out. This precaution is important, as the paper-thin dough can very quickly dry out and become too brittle to work with. Flaky pastry may be used as a rather less suitable substitute.

2 To fold Baklava triangles, illustration.

3 Unbaked Baklava can be frozen, tightly wrapped, up to 3 months.

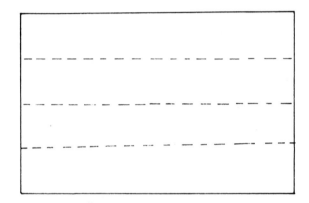

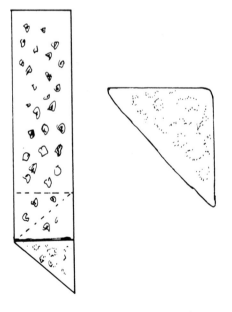

# Fillo pastry shells

Total Preparation Time: 23–5 min
Microwave Time: 4–5 min
Makes: 6 shells

*These crisp pastry shells are enormously versatile. Fill them with ice cream or Pastry cream and fresh fruit. Substitute them for Pie pastry to make individual Coconut-banana cream pies. And use them to highlight entrées, such as Chicken and shrimp in fillo shells, or your favourite seafood salad. (See Index for recipes.)*

5–8 sheets fillo pastry
50g (2oz) butter or margarine

Cut fillo into thirty 11.25cm (4½in) squares. Microwave butter in cup, uncovered, at High until melted. Brush 1 square fillo with butter; top with 1 square fillo. Repeat with butter and 3 more squares fillo; shape around bottom of inverted cup or ramekin. Repeat with remaining fillo and butter to make 5 more shells. Place 3 in oven; microwave uncovered at High until crisp, 1–1½ minutes (pastry should NOT turn brown). Let stand 2 minutes; remove shells from cups and cool on wire rack. Repeat with remaining 3 shells. Store at room temperature in airtight container.

*Tips*
1 See previous recipe for tips on handling fillo pastry.
2 To cut squares of fillo, leave the sheets in a stack and cut straight down through the layers with a sharp slicing or serrated knife (don't drag the knife or you will risk tearing the pastry). You can also cut pastry with kitchen scissors.

# Viennese chocolate

Total Preparation Time: 16–18 min
Microwave Time: 5–7 min
Serves: 6

*The world's most luxurious beverage—a custom imported from European pastry shops. Serve it with biscuits or all by itself, after dinner or at teatime. Dribble a small amount of chocolate or coffee liqueur into each mug, if you wish.*

225ml (8fl oz) whipping cream
50g (2oz) plain chocolate, broken into pieces
400ml (16fl oz) milk
2 × 15ml tbsp (2tbsp) sugar
few drops vanilla essence
freshly grated nutmeg

Process (Steel Knife) cream until stiff; transfer to small bowl. Place chocolate in food processor bowl without Steel Knife; microwave uncovered at High until chocolate is soft but not melted, about 2 minutes, stirring after 1 minute. Insert Steel Knife. Microwave milk, sugar and vanilla in glass measure, uncovered, at High just until boiling. With machine running (Steel Knife), pour milk mixture through feed tube, processing until completely mixed with chocolate. Add whipped cream to bowl; process using on/off technique just until blended. Serve in small mugs; sprinkle with nutmeg.

*Tip*
Cream will whip more quickly if the food processor workbowl and Steel Knife are both chilled before processing.

# Flavoured coffees

*For convenient brewing, process instant coffee with sugar and spices and keep the mixture on hand. All of these coffees can be served over ice or laced with a complementary liqueur.*

# New Orleans coffee

Total Preparation Time: 5–7 min
Microwave Time: 1–2 min
Serves: 12

40g (1½oz) instant coffee granules
50g (2oz) light brown sugar
pinch of ground cardamom
water
whipping cream (optional)
cinnamon sticks (optional)

Process (Steel Knife) coffee sugar, and cardamom until mixed; store in airtight container. For each cup of coffee, measure 125ml (5fl oz) water into coffee cup; microwave uncovered at High until boiling; stir in scant 1½ × 15ml tbsp (1½tbsp) coffee mixture. Process (Steel Knife) cream until stiff. Garnish coffee with dollop of cream; serve with cinnamon stick for stirring.

# Coffee mocha

Total Preparation Time: 8–9 min
Microwave Time: 1–2 min
Serves: 12

40g (1½oz) instant coffee granules
100g (4oz) sugar
25g (1oz) cocoa
1½ × 15ml tbsp (1½tbsp) ground cinnamon
pinch of ground nutmeg
milk
water
plain chocolate (optional)
whipping cream (optional)

Process (Steel Knife) coffee, sugar, cocoa, cinnamon and nutmeg until mixed; store in airtight container. For each cup of coffee, measure 65ml (2½fl oz) milk and 65ml (2½fl oz) water into coffee cup; microwave uncovered at High until boiling; stir in 2 × 15ml tbsp (2tbsp) coffee mixture. Shred (Shredding Disc) chocolate; remove. Process (Steel Knife) cream until stiff. Garnish coffee with dollop of cream; sprinkle with chocolate.

## Orange spiced coffee

Total Preparation Time: 6–8 min
Microwave Time: 1–2 min
Serves: 12

40g (1½oz) instant coffee granules
50g (2oz) sugar
2 × 15ml tbsp (2tbsp) sweetened orange drink
    concentrate
1 × 5ml level tsp (1 level tsp) mixed spice
pinch of ground cloves
milk
water
1 small orange, cut to fit feed tube (optional)

Process (Steel Knife) coffee, sugar, orange drink, mixed spice and cloves until mixed; store in airtight container. For each cup of coffee, measure 65ml (2½fl oz) milk and 65ml (2½fl oz) water into coffee cup; microwave uncovered at High until boiling; stir in 1½ × 15ml tbsp (1½tbsp) coffee mixture. Slice (Slicing Disc) orange; garnish each cup of coffee with orange slice.

# Miscellaneous

## Chocolate rum truffles

Total Preparation Time: 19–22 min
(plus chilling time)
Microwave Time: 4–6 min
Makes: about 3 dozen

*An elegant chocolate prepared almost entirely in the food processor bowl. A grand menu finale, these make a fitting gift for a dinner host or hostess.*

125g (5oz) blanched almonds
50g (2oz) digestive biscuits, broken into pieces
50g (2oz) gingersnaps, broken into halves
2 × 15ml tbsp (2tbsp) light rum
150g (6oz) chocolate chips or pieces
100g (4oz) cold butter or margarine, cut into pieces
50g (2oz) caster sugar
few drops vanilla essence
75ml (3fl oz) whipping cream

Process (Steel Knife) almonds until finely chopped. Microwave almonds on a plate uncovered at High until toasted, about 3 minutes, stirring after 1½ minutes; reserve.

Process (Steel Knife) digestive biscuits and gingersnaps using on/off technique until finely ground. Add rum to bowl; process using on/off technique until blended. Add chocolate, butter, sugar and vanilla to bowl. Microwave cream in a small bowl, uncovered, at High until boiling; with machine running (Steel Knife), add boiling cream through feed tube, processing until mixture is smooth and scraping bowl with rubber spatula if necessary. Refrigerate mixture in food processor bowl until firm enough to hold shape.

Spoon chocolate mixture into pastry bag fitted with medium plain tip. Pipe mixture in 1.25cm (½in) mounds onto baking sheet; refrigerate until firm. Roll in chopped almonds. If mixture becomes too soft at room temperature, refrigerate in container.

*Tips*
1 The chocolate pieces will melt when you pour the boiling cream through the food processor feed tube with the machine running.
2 You can spoon the chocolate mixture onto the baking sheet instead of piping it through a pastry bag, if you wish.

## Coconut walnut caramels

Total Preparation Time: 41–6 min
Microwave Time: 31–4 min
Makes: 4 dozen pieces

*Deliciously creamy caramels, with the chewiness of coconut and the crunch of walnuts.*

40g (1½oz) grated coconut
100g (4oz) walnuts
225g (8oz) granulated sugar
175g (7oz) light brown sugar
150ml (6fl oz) golden syrup
75g (3oz) butter or margarine
400ml (16fl oz) whipping cream
salt
1 × 5ml tsp (1tsp) vanilla essence

Microwave coconut on a plate, uncovered, at High until toasted, 1½–2 minutes, stirring every 30 seconds. Process (Steel Knife) walnuts using on/off technique until finely chopped. Microwave walnuts on a plate, uncovered, at High until toasted, about 3 minutes, stirring after 1½ minutes.

Combine sugars, syrup, butter, half the cream and the salt in a glass bowl. Microwave uncovered at High 10 minutes, stirring twice. Gradually stir in remaining cream. Microwave uncovered at High until mixture registers 120°C (250°F) on sugar thermometer, 16–19 minutes; stir 3 times during first 12 minutes of cooking time and every minute thereafter, checking temperature every minute. Stir in coconut, walnuts and vanilla; pour into greased 20cm (8in) square dish. Cool; cut into squares.

*Tips*
1 Do not leave the thermometer in the mixture unless it is specially designed for microwave ovens. It is very important to check the temperature every minute towards the end of cooking time, as the temperature can increase suddenly; if the mixture gets too hot, it will become brittle. It is possible, but quite inconvenient, to make caramels without a thermometer. If you do not have a thermometer, use the water test: drop a little of the syrup into a cup of cold water; it should form a firm ball that does not flatten upon removal from the water.

2 To save washing-up time, add water to the cooking bowl and microwave at High to dissolve the sugar mixture, scraping the sides of the bowl occasionally.

## Candied walnuts

Total Preparation Time: 15–20 min
Microwave Time: 8–12 min
Makes: about 250g (10oz)

*An after-dinner confection or snack for those who prefer something not too sweet.*

250g (10oz) walnut halves
2 egg whites
2 × 15ml tbsp (2tbsp) water
50g (2oz) caster sugar
pinch of cream or tartar
pinch of ground cinnamon

Microwave walnuts in a baking dish, uncovered, at High until toasted, about 3 minutes, stirring after 1½ minutes. Cool to room temperature.

Process (Steel Knife) egg whites, water, sugar and cream of tartar until egg whites form stiff peaks. Add cinnamon to bowl; process using on/off technique until blended. Fold egg whites into walnuts in baking dish until nuts are evenly coated with egg mixture. Microwave uncovered at High until nuts are glazed, 5–7 minutes, stirring every 1½ minutes (nuts will be sticky). Cool to room temperature. (Nuts will become dry. If not completely dry, microwave uncovered at High 1–2 minutes longer.) Store in airtight container.

## Chocolate peanut butter cups

Total Preparation Time: 32–4 min
(plus freezing time)
Microwave Time: 2–4 min
Makes: 1½ dozen

*These mouth-watering sweets make ideal gifts and are almost too easy to make!*

300g (12oz) plain chocolate
40g (1½oz) butter or margarine
125g (5oz) salted peanuts
1½ × 5ml tsp (1½tsp) honey
50g (2oz) caster sugar
40g (1½oz) butter or margarine, softened
assorted jams (any flavour)

Microwave chocolate and 40g (1½oz) butter in glass measure, uncovered, at High until melted, 2–4 minutes; stir well. Spread chocolate on sides and bottoms of 18 double thickness paper cake cases with small spatula or brush (you should have 2–3 × 15ml tbsp [2–3tbsp] chocolate left over); place in freezer until firm, about 10 minutes.

Process (Steel Knife) peanuts until smooth butter is formed, 5–6 minutes, scraping bowl with rubber spatula if necessary. Add honey, half the sugar and 40g (1½oz) softened butter to bowl; process (Steel Knife) until smooth. Add remaining sugar; process until smooth.

Spoon a generous teaspoon of desired jam in bottom of each chocolate cup; fill each almost to top with peanut butter mixture. Brush remaining chocolate over each cup to seal in filling; freeze until firm, about 10 minutes. Carefully peel off paper. Store in airtight container at room temperature.

## Vegetable antipasto

Total Preparation Time: 24–6 min
Microwave Time: 9–11 min
Makes: 1 litre (1¾pt)

*Low-calorie hors d'oeuvre, ideal picnic fare and a bright garnish for plates of cold meats and cheese are all packed in colourful jars of Vegetable antipasto. The mixture can be prepared so quickly that you may want to make several batches, especially when there's a good supply of ripe peppers.*

2 medium carrots, peeled, cut to fit feed tube
¼ small cauliflower, broken into florets
50ml (2fl oz) water
2 medium red or green peppers, seeded, cut to fit feed tube
100g (4oz) mushrooms
75–100g (3–4oz) olives, stoned
125ml (5fl oz) olive oil
100ml (4fl oz) water
100ml (4fl oz) white wine vinegar
50ml (2fl oz) lemon juice
1 × 5ml tsp (1tsp) dry mustard
12 peppercorns
1 × 5ml tsp (1tsp) dried tarragon
pinch of dried thyme
1 bay leaf, crumbled

Slice (Slicing Disc) carrots and cauliflower; microwave in 2 separate bowls with 2 × 15ml tbsp (2tbsp) water, covered with clingfilm, at High until crisp-tender, about 4 minutes. Drain. Slice (Slicing Disc) fresh peppers, mushrooms and olives separately. Layer vegetables in sterilised 1 litre (1¾pt) glass jar.

Microwave oil and remaining ingredients in a bowl, uncovered, at High until boiling, about 5 minutes. Pour over vegetables. Cool to room temperature; cover and refrigerate up to 1 month.

# Peach chutney

Total Preparation Time: 32–9 min
Microwave Time: 20–5 min
Makes: about 300ml (12fl oz)

*It's so easy to processor-chop and microwave your own chutney that there's little reason to settle for the inferior taste of commercial products. To keep up with the seasons, substitute other fruit when peaches are not available. Serve chutney with poultry, lamb or ham, as well as Indian curries.*

1 clove garlic, peeled
4 medium peaches, skinned, stoned, cut into 2.5cm (1in) pieces
1 green pepper, seeded, cut into 2.5cm (1in) pieces
1 small onion, peeled, cut into 2.5cm (1in) pieces
1 hot chilli pepper, seeded, cut into 2.5cm (1in) pieces
125g (5oz) light brown sugar
75g (3oz) raisins

100ml (4fl oz) cider vinegar
2 × 15ml tbsp (2tbsp) lime juice
1 × 5ml tsp (1tsp) ground ginger
$\frac{1}{2}$ × 5ml tsp ($\frac{1}{2}$tsp) dry mustard
$\frac{1}{2}$ × 5ml tsp ($\frac{1}{2}$tsp) salt

With machine running (Steel Knife), drop garlic through feed tube, processing until minced. Add peaches, green pepper, onion and hot pepper; process using on/off technique until coarsely chopped.

Combine peach mixture and remaining ingredients in a casserole. Microwave uncovered at High until thickened, 20–25 minutes, stirring every 10 minutes. Spoon into sterilised jar; cool to room temperature. Cover and refrigerate up to 1 month.

*Tip*
Four medium pears or one small cantaloupe or honeydew melon can be substituted for the peaches; peel, core or seed and cut fruit into 2.5cm (1in) pieces.

## Orange flowerpot breads

Total Preparation Time: 69–73 min
Microwave Time: 26–7 min
Makes: 8 loaves

*A novel way to bake individual loaves of bread. These rich, raisin-walnut loaves make original gifts, too.*

50ml (2fl oz) orange juice
7g ($\frac{1}{4}$oz) active dry yeast
3 × 15ml tbsp (3tbsp) granulated sugar
450g (1lb) strong plain flour
1 × 5ml tsp (1tsp) salt
65g (2$\frac{1}{2}$oz) frozen butter or margarine, cut into pieces
40g (1$\frac{1}{2}$oz) walnuts
40g (1$\frac{1}{2}$oz) raisins
1 × 5ml tsp (1tsp) grated orange rind
2 eggs
65g (2$\frac{1}{2}$oz) caster sugar
a few drops vanilla essence
1–2 × 5ml tsp (1–2tsp) orange juice
3 × 5ml tsp (3tsp) grated orange rind

Microwave orange juice in a small bowl until warm (43°C [110°F]); stir in yeast and granulated sugar. Let stand 5 minutes. Insert Steel Knife in food processor bowl. Measure flour and salt into bowl; add butter, walnuts, raisins and 1 × 5ml tsp (1tsp) orange rind. Process using on/off technique until butter is incorporated into the flour. Add eggs to bowl; process until dough forms a ball. Let ball of dough spin around bowl 5 times. (If dough is too moist, sprinkle 1–2 × 15ml tbsp [1–2tbsp] flour over dough and process until blended.) Remove Steel Knife; cover food processor bowl with clingfilm.

Place food processor bowl in shallow glass baking dish; fill baking dish halfway with warm water. Microwave at 10% (Low) 10 minutes; let stand covered 10 minutes. Shape dough into 8 equal-sized balls. Generously grease 8 clean clay flowerpots, 6.25 × 6.25cm (2$\frac{1}{2}$ × 2$\frac{1}{2}$in). Place dough in flowerpots; cover loosely with clingfilm. Place flowerpots in a circle in the oven; place 2 small cups filled with warm water in diagonal corners of oven. Microwave at 10% (Low) 10 minutes; let stand covered 10 minutes or until doubled in bulk. Remove clingfilm and cups; rearrange flowerpots. Microwave uncovered at 50% (Medium) until tops of breads are no longer moist, 5–6 minutes, rearranging flowerpots after 3 minutes. Let stand on worktop 5 minutes.

Mix caster sugar, vanilla and 1–2 × 5ml tsp (1–2tsp) orange juice to make glaze consistency. Spoon glaze over breads; sprinkle with 3 × 5ml tsp (3tsp) orange rind.

*Tips*
1 Make sure orange juice is no warmer than 43°C (110°F) when you stir in the yeast. Scrape down side of bowl, when processing the dough.
2 Breads can be baked in 8 greased 75g (3oz) cups, if desired; proceed as above.

## Bread and butter pickles

Total Preparation Time: 30–5 min
(plus standing time)
Microwave Time: 15–20 min
Makes: about 1¾ litres (3pt)

*A welcome addition to all kinds of sandwiches. Give extra jars as gifts.*

1kg (2lb) cucumbers, ends trimmed, cut to fit feed tube
2 medium onions, peeled, cut to fit feed tube
150g (6oz) salt
1.1 litres (2pt) water
225ml (8fl oz) cider vinegar
225g (8oz) sugar
1 × 5ml tsp (1tsp) mustard seeds
½ × 5ml tsp (½tsp) dill seeds
½ × 5ml tsp (½tsp) ground turmeric
pinch of mixed spice

Slice (Slicing Disc), cucumbers and onions; transfer to 3 litre (5pt) bowl. Sprinkle with salt; pour in 1 litre (1¾pt) of the water. Let stand 2 hours. Drain and rinse thoroughly.

Microwave remaining water, the cucumber mixture, and remaining ingredients in 3 litre (5pt) casserole, covered, at High until vegetables are crisp-tender, 15–20 minutes, stirring after 8 minutes. Spoon pickles into sterilised jars; cool to room temperature. Cover and refrigerate up to 1 month.

*Tip*
The above recipe can easily be doubled, but don't microwave more than 1½ litre (2½pt) at a time.

# Index